A
World
Religions
Bible
Robert Van de Weyer

BOOKS

A World Religions Bible
Robert Van de Weyer

First published by O-Books, 2003
O-Books is an imprint of John Hunt Publishing Ltd., Laurel House, Station Approach,
Alresford, Hants, SO24 9JH, UK
office1@o-books.net
www.o-books.com

For distributor details and how to order please visit the 'Ordering' section on our website.

ISBN: 978 1 84694 501 4

A CIP catalogue record for this book is available from the British Library.

Printed in the UK by CPI Antony Rowe
Printed in the USA by Offset Paperback Mfrs, Inc

Contents

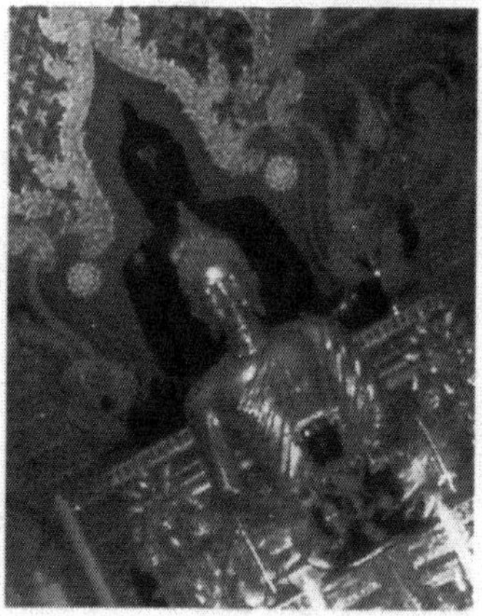

Preface

From as far back in time as history records human beings have sought the 'truth' – some order or entity that unifies all existence. This search has followed two paths, which may be called religion and philosophy. Religion uses the faculty of intuition; and it cultivates this by means of rituals and symbols, meditation and asceticism. Philosophy uses the faculty of reason; and it cultivates this by means of argument and debate, study and reflection. The external forms of religion differ hugely across the world; but there is remarkable similarity in the insights of the various main traditions. Equally the styles of philosophy vary greatly; but the insights of the different movements overlap and complement one another.

Religion has a terrible record of bigotry and conflict; and the source is idolatry – the tendency to turn human doctrines and institutions into objects of worship. Philosophy, in its urge to question every concept and idea, easily leads to cynicism and despair; and many philosophers have concluded that the search for truth is vain, either because there is no unifying order or entity, or because it is beyond human knowledge. Nonetheless the search continues, with as much ardor as ever.

And it has produced much great literature – the greatest of which is contained in this book, ***A World Religions Bible*** and its sequel ***A World Philisophy Bible***. Of course, the division between religion and philosophy is, and should be, blurred, since intuition and reason enhance one another. Moreover, philosophical movements often emerge from religious traditions.

Religion has over the past three millennia been strongest in Asia, while philosophy has been strongest in Europe; and these books inevitably reflect this. But in the new millennium, as global communications rapidly improve, any sincere seeker of truth will look for inspiration throughout the world.

Introduction

Some religious traditions have powerful institutions; and typically these institutions approve certain writings as 'scriptural'. Some religious traditions have a multiplicity of schools and communities led by spiritual teachers; and typically these will have collections of the sayings of outstanding teachers, and stories about them. And some religious traditions are tribal; and their ideas and insights are typically passed from one generation to another by word of mouth – and are only recorded by interested visitors.

All three types of religious traditions are represented in this book, so the form and style of the writings vary hugely. Yet there are many common insights; and the distinctive features of each tradition do not contradict those of other traditions, but complement them. Thus open-minded seekers can learn from all of them.

Each chapter is devoted to a particular religious tradition. A chapter begins with a brief account of the origins, teachings and distinctive features of the tradition, and a suggestion of how its insights may apply to our own lives. Then there are 31 sections of the greatest literature of that tradition, rendered into modern language. The book may serve as an annual cycle of religious readings; it may be dipped into at any time for inspiration; or it may be used as a means of education.

At the end of each reading is a reference to the book from which it comes. In many cases there are several editions available of the full text, to which interested readers can refer. The pieces are mostly abridged from the original, and are occasionally paraphrased in order to try and eliminate obscurities.

The Editor

The editor is Robert Van de Weyer. He was raised by atheist parents who were active socialists; he was introduced to religion by Hindus and Muslims in India; he studied Christianity in Ethiopia, and became a priest in England. He now serves a church committed to global spirituality. He also lectured for twenty-five years in Cambridge on economics, philosophy and religion, and has written and edited over 50 books on those subjects.

MONTH

1

HINDUISM

Introduction

Origins

A great civilization flourished in the valley of the river Indus, in the north-west of the Indian subcontinent, four thousand years ago; and statues have been excavated of a spiritual leader similar to much later figures. Around 1600 BCE the civilization went into decline; and at around the same time Aryan tribes from central Asia arrived. These tribes seem to have adopted the religion of the Indus valley – and came to be called 'Hindus', after the river.

By the middle of the second millennium BCE specialist spiritual teachers *(gurus)* began to emerge; and through the following millennium their number and importance gradually increased. They were treated with great respect, and people came to them for advice. People aspiring to become gurus themselves, as well as older people whose families had left home, often formed a community (*ashram*) around a particular guru.

The words of these gurus were passed down from one generation to another, and eventually written down. The first major collection, possible made as early as the thirteenth century BCE, was the *Rig Veda* (eternal truth). The greatest collection, the *Upanishads* (lessons), was made around the fourth century BCE.

The most famous figure in Hinduism, Krishna, is regarded as a divine incarnation (*avatar*). He appears in several books, and plays a variety of roles. His most important role is that of spiritual counselor; and the *Bhagavad Gita*, his advice to a warrior called Arjuna on the eve of a great battle, is a summary of Hinduism.

Teachings

The Rig Veda and the Upanishads teach that there is a single soul (*atman*) within every plant and tree, every animal and bird, and also every man and woman. The soul is identical in essence with God (*Brahman*). Thus in order to find God, people should look inwards to the soul – and the primary means of this spiritual introspection is meditation. When people succeed in discovering their own soul, they also discern the universality of the soul, and thus come to love all living beings with the same love as they have for themselves.

This belief in the universality of the soul led the Hinduism to reject from the outset any notion of religious exclusivity. The Rig Veda declares that all religions are one, differing only in the name they use for God.

The Upanishads relate the spiritual journeys of a number of men and women. Many start in their youth by spending a few years with a guru. Then they return home to get married and raise children. And after the children have grown up, they leave home again to live in seclusion, and devote themselves entirely to meditation.

The Bhagavad Gita teaches that there are two main methods (*yoga*) of seeking God. The first is the yoga of action *(karma-yoga)*, which consists of serving others to the best of your ability, without thought for your own gain. The second is the yoga of knowledge (*jnana-yoga*), which consists of attaining direct awareness of the soul through meditation. The third is the yoga of devotion *(bhakti-yoga)*, in which the passions are directed to God.

Expression

In addition to the major scriptures, Hinduism has produced a huge volume of religious literature. This includes popular epics and stories, including fables from which Aesop may have drawn inspiration; and mystical poetry, much of which is highly erotic in its devotion to Krishna and other avatars. During the first millennium CE several schools of religious thought emerged, each of which developed its own interpretation of the Upanishads. One of these schools, founded by Patanjali, was especially concerned with the techniques of meditation; and since the late nineteenth century these techniques have been taught throughout the world.

Hinduism has also excelled in the arts of painting and sculpture; and the main subjects are Brahma, Vishnu and Shiva, who represent three aspects of God. Brahma is the creator; he is usually depicted in royal garb, with four heads that look to the four corners of the universe. Vishnu is Brahma's agent in the act of creation, and sustains the universe; he is usually portrayed as a king with four arms. Shiva is the power of destruction and renewal; he is dressed in a loin cloth, has a third eye in the center of his forehead, and dances within a ring of fire.

Most Hindu temples are dedicated to either Shiva or Vishnu. People visit the temples of their choice when it is convenient for them, or at times of spiritual need. Some of the major temples, such as those at Varanasi and Madurai, are popular places of pilgrimage. There are numerous festivals through the year, of which Diwali and Holi are the most prominent. Diwali is marked by the lighting of lamps, to symbolize virtue and good fortune. Holi celebrates Krishna's playfulness with singing and dancing.

Us

We naturally see ourselves as separate from one another, and from animals and plants. Hinduism teaches that this separateness is illusory, since the same soul animates all living beings; and it also teaches that the soul is divine.

The moral implication is that we should treat all living beings as we would wish to be treated ourselves. Violence against animals, which includes slaughtering them for meat, is as abhorrent as violence towards other humans. And, although humans must eat plants in order to survive, they too should be treated with respect and reverence.

The spiritual implication is that personal fulfillment consists in knowing the soul. Most of us have occasional mystical experiences, when we sense the divine presence in all living beings, and are overwhelmed by their beauty. The purpose of meditation is to make this experience constant.

In passing through the four stages of life, the hardest transition is the withdrawal from worldly affairs; our inclination is to cling to our profession and status. But by making that change, we turn old age into the time of greatest happiness.

1

Many names for God

The gurus never cut their hair. Apart from a few hours of sleep at night, and a short period in the middle of the day collecting wild roots and berries to eat, they spent their time meditating. They covered themselves with only thin rags. Just as their bodies were exposed to the earthly wind, their souls were exposed to the divine wind; so their souls blew in whatever direction God wanted. Sometimes the divine wind made them mad and passionate, and sometimes it made them serious and calm. These gurus could read the mind of every person they met, and they excited the minds of all to whom they spoke.

A guru said: 'Some say that the creator of the universe is male; some say that the creator of the universe is female. If you have eyes that can see beneath the surface of things, you can discern that the creator of the universe is both male and female. But if you are blind, you will remain convinced that the creator is either male or female.'

Another guru said: 'The whole universe is sustained by a divine syllable, Aum. If you have ears that can hear beneath the surface of things, you can listen to this syllable everywhere.'

Another guru said: 'People refer to God by many different names. God is like a bird that flies anywhere and everywhere. The wise know that God is one, and that God appears in many forms. So they know that all the names for God have the same meaning.'

Another guru said: 'People often ask where God is located. But if you look for God in one particular place, you will not find him.'

Rig Veda

2

The Truth of God

Another guru said: 'God could destroy the world as quickly as a gambler can lose his money. And he could create it again as quickly as a gambler can regain his money.'

Another guru said: 'God gives strength to the weary, comfort to the sick, and food to the hungry. Every horse and every cow is under his command. He made the villages in which people live, and the chariots on which warriors ride. At dawn each morning he gives birth to the sun. Each day he causes the sea to rise and fall.'

Another guru said: 'When two armies confront each other in battle, the warriors of both armies invoke God. No army can win victory without his approval and help; so he decides which army will win. But he himself can be defeated by no one and nothing.'

Another guru said: 'You may try to understand God; but as you think that you are grasping him with your mind, he slips away. He may try to gain power over God; but the more you assert yourself, the greater becomes his power over you. God possesses all the wisdom of the wise, and all the visions of the poets.'

Another guru said: 'If you seek God with all your heart and mind, eventually you will find him.'

Another guru said: 'If you are generous to others, God will be generous to you. But if you are mean and stingy with others, you should expect nothing from God.'

Another guru said: 'God is my closest friend, and your closest friend. So love him with more love than you have for any human being.'

Rig Veda

3

Different abilities

Another guru said: 'Our different abilities suit us for different occupations, and cause us to seek different opportunities. Those with ability in carpentry seek furniture that is broken, so they can mend it. Those with ability in healing seek bones that are fractured, so they join them together. Those with ability in spiritual matters seek places of solitude, so they can pursue wisdom without distraction. They all serve God is different ways.'

Another guru said: 'The harnessed horse longs for a light cart, and the seducer longs for a woman's smile. Everyone longs for God.'

Another guru said: 'Words are the greatest human invention: they enable us to make plain the deepest mysteries of the world, and to express love for one another. But they also enable us to tell lies and to spread slander. So treat words with care.'

Another guru said: 'Friends should help and encourage one another on the path of life. They should save one another from error by sharing knowledge – just as they would save one another from hunger by sharing food.'

Another guru said: 'There are many ways of sharing knowledge. Some can compose poems; a good poem is like a tree, in which each line is a branch bearing the blossom of divine truth. Some can sing songs, whose melody and rhythm form the music of divine love. Some can remember and repeat the words of ancient gurus.'

Another guru said: 'Some gurus are shallow ponds, while others are deep lakes. Find a deep lake in which to swim.'

Rig Veda

4

Good friends

Another guru said: 'God did not ordain hunger as the way for people to die; God ordained that people should be well-fed, and die by other means. Thus God wants the wealthy to share their wealth with the poor, so all have enough. The wealth of the generous person never runs out, whereas the miser's wealth is soon exhausted.'

Another guru said: 'When the poor come to you in need, do not harden your hearts against them. Remember that the poor may once have been rich, and that you may one day be poor.'

Another guru said: 'When you see people who are thin for lack of food, do not wait for them to beg for your help; on the contrary, beg them to accept your help. Put yourself at the service of those who call at your house in need.'

Another guru said: 'If your friends refuse to share their food with you, they are not genuine friends. If your companions refuse to share their knowledge with you, they are not true companions. Drive away mean friends, and rid yourself of false companions; seek new friends and companionship whose generosity and honesty you can trust.'

Another guru said: 'The sun, which moves without feet, is greater than any man or woman, who moves on two feet. The young person on two feet walks faster than the old person on three feet. Babies on four feet depend on their mothers with two feet. So it is clear that those with fewer feet should protect and care for those with more. It follows that human beings should protect and care for animals and insects.'

Rig Veda

5

THE SINGLE SOUL

Another guru said: 'There is only one soul, from which the souls of all living beings are derived. In the beginning the soul looked around, and saw nothing but itself. It realized that without company it could enjoy no pleasure. So it split into two, and became husband and wife. The husband and wife had sexual intercourse, and from their union human beings were born. It then occurred to the wife that, since she and her husband came from a single soul, it was wrong to have sexual intercourse; so she hid herself by becoming a cow. But he became a bull, and they had intercourse; and from their union cattle were born. Then she became a mare, and he a stallion; and from their union horses were born. In this way all types of living being were born, down to the smallest insect.'

Another guru said: 'If you had eyes to see beneath the surface of all living beings, you would see that their source of life is the same; and the source of life is what we call the soul. The soul is dearer to you than a son or a daughter, dearer than wealth, dearer than all material things. When people recognize that only the soul is truly dear to them, then they know that the object of their dearest love will never perish.'

Another guru said: 'The universe is a trinity: name, form, and action. Names are given through speech; and all speech is an echo of the soul's speech. Forms are discerned by means of sight; and all sight comes from the light of the soul. Actions are performed by bodies; and all bodies are moved by the soul's power. Thus, since there is a single soul, the universe is also a unity.'

Brihadaranyaka Upanishad

6

The divine syllable

Another guru said: 'God speaks the syllable Aum throughout the universe. He also speaks it within the soul. So if you pronounce the syllable Aum over and over again, and meditate upon the sound that you make, you will find that you are listening to the soul within you; and when you are listening to the soul within you, then you are hearing God throughout the universe.'

Another guru said: 'The earth emerged from the waters. Plants rise out of the earth. Animals live by eating plants. Humans are a particular type of animal. Words come from humans. Aum is the word that includes all words; so it embraces all that exists. So when you pronounce, you express universal love.'

Another guru said: 'The sound of Aum signifies assent. So when you utter this sound, you are giving assent to all that lives.'

Another guru said: 'The syllable Aum expresses the desire for enlightenment, and is the means of becoming enlightened. When you pronounce this syllable, you say that you want to know God and the soul, and you come to know God and the soul.'

Another guru said: 'Those who want to know the soul, and those who do not care whether they know the soul, may sit side by side reciting this syllable. But the desire for knowledge and indifference to knowledge are quite different. When Aum is recited with the mouth only, it is impotent; but when it is recited with the heart and mind as well, its potency is boundless.'

Chandogya Upanishad

7

THE LIGHT OF TRUTH

Another guru said: 'There are three ways of striving for truth. First, you may visit temples and shrines, sing hymns, and strive to help the needy. Secondly, you may abstain from all bodily pleasures. Thirdly, you may become the disciple of a guru. Follow whichever way seems to suit you best; change from one way to another as your spiritual needs change; and follow more than one way at a time, if you have the inclination.'

Another guru said: 'There are five ways in which you may perceive the truth. The first is sight; if you train the faculty of sight through meditation, you see the spiritual unity amidst material diversity. The second is hearing; if you train the faculty of hearing through meditation, you hear the spiritual harmony amidst material cacophony. The third is speech; if you meditate on words, you hear and understand the word that embraces all words. The fourth is thought; if you think only about thought itself, subject and object merge. The fifth is breathing; if your breath is slow and calm, you can enter the presence of the soul.'

Another guru said: 'There is a divine light, which shines from above the highest point in the universe. It illuminates all beings, and warms them. It is the same light that shines in the heart of every human being. When we touch a human body, we feel warmth; this heat comes from the divine light. When we press our ears shut, we hear the crackle of a blazing fire; this sound comes from the divine light. We should venerate this light, as we feel it and hear it. When the light shines brightly within us, our faces become radiant.'

Chandogya Upanishad

8

THE UNIVERSE AND THE SOUL

Another guru said: 'The universe emerges from God, and will return to God; he is the beginning and the end. God is all, and all is God.'

Another guru said: 'You are your deepest desire. Your entire life is shaped by your deepest desire. So let your deepest desire be knowledge of the soul.'

Another guru said: 'The soul can be known by those who are pure in heart. The soul is light and life, truth and space. The soul is the source of all activity, all desires, all fragrances and tastes. The soul is beyond words. From the soul comes eternal joy - and the soul dwells within every heart.'

Another guru said: 'The soul is smaller than a grain of rice, smaller than a grain of barley, smaller than a mustard seed, smaller than a grain of millet, smaller even that the kernel of a grain of millet. Thus the heart has room for the soul. The soul is also larger than the earth, larger than the sky, larger than the entire universe.'

Another guru said: 'In the heart there is a tiny lotus; in this lotus there is a tiny dwelling; and in this dwelling is the soul. Yet that lotus, and that dwelling, and the soul itself are as vast as the space that contains the earth and the sky, the sun and the moon.

Another guru said: 'Do not be anxious that sickness will ever infect the soul, or that old age will come upon it. Time does not touch the soul; it only touches the body'.

Another guru said: 'The soul only desires what is real, and it only thinks what is true.'

Chandogya Upanishad

9

The Bridge of Healing

Another guru said: 'The soul is the bridge by which people may pass from darkness to light, from mortality to immortality, from the world to the city of God. If you are blind as you approach the bridge, your eyes will be opened as you cross it. If you are wounded or sick as you approach the bridge, you will be healed as you cross it. If you are sad as you approach the bridge, you will be made happy as you cross it. But first you must become pure; the bridge is only open to those who have purified their minds of all evil thoughts, and purified their hearts of all evil emotions.'

Another guru said: 'When words try to approach God, they are forced to turn back. Human thought can never reach God. Yet human beings can know the bliss of God, and thereby be freed from all fear.'

Another guru said: 'The soul and the sun are one. If you understand this, you see the world as it really is; you understand the unity of all existence. You do not agonize about right and wrong, because you know what is right and wrong. Thus you are utterly free.'

Another guru said: 'When you have moved forward in spiritual undertanding, do not allow yourself to slide backwards. Learn from those who are wiser than you, and teach those who are less wise. And when you teach others, be aware of the effects of what you are saying; listen to yourself as others are listening to you. Look for that which is divine in your mother and your father, in friends and in strangers.'

Chandogya Upanishad and Taittiriya Upanishad

10

Fullness of love

A successful merchant called Yajna, when his children had grown up, decided to dedicate the rest his life to the pursuit of wisdom. He went to his wife, Maitreyi, and offered to give her all his wealth. 'If I were to possess all the wealth in the world,' she asked, 'would it help me to attain immortality?' 'No,' Yajna replied. 'In that case,' she declared, 'I should prefer to join you in the pursuit of wisdom.' So together they went into the forest, and built a small hut for themselves; then they spent their time in meditation. Eventually, just before they both died, they wrote down the insights they had gained:

A wife holds her husband dear, not out of love for him, but out of love for the soul within her. A husband holds his wife dear, not out of love for her, but out of love for the soul within him. Parents hold their children dear, not of love for the children, but out of love for the soul within them. People hold the entire world dear, not out of love for the world, but of love for the soul that permeates the world. Thus when you come to know the soul in its fullness, you love fully.

When you throw a lump of salt into water, it dissolves; you cannot take it out again, and hold it in your hands. Yet if you sip any part of the water, the salt is present. In the same way the soul can be perceived anywhere and everywhere; the soul has no limit.

At present there is duality. You are the subject, and through your senses you perceive other beings as objects. But when you know the soul, the duality of subject and object ceases, because you discern that all are one.

Brihadaranyaka Upanishad

11

THE SUPREME GOAL

If every physical light were to go out, plunging the world into total darkness, the soul would still shine. The soul is consciousness, and it shines as the light within the heart. While remaining unchanged, the soul causes the mind to think and the body to move. The soul is in the world of waking life, and in the world of dreams. When the soul takes on a body, it seems to assume the body's frailties and limitations; but when the soul sheds the body at death, it leaves all these behind.

The soul in itself is free from desire, free from evil, and free from fear.

When a man is in the arms of his beloved, he is oblivious to what is happening around him and within him. In the same way when we come to know the soul, we are oblivious to what is happening around us and within us.

In this state there are no parents, no worlds, no spiritual forces, and no sacred texts. In this state there is neither thief nor murderer; there is no low class or high class; there is neither teacher nor pupil. The soul is beyond good and evil, and beyond all sorrows.

In this state we sense without sensing, perceive without perceiving, and think without thinking. Nothing is separate from us, because there is no subject or object; subject and object have merged.

Through knowing the soul, we know God, because God and the soul are one. This is the supreme goal of life, the supreme treasure, and the supreme joy.

Brihadaranyaka Upanishad

12

Da, Da, Da

A young man, as soon as he reached adulthood, decided to leave home, and spend his life seeking wisdom. He walked for many days until he found a guru living in a cave. After twenty years with the guru he departed, and lived in another cave. After a further twenty years he felt ready to teach others.

His first disciples were three young men. For many months he said nothing at all to them. The young men felt frustrated at this silence, but thought it would be rude to ask questions.

Finally one of the young men could not contain himself any longer. 'Teach us something,' he blurted out. The guru put his hand on the young man's heart, and said: 'Da!' 'What does that mean?' he asked. 'Be brave,' the guru replied.

Then the second young man said: 'Teach us something.' The guru held out his hand to him, with his palm open, and said: 'Da!' 'What does that mean?' he asked. 'Be generous,' the guru replied.

Then the third young man said: 'Teach us something.' The guru embraced the young man, kissing him on both cheeks, and said: 'Da!' 'What does that mean?' he asked. 'Be kind,' the guru replied.

The guru then said to the three men: 'Whenever the thunder rolls, you can hear the sound, "Da! Da! Da!" That is God saying: "Be brave. Be generous. Be kind."' The young men returned home, and led good and happy lives.

Chandogya Upanishad

13

A SINGLE MOTHER

A young man called Satya heard about a particular guru, and decided he wanted to become a disciple. Satya was his mother's only child, and she was unmarried; so he knew she would feel very lonely if he went away. Nonetheless he asked her permission; and with a weak smile she gave it.

Then Satya broached a subject that had never been mentioned: 'The guru is bound to ask about my parents. So what shall I say about my father?' His mother blushed with shame, and said: 'I do not know who your father is. When I was a young woman, I was very poor, and worked as a prostitute. Then I became pregnant with you. And I continued to work as a prostitute in order to support us both – until you were old enough to work.' Satya burst into tears. He felt utterly ashamed of his mother; and without saying another word he left the house, and set out for the guru's hut.

He walked for three days and three nights, resting only in snatches by the side of the road. He wept so much that his eyes grew red, and his face became lined with tears. Finally he reached the guru's hut. He begged the guru to receive him as a disciple, let him live in his hut. Then he told him about his mother's past, and added: 'Now that I know about her disgrace, I never want to see her again.'

The guru said: 'I receive you gladly as my disciple. And I give you one instruction: return home, look after your mother, and learn to love her even more than before. As a result you will come to know the soul which you and she share.'

Chandogya Upanishad

14

Knowing the Unknown

Aruni was a man of great wisdom. But rather than teach his son himself, he sent him at the age of thirteen to a guru. The son stayed with the guru for twelve years, and the guru gave him a lesson every day. The son learnt the guru's words by rote; but he did not truly understand them with his heart. Finally the guru sent the son, who was now a young man, back to Aruni.

The young man was very proud of all he knew, and thought himself superior to all the other young people in the neighborhood. He also thought himself superior to his own parents.

One day Aruni said to him: 'Your head has grown very large with all the knowledge you have acquired. But did you ask the guru to teach you the special wisdom?' 'No,' the young man said; 'what wisdom is that?' Aruni replied: 'It is the wisdom that enables you to hear what cannot be heard, to see what cannot be seen, to think what cannot be thought, and to know what cannot be known.' The young man looked anxious. 'I never asked the guru for that wisdom,' he said; 'give it to me yourself.'

Aruni stooped down. An ant was moving across the ground, and Aruni put his hand in front of it, so it crawled onto his palm. 'By understanding a single ant,' Aruni said, 'you understand all ants. And by understanding ants, you understand living beings. And then you realize that all living beings are one.' The young man replied: 'I don't understand; tell me more.'

Chandogya Upanishad

15

BEES, RIVERS, AND TREES

Aruni said to his son: 'Bees suck nectar from many different flowers, and then make honey. You cannot say one drop of honey came from one flower, and another drop came from another flower; all the honey is one. Likewise all living beings are one - even though they are not all aware of it. The tiger and the lion, the wolf and the fox, the worm and the moth, the gnat and the mosquito - they all come from the one soul, and they all contain the one soul.'

'Tell me more,' the young man said.

Aruni continued: 'Rivers flowing east and rivers flowing west all flow into the sea; and their waters merge with the waters of the sea. You cannot say one drop of sea came from one river, and another drop came from another river; all the sea is one. Likewise all living beings are one.'

'Tell me more,' the young man said.

Aruni continued: 'Hack at the root of a tree, and its sap will flow; hack at the middle of a tree, and its sap will flow; hack at the top of a tree, and its sap will flow. The sap supports and nourishes the tree. Likewise the soul supports and nourishes all that exists. If the sap were to leave a branch of a tree, the branch would die; if it were to leave the whole tree, the tree would die. Likewise, when the soul leaves any living being, that being dies. But the soul never dies.'

'Tell me more,' the young man said.

Chandogya Upanishad

16

THE PAPAYA AND THE BLIND-FOLD MAN

'Bring me a papaya fruit,' Aruni said to his son. His son went out into their orchard, picked a papaya, and brought it to Aruni. 'Cut it in two,' Aruni said. The young man did as his father asked. 'What do you see in the middle of the papaya?' Aruni asked. 'I see lots of seeds,' the young man replied. 'Take a seed, and cut it in two,' Aruni said. 'They are too small to cut in two,' his son answered.

Aruni said: 'Within each seed is an entire tree; you could plant any of those seeds in the ground, and it would grow into a tree, bearing many other papayas. Likewise within the soul, which dwells in every living being, is the entire universe; from the soul, which is divine, the entire universe came into existence.'

'Tell me more,' the young man said.

Aruni continued: 'A man was once blindfolded, taken away from his village, and abandoned. The man wandered to the east and west, to the north and south, but he had no idea which way he was going. So he called out for help. Eventually someone heard his call, and took off the blindfold. The man could now find his way home. In the same way good teachers take the blindfold from the minds of their disciples, and allow them to discern the soul within themselves – hence they are enlightened.'

'You have said enough,' the young man said to his father; 'I shall return to the guru. This time I shall not merely listen to his words, but try to understand the truth that lies behind his words.'

Chandogya Upanishad

17

THE CRUEL KING

An evil king called Kamsa once ruled northern India. He imposed very heavy taxes on the rich and poor alike, in order to build great palaces for himself, and to entertain his friends with sumptuous banquets. And when people protested, he ordered them to be tortured and killed.

Kamsa had a half-sister called Devaki, who was both good and brave, and frequently protested at the injustice of Kamsa's rule. He was anxious that she might encourage the people to rebel, and make herself queen. But since Devaki was a close relation, Kamsa could not bring himself to kill her; so he imprisoned Devaki and her husband in the wing of one of his palaces. They had every material comfort, but the king's guards prevented them from ever going outside.

One day an old man, who was renowned for his wisdom, came to see Kamsa. 'Devaki will bear eight children,' the old man said; 'and one of these will assassinate you.' Kamsa was terrified. He ordered his guards to kill at birth any child born to Devaki.

Soon afterwards Devaki became pregnant, and bore a son. The guards immediately seized the baby, and hacked him into little pieces. Devaki bore six more children, and each one was hacked to pieces by Kamsa's guards.

God took pity on Devaki in her misery; and he also took pity on the people living under Kamsa's cruel rule. He decided to send a leader who would set people free, and show them how to be happy.

Bhagavata Purana

18

THE BIRTH OF KRISHNA

When Devaki became pregnant for the eighth time, God decided that this baby would survive; he also decided that the baby would have dark skin. Immediately after the birth, Devaki's husband took the baby into his arms, climbed out of a window, and ran away. The baby had been born at precisely midnight; and in the darkness none of the guards saw the escape.

Devaki's husband arrived at the river Jamna at a point where the waters are very shallow. He lifted the baby above his head, and waded across; and when he reached the other side, he met a cowherd called Nanda, and his wife Yasoda. He could see from their expressions that they were kind and gentle. 'This baby will grow up to be a great leader and teacher,' he said to Nanda and Yasoda; 'I want you to adopt him, and raise him as if he were your own son. But you must take him far away from here, because King Kamsa will try to kill him.'

Yasoda took the baby from his father. By now the sun had risen, and they could see the baby's dark skin. They decided to call him 'Krishna', meaning 'the dark one.'

Nanda and Yosada then set off with Krishna along the bank of the river. When they had been walking for many days, they came to a place where the grass was especially lush and green. Cows were grazing peacefully as far as the eye could see; and cowherds and dairymaids were looking after them. Nanda and Yasoda decided to settle there; and Nanda worked as a cowherd for one of the landowners.

Bhagavata Purana

19

THE MASSACRE OF BABIES

When Kamsa learnt that Devaki's husband had run away, he guessed at once the reason. So Kamsa ordered that all babies in his kingdom under the age of one be slaughtered. His soldiers went to every town and village, searched every house, and hacked every baby to pieces. Mothers and fathers, grandmothers and grandfathers, cried out in horror and grief; the whole kingdom seemed to shake with the noise.

But Krishna escaped the massacre, because the new home of Nanda and Yasoda was outside Kamsa's kingdom.

Each morning Yasoda put Krishna on a cot outside her hut, where he could enjoy the songs of the birds in the nearby trees. One day an evil woman called Putana was walking past; she saw Krishna's dark skin, and concluded that he must have been adopted. A few days later she heard that Kamsa had ordered his soldiers to murder every baby in his kingdom, with the intention of slaying Devaki's son. Putana wondered if this dark infant was the baby Kamsa wanted to kill. So she went to Kamsa, and told him about Krishna.

Kamsa gave Putana the most beautiful clothes to wear, and a bottle of poison to smear on her breasts. At Kamsa's instruction Putana returned to Krishna. She said to Yasoda: 'Allow me to feed your baby with my own breasts.' Yasoda was so enthralled by Putana's beauty, that she nodded. Putana picked up Krishna in her arms, and offered him her left breast. Krishna refused to suck, and instead bit the breast hard. Putana screamed in agony, and fled.

Bhagavata Purana

20

The Boyhood of Krishna

Krishna grew into a strong and healthy boy. He was also naughty and headstrong. He loved fruit, and frequently raided the local orchards to satisfy his appetite; he also loved milk and butter, and raided both local dairies and his adopted mother's larder. Once, when she had found that all the milk in her larder had gone, Yasoda was so angry that she tied a rope around his belly, and attached the rope to a heavy earthenware jar. But he dragged the jar between two trees, and smashed it.

From time to time both Nanda and Yasoda had visions of Krishna's greatness. On one occasion Yasoda ordered Krishna to open his mouth, to see if he were eating stolen fruit. She looked into his mouth, and saw inside an image of him as king on a great throne, with the entire universe at his feet. But whenever Nanda or Yasoda had such a vision, they forgot it soon afterwards. As a result they treated him as any other boy: they punished him when he was naughty, and encouraged him to be good.

As a teenager he was exceedingly handsome, and the local dairymaids all admired him. And he loved to flirt with them, as well as play tricks on them. One morning a group of dairymaids were bathing in the river. Krishna took their clothes, which they had left on the bank, and climbed up a tree. When they realized what he had done, they screamed at him, and begged him to return their clothes. But he insisted that they come out of the water, and dance naked around the tree. At first they were embarrassed, but soon they were enjoying themselves. When they collapsed with exhaustion, he gave them their clothes.

Bhagavata Purana

21

The Defeat of Kamsa

As Krishna grew up, his uncle Kamsa, the evil king, became more and more anxious that Krishna would come and assassinate him - as the old man had predicted. He heard that Krishna was a brilliant athlete. So he organized at one of his palaces a great tournament, and invited Krishna to come. Krishna, who was eager to show off his prowess, eagerly accepted.

At the start of the tournament there were races, as well as high-jump and long-jump competitions. The finest athletes in the kingdom competed against Krishna; but Krishna beat them all. Then Kamsa announced that there would be a wrestling contest; and he ordered the four largest and strongest men of the kingdom to take on Krishna - in the hope that one of them would kill him.

The first man tried to strangle Krishna; but Krishna took him by the throat, and squeezed so hard that the man's eyeballs popped out. The second man tried to punch Krishna on the head; but Krishna knelt down, grabbed him by the ankle, and hurled him into the crowd. The third man had a knife, and tried to stab Krishna; but Krishna seized the hand in which he held the knife, and forced him to stab himself. The fourth man was so frightened that he ran away

Kamsa was now purple with rage. And in his fury he drew his sword, and attacked Krishna himself. But Krishna pulled him down by his hair, hauled him into the river, pushed his head under the water, and drowned him.

Bhagavata Purana

22

On the Eve of Battle

Krishna now decided to seek enlightenment. So he went to live in a forest, and for a year he meditated on God and the soul. He also took a vow never again to engage in acts of violence.

Meanwhile there was a dispute over who was the rightful king. Two rival claimants to the throne were cousins; each assembled a vast army, and prepared for battle. The brother of one of them, called Arjuna, sent a message to Krishna, begging for his help; Krishna offered to be Arjuna's charioteer.

On the eve of the battle Arjuna asked Krishna to drive him in his chariot across the land that lay between the two armies, so that he could see his opponents. When he saw members of his own family on the other side, including his own uncle who was blind, Arjuna was appalled. 'I'm weak at the knees,' he said to Krishna, 'my mouth is dry, my body trembles, and my hair is bristling. I can hardly stand, and my head is swimming. What good can come from killing our own flesh and blood in battle? If we win tomorrow, there will be no pleasure, but only sadness.'

'This despair and weakness is unworthy of you,' said Krishna; 'I'm astonished that you have allowed your emotions to overcome you. Tomorrow courage must fill your heart, and you must destroy your enemy.' Tears welled up in Arjuna's eyes. 'I should rather be a beggar in the street than kill cousins whom I love and respect,' he exclaimed - and then fell silent.

Bhagavad Gita

23

LIFE, DEATH AND DUTY

Krishna stopped the chariot. Some distance to the left the army led by Arjuna's brother was camped; and to the right was the enemy army. It was now dusk, and amongst the tents thousands of fires were burning, on which the soldiers were cooking their dinner.

'You speak honestly,' Krishna said to Arjuna, 'but your sorrow is foolish. In the battle tomorrow you may be killed, or you may kill. Your body may die tomorrow, or it may die in many years time when you have grown old; every body must eventually die. But the soul can never be killed; not even the longest and the sharpest sword can pierce it. So why should you worry about being killed, or about killing?

'While your body lives, you should do your duty. If you were a carpenter, your duty would be to make furniture and build houses. If you were a shopkeeper, your duty would be to sell goods that people want. If you were a farmer, your duty would be to grow food for people to eat. If you were a priest, your duty would be to perform religious rituals. But you are a warrior; so your duty is to train for battle - and, when confronted by an enemy, to fight with skill and courage. If you refuse to fight this battle, you will be neglecting your duty - and so dishonoring the soul.'

'You are right, dear Krishna,' Arjuna said; 'I shall fight tomorrow as a true warrior. If I am to die, I should like to hear about God and the soul before my death; and if I am to survive, I should like to live in unity with God and the soul. So tell me what you know.'

Bhagavad Gita

24

The Yoga of Action and Devotion

Krishna climbed down from the chariot, followed by Arjuna, and they sat together on the ground. Krishna spoke:

In order to become enlightened, and live in unity with God and the soul, you must practice yoga. There are three forms of yoga. The first is the yoga of action; and this consists in doing your duty. This does not mean merely performing tasks set by others. Rather it means serving others, according to your particular abilities and skills, with the same devotion as you serve yourself. Foolish people, who despise yoga, work only for their own profit; they think this will make them happy, but in fact it makes them miserable. Wise people, who practice yoga, work for the welfare of all people; and by making others happy, they make themselves happy also.

In order to serve others, you must control your own selfish desires. A fire may be covered by smoke, and a mirror may be covered by dust; likewise selfish desires obscure the soul - both the soul within you, and the soul within others. But when you conquer selfish desires, you see the soul clearly. And since the soul within yourself is the same as the soul within others, you wish to serve yourself and others with equal care.

As you practice the yoga of action, a moment will come when you think: "I am not performing these actions. My body is merely acting as the soul requires."

The second form of yoga is the yoga of devotion. This consists in becoming aware of God's beauty, and loving him with all your heart.

Bhagavad Gita

25

THE YOGA OF KNOWLEDGE

The third form of yoga is the yoga of knowledge. This does not mean knowledge of facts. It means direct knowledge of the soul, attained through quiet meditation; and this leads to knowledge of God.

In order to meditate, you must free yourself from all feelings of anger and hatred. When you are angry and hateful, your mind is obsessed with the objects of your anger and hatred; so you cannot turn your mind inwards to the soul. Thus day by day, and moment by moment, watch over your heart; and whenever an angry or hateful emotion arises, banish it immediately.

Meditate at least once each day. Go to a place where you will not be disturbed; then sit down, and relax. Hold your body, neck and head upright in a straight line. Breathe steadily, with an unchanging rhythm. Calm your mind by focusing your attention on a single point. You may keep your eyes open, staring at a candle or a mark on the wall in front of you; or you may close your eyes, fixing your mind on the center of your forehead.

From time to time your mind will wander, thinking of various pleasures. When this happens, grasp your mind firmly, pulling its attention back to the single point. Banish at once any evil or impure thoughts that enter your mind.

Through meditation you will gradually become aware of the soul within you; and as you become aware of the soul within you, you will become aware of the soul within all living creatures. As this knowledge deepens, so meditation grows easier.'

Bhagavad Gita

26

THE MOUNTAIN AND THE CAVE

As you practice the yoga of action and of knowledge, you will climb the mountain of oneness. At the summit of this mountain there is perfect unity with the soul and God; and you experience peace and joy beyond description.

As you practice the yoga of action and of knowledge, you will enter the cave of light. In this cave the soul appears before you as a lamp, whose brightness is beyond imagination, and whose flame is utterly steady.

Nothing can now disturb your serenity. You are not elated by good fortune or success, nor are you upset by misfortune or failure. You have no desire to excel over others in your various tasks, nor are you upset by others excelling over you. You do not regard one person as more important than another, but treat all people with courtesy. You do not look for pleasure, but are grateful when it comes; you do not dread pain, but seek to remove it when it comes. You are kind to friends and enemies equally. Praise does not swell your head, nor does blame depress you. You perform your duties without complaint or resentment; but you do not condemn those who fail to perform their duties.

Death no longer has any power of you. You are happy to be alive in this body. But the prospect of death through injury, illness or old age does not frighten you, because you know that after death you will enter heaven.

This is the state of enlightenment. And others will be aware of your state, because your face will be radiant.'

Bhagavad Gita

27

The Equality of All Religions

Since every living being contains the soul, and since the soul is divine, every living being is the body of God. Every man and woman, and every boy and girl, embodies God. Every animal and insect, and every bird and fish, embodies God. Every tree and shrub, and every flower and blade of grass, embodies God.

Since every religion aims to enlighten people, and since enlightenment is divine, every religion comes from God. Every ritual and sacrifice, and every prayer and hymn, is guided by God. Every holy book and wise sermon, and every parable and miracle, is inspired by God. Every sincere prophet and priest, and every honest preacher and teacher, is prompted by God.

God does not love one living being more than another; he loves all equally. God does not love one religion more than another; he loves all equally. So you should show equal kindness to all the living beings in your care. And you should show equal respect to all religions. You may practice the religion whichever you like, in the manner that suits you; but never despise the religions which others practice.'

Krishna now fell silent. His words had satisfied Arjuna, so he too was silent. They climbed back onto the chariot, and rode to their tent. On the following day Arjuna's side was victorious, and his brother became king.

Krishna returned to the forest, where he lived alone; many people came to him for wisdom, and he taught them as he had taught Arjuna.

Bhagavad Gita

28

YOGA TECHNIQUE

Inspired by the teachings of Krishna on the yoga of knowledge, a guru called Patanjali developed a technique for practicing this form of yoga:

The purpose of yoga is to become free from spiritual disturbance, and to attain perfect knowledge of the soul. Through yoga the soul becomes perfectly tranquil and serene; without yoga the soul is contantly subject to disturbance.

In order to attain perfect knowledge, you must climb up the seven steps of yogic practice. The seven steps are abstinence, correct posture, correct breathing, control of the senses, steadiness of mind, concentration, meditation, and integration.

Abstinence has five aspects. The first is abstaining from violence. The second is abstaining from falsehood. The third is abstaining from theft. The fourth is abstaining from sexual immorality. And the fifth is abstaining from avarice. These five aspects of abstinence are universal, and must be practiced regardless of time, place and circumstances.

The correct posture for yoga is one that enables your body to be both firm and relaxed. The purpose of the correct posture is to keep your mind alert and attentive, without effort. Any tensions in the body upset alertness and attentiveness.

The correct breathing for yoga is regular and calm. The length or shortness of each breath does not matter, so long as it is steady. The purpose of correct breathing is to keep your mind alert and attentive, without effort.

Patanjali: Yoga Sutra

29

UNIFIED CONSCIOUSNESS

Control of the senses requires you to make your senses unresponsive to stimuli. You should watch over your sense organs, suppressing every feeling of excitement that comes from them.

There are various methods of learning to hold the mind steady. One method is to become aware of your own awareness of sensory objects - to focus your attention on the senses themselves, rather than on the objects of the senses. Another method is to focus your eyes on a source of light. Another method is to hold your attention steady during a dream, or in that state between waking and sleeping. Another method is to fix your attention on some particular external object.

Concentration means holding consciousness steady, in a single position.

Meditation means allowing knowledge to flow without interruption through consciousness.

Integration occurs when consciousness ceases to regard even itself as an object of consciousness.

When there is concentration, meditation and integration, there is complete unity of consciousness, which is perfect knowledge of the soul. The soul transcends time and place, and enters eternity and infinity.

When you have mastered the practice of yoga, you may enter this state of unified consciousness whenever you wish.

Patanjali: Yoga Sutra

30

Devotion to Krishna

Inspired by Krishna's teachings on the yoga of devotion, a poet called Mirabai wrote verses in honor of Krishna himself:

Krishna is my life; the world tastes bitter to me. I love Krishna only; let my eyes see no one and nothing but him.

Krishna is divinity in the form of a man, and his beauty enraptures me. If he sees me in the bazaar or on the street, he teases me. His eyes are like lotus flowers; and when he glances at me, I feel weak. He has a herd of cattle that graze by the river; and he sits nearby playing his flute. I shall throw myself at his feet, and surrender myself - my heart and my body - to him. He is my lord.

When my lord goes away, I look out for him constantly; I long for him to return. My eyes ache from staring at the horizon. I cannot rest, and every night seems like half a year. No-one can understand the pain of my separation; no-one listens to my sorrow. I cry out: 'My Lord, when shall I see you? When will you make me happy again?'

When my lord returns, he dances for my pleasure; yes, I have seen him dance. In his presence I feel no hunger or weariness; I want neither food nor sleep. People mock me for my devotion to him; my relatives swarm around me like bees, and tell me I am foolish. But I do not care. I am the servant of my lord; and serving him is my only desire.

My Lord, remain always by my side, for I am your most ardent lover. Nothing pleases my heart except your presence. When you talk and laugh with me, I am happy.

Mirabai: Poems

31

THE GURUS' PRAYER

The gurus of India taught at the beginning of any act of worship, or when settling down to meditate, people should recite this prayer:

From falsehood lead me to truth.
From darkness lead me to light.
From death lead me to eternity.

They said that if you understand these words, you have conquered the world; and if you have conquered the world, you are free from all fear.

Brihadaranyaka Upanishad

MONTH

2

BUDDHISM

Introduction

Origins

In northern India in the middle of the first millennium BCE there were numerous religious sects and monastic communities. They mostly claimed to be following the ancient Hindu wisdom. But some were materialistic, with their leaders bent on accumulating wealth and power for themselves. And others advocated extreme asceticism; they believed that by starving the body, and even renouncing clothes and shelter, the soul would be liberated. The Buddha taught a middle way between materialism and asceticism, which he summarized in a few simple principles.

He was born around 560 BCE, and was given the name Gautama. His father was probably a minor ruler, controlling an area near the border with Nepal. His mother died when he was young; and his doting father tried to protect him from all suffering. But when as a young man he encountered disease, old age and death, he was overwhelmed with sadness. He left his father's palace, in order to find the cause of suffering and eliminate it.

At first he believed that the body was the cause of suffering; and he devoted six years to asceticism in order to detach the soul from the body. But he was still inwardly in turmoil, so he resumed a normal diet. He now found he could meditate for long periods. And finally, in the course of a single night, he attained enlightenment (***bodhi***) – and was utterly at peace within himself.

He spent the rest of his life teaching others what he had learnt that night. And he formed a community (***sangha***) of monks and nuns to share this task.

Teachings

Gautama's first disciples gave him the title ***Budha***(enlightened one), and he taught that all people could become buddhas.

The core of the Buddha's teaching is the four Truths: that there is suffering in world, to which all living beings are subject; that desire is the cause of suffering; that suffering would cease if desire ceased; and that there is a path leading to the cessation of suffering.

This path is the eightfold Way. The first part is right vision, which consists in grasping the four Truths. The next four parts concern morality: right purpose, which consists in never deliberately harming another living being; right speech; right action; and right livelihood. The final three parts concern spirituality: right effort, which involves controlling the mind; right vigilance, which consists in controlling the emotions; and right meditation. At the end of the eightfold Way the soul is enlightened.

Right effort and vigilance comprise the first stage of meditation. The second stage involves focusing the mind on a single point. The third and fourth stage consist in emptying the mind of all feeling, even feelings of joy and tranquility.

The Buddha accepted the prevailing belief in reincarnation; so a person may follow the eightfold Way over many hundreds and even thousands of lives before attaining enlightenment – and hence becoming a buddha. At death buddhas are not reborn but enter eternal bliss (***nirvana***).

EXPRESSION

Soon after the Buddha's death the senior monks met, and began the task of recording his teachings. But it was not until about 240 BCE, when an emperor of India called Asoka converted to Buddhism, that a written collection of the Buddha's teachings was agreed; it is referred to as the Pali Canon, after the language in which it is written. The Canon shows the Buddha as an eloquent preacher; but it contains many dialogues, in which he responded to individual needs. It contains almost no information about him prior to his enlightenment; the stories about his early life come from a biography written by Ashvagosha in the first century CE.

After the Buddha's death his body was divided; and each part was buried under a large mound (***stupa***) that was covered with stone. Subsequently stupas were built across India and beyond. Most stupas have a platform around the base, where people may walk and meditate; and at the top they have a spire.

The Pali Canon records that the Buddha wanted people to visit places associated with his life, as a means of remembering his teaching. The four main sites of Buddhist pilgrimage are his place of birth, Kapilavastu, where Asoka erected a pillar; Bodh Gaya, where the tree, under which he was enlightened, still grows; the park of Varanasi, where he first preached; and Kusinara, where he died and entered nirvana.

The main subject of Buddhist art is the Buddha himself. He is usually depicted sitting with his legs crossed in the full lotus position – his feet turned upwards on his thighs.

Us

When we suffer any kind of pain, physical or emotional, we naturally regard it as an aberration from our proper condition; and our response is to look for its cause externally. The four Truths teach us that suffering is central to the human condition; and that we should look for its cause within ourselves.

In the eightfold Way the Buddha offers a practical means of changing ourselves, to rid ourselves of all suffering, and to attain a form of joy that no external events can disturb. The Way carries an implicit warning to those who want immediately to engage in spiritual activity: we must first learn to live according to the highest standards of morality – or else our spirituality will be vain. The Buddha himself demonstrated this, with his unfailing compassion and kindness.

Unless we are exceptional, we should not expect to pass beyond the first stage of meditation in this life. But this brings great benefits: we shall know how to relax; and we shall be free of negative thoughts and feelings, which are the source of much pain.

The Buddha asks us to believe nothing on his authority. In the four Truths he seeks to open our eyes; and the proof of the Way is people's experience of following it.

1

The Birth of Gautama

There was once a king who was renowned for his kindness to all his people. Whenever poor people came to his palace for help, he gave them food and clothing. Whenever someone died in his kingdom, he rode out from his palace to visit the grieving family, and offered words of comfort. And whenever people quarreled, he tried to reconcile them. This king had a wife whose beauty was famous throughout the world; and her gentle, generous character matched her outward appearance.

One afternoon, when she was having a nap, she dreamt that a white elephant entered her body. That night she conceived a child. During the following months she suffered none of the nausea, tiredness and depression that often afflict pregnant women. Every morning she rode out into the forest near the palace, sat beneath a tree, and meditated. As she meditated she came to realize that the child within her was destined for greatness. And although she had no idea what form this greatness would take, she assumed that, if the child were male, he would be a great king, like his father; or if the child were female, she would be a great queen.

As the time of birth approached, the king assembled nurses from throughout his kingdom to assist. A special bed was made by the finest craftsman, and put in the center of the great hall of the palace; and a massive awning was spread above it. The baby was male; and he was born without his mother suffering any pain. The king and queen named him Gautama.

Ashvagosha: Buddhacarita

2

ASITA'S PROPHECY

At the moment of Gautama's birth a wise old man, called Asita, was meditating in the forest near the palace. He saw within his mind a baby whose limbs shone like gold, and who was surrounded by a bright light. He hurried to the palace, went to the couch where Gautama and his mother lay, and knelt down.

Then his whole body began to shake. 'What is upsetting you?' the king asked anxiously. 'It's not for the baby that I am upset,' Asita replied, 'but for me. I have searched all my life for someone to show me how all misery and suffering can be ended, and how perfect happiness can be attained. Your son is destined to show the path to true happiness. But I am now so old, that I shall be dead long before he reaches adulthood; so I shall never hear his words. That is why I weep with sadness.'

Asita returned to the forest, and resumed his meditation. He thought of all the people whose lives would be transformed by Gautama's teaching – whose misery would be turned into joy. And this thought brought him great joy. That night he died, with a happy, peaceful smile on his lips.

A few weeks later Gautama's mother also died. She suffered no illness, but simply stopped breathing; and, like Asita, she had a happy, peaceful smile on her lips. The king placed Gautama in the care of the queen's sister, and urged her to treat him as if he were her own son. Since she had no children of her own, her grief at the queen's death was turned into joy; so she was the first person whom Gautama made happy.

Ashvagosha: Buddhacarita

3

THE OLD MAN

The king could not forget Asita's prophecy; and he dreaded that Gautama would one day leave the palace, and go in search of the path to perfect happiness. So the king turned the top storey of his palace into a luxurious apartment for his son. The walls were painted white and gold; the floor was marble, covered with finely woven carpets; and everywhere there were cushions covered in silk. A team of chefs cooked the finest food; and beautiful young women played flutes and harps. Gautama enjoyed life in his apartment so much that for the first twenty years of his life he never left it.

But one day the musicians told Gautama about the trees that grew in the forest; they described the thick trunks, the slender branches, and the leaves and blossoms that sprouted from the branches. Gautama was determined to see these trees for himself. The king heard of his son's intention; and he ordered that every old, poor and disabled person be banished from the area between the palace and the forest, so Gautama's mind would not be disturbed by the sight of human suffering.

Gautama set out in a golden carriage, drawn by six white stallions. The young and healthy people of the kingdom lined his route, eager to catch a glimpse of the young prince. When they reached the forest, Gautama climbed out of the carriage. At that moment an old man, who had not heard the king's order, appeared; his face was wrinkled and his back bent. Gautama was so shocked at the sight of him, that he hurried back into the carriage, and ordered the driver to take him back to the palace.

Ashvagosha: Buddhacarita

4

The Disabled Woman

As he rode in the golden carriage back to the palace, Gautama asked the driver about the old man he had seen. The driver explained to Gautama how every human being grows old: the skin becomes wrinkled, the hair turns gray, the limbs weaken, the joints of the bones ache, the back bends, and the body becomes prone to every kind of disease. 'So the vigor and beauty of youth do not last forever!' Gautama exclaimed.

In his apartment Gautama could no longer enjoy the fine food that the chefs cooked for him, and the music that the young women played; the image of the old man in the forest filled his mind and troubled his heart. After a few days he decided to return to the forest, in the hope that the trees would bring tranquility. Again the king ordered that every old, poor and disabled person be banished from the area; and again the young and healthy people lined Gautama's route, eager to catch another glimpse of his handsome face.

When they reached the forest and Gautama climbed down from his carriage, a disabled woman appeared. One of her legs was missing, and her skin was covered in a red rash. Gautama was even more horrified than at the sight of the old man; he hurried back into the carriage, and ordered the driver to take him home.

As they returned to the palace, the driver explained to Gautama how many people are born with disabilities. 'So the vigor and beauty of youth is permanently denied them!' Gautama exclaimed.

Ashvagosha: Buddhacarita

5

THE DEAD WIFE AND THE GRIEVING HUSBAND

Gautama now found every kind of pleasure repulsive. When he tried to eat the fine food that the chefs prepared, he felt sick; and when the young women played, their music sounded to him like the screams of people in agony. Again he decided to return to the forest, in the hope that the trees would restore his tranquility.

On his way to the forest he saw a man weeping, with a woman lying on the ground beside him. Gautama asked his driver to stop the carriage, and he stepped down. 'Why are you weeping?' Gautama asked. 'My wife and I were waiting here for you,' the man replied, 'so we could see your handsome face. But then suddenly she put her hands to her chest, and fell to the ground. A few minutes later she was dead.'

Gautama knelt down beside the woman, and saw a look of pain on her face. He touched her forehead, and already it was cold. Then looked up to the sky, and exclaimed: 'Does all life come to this? Must every living being eventually die? Are we all destined to grieve over the deaths of those we love?' He too began to weep.

The driver of the chariot helped Gautama to his feet, led him to the carriage, and took him back to the palace. That night Gautama could not sleep; the images of the old man, the disabled woman, the grieving husband, and his dead wife haunted him. He felt like a lion whose heart has been pierced by a poisoned arrow. It seemed to him that the world outside his apartment was full of suffering and misery; and he had no idea how it could be relieved.

Ashvagosha: Buddhacarita

6

Injured animals and insects

The following day he decided to go out into the countryside, in the hope that the sight of fields and hedges and livestock would ease his mind and heart. He took with him in his carriage three young men who were gifted at telling funny and entertaining stories.

At first the combination of the young men's stories, and the sight of men plowing the fields and women milking cows, brought Gautama relief. For the first time since his initial trip from the palace he found himself smiling and laughing. Then he asked the driver to stop the carriage, so he could walk freely in the fields.

He followed a man who was plowing. He looked closely at the man's face, and saw how the skin had been roughened and worn by the sun and the wind. He looked at the oxen pulling the plough, and saw how their backs were sore from the yoke. And he looked down at the earth, and saw the worms and insects that had been injured and killed as the plough cut through the turf. He fell to the ground, overcome with sadness.

As he lay there, an intense desire for solitude rose up within him. Eventually he rose to his feet. Then he ordered the driver of the carriage to take the three young men back to the palace, and leave him behind. The driver protested, saying that the king, Gautama's father, would be angry and upset. But Gautama was insistent.

He walked away from the fields, where people were working, towards an orchard; and he sat down beneath an apple tree, whose branches shaded him from the sun. For the first time in his life Gautama was alone.

Ashvagosha: Buddhacarita

7

THE OLD HERMIT

As Gautama sat beneath the apple tree, he reflected that all suffering derives from people's desires and attachments. It is because people desire the vigor and beauty of youth, that they become distressed at old age. It is because they desire physical agility, that they are frustrated by disability. It is because they desire pleasure, that they dread pain. It is because they are emotionally attached to relatives and friends, that they are stricken by grief at the death of a relative or friend. It is because they are attached to living, that they fear dying. To his surprise these thoughts eased his mind, and he felt peaceful.

An old man appeared; he wore only a dirty cloth round his face, and his body was so thin that every bone was visible through his wrinkled skin. 'Who are you?' Gautama asked. 'I am a hermit,' the old man replied, 'who is terrified by pain and death – like most other living beings. And I have dedicated my life to seeking freedom from pain and death.' 'How have you undertaken that search?' Gautama asked. The old man answered: 'Long ago I gave away my home and my all possessions. Since that time I have wandered from place to place. I have eaten whatever food people may give me, and rested at night under trees and hedges.' 'Why have you chosen to live in this way?' Gautama asked. 'By denying myself all pleasures,' the man said, 'I hope to become free from all pain.' 'Have you found this freedom?' Gautama asked. 'Not yet,' the old man said; 'but I continue my search. And with these words the old man left.

Gautama knew that he too must abandon his home and his possessions.

Ashvagosha: Buddhacarita

8

FLIGHT FROM THE PALACE

It was now almost dusk. Gautama walked back to the palace, and went up to his apartment. The musicians and the chefs were lying asleep on cushions; and as he looked at them, he felt both intense love, and also repulsion for the way of life that they had provided for him. 'Farewell, brothers and sisters,' he whispered. Then he looked into a cupboard, where he found a large yellow piece of cloth; he put it into a bag, and left.

He went to the cottage next to the stables, where the driver of the carriage lived. He knocked on the door; and when the driver opened it, he was astonished to see the young prince. 'I want you to take your strongest horse,' Gautama said, 'and ride out of the palace, with me sitting behind you. I shall direct you where to go.' The driver was perplexed, but did as Gautama commanded. The two men rode throughout the night, and crossed the border into another kingdom; and at dawn they arrived at the bank of a river.

Gautama dismounted. He took off all his fine clothes, which were made of silk and studded with diamonds and rubies. He took out the yellow cloth from his bag, and wrapped it round himself. Then he put his princely clothes into the bag, and handed it to the driver.

'This is the last order I shall ever give you,' Gautama said, ' and I want you to obey it without protest. Return to the palace, and tell my father, the king, that I have renounced the life of a prince, in order to search for true and lasting happiness. Tell him not to grieve, because all human attachments must eventually be broken.'

Ashvagosha: Buddhacarita

9

SELF-TORTURE

The driver wept, but said nothing. He turned the horse round, and rode slowly back to the palace.

Gautama spent the next six years living as a hermit, and denied himself every pleasure and comfort. He ate each day only one piece of fruit, a few grains of rice, and a few sesame seeds; he allowed himself only a few hours of sleep each night, and often did not sleep at all; he never washed; and he had no shelter from the sun and the rain apart from the trees of the forest. His body gradually wasted away, so that it became little more than a skeleton. He believed that the body was the source of suffering; so he hoped to make himself numb to all bodily feelings – and then attain inner happiness.

Nearby there were five other men living in a similar fashion, who also hoped to attain inner peace and happiness. They were astonished at Gautama's capacity to forgo food and sleep; they each ate and slept far more than he did. So they asked him to be their teacher. 'I am honored by your request,' Gautama replied; ' but I am not yet worthy to be anyone's teacher. Although I eat and sleep little, my mind and my heart are still in turmoil.'

Eventually Gautama realized that torturing his body in this fashion was useless. He said to himself: 'I enjoyed greater tranquility when I first meditated under the apple tree, than I do now. In fact I am now so weak that I can't meditate at all. So I must start to nourish my body again.'

Ashvagosha: Buddhacarita

10

Eating and meditating

To prepare himself for food Gautama bathed in the river. But he was so weak that he had great difficulty in pulling himself out of the water; he grabbed hold of an overhanging branch with both hands, and dragged himself onto the bank.

A milkmaid walked each morning and evening along the bank, between her home and her cattle. As she passed that morning, Gautama beckoned to her; she came over to him, and he begged her for food. She was appalled to see his emaciated state; and she willingly gave him her midday meal, packed in a cloth; it consisted of rice boiled in milk. From then onwards she prepared food especially for him, and gradually his body regained its normal shape.

When the five other men saw that Gautama was eating a full meal each day, and was putting on weight, they were disgusted. 'You have betrayed us and our way of life,' they said to him; 'you should be ashamed of yourself.' Gautama said nothing.

Gautama now found that he was able to meditate again; and he sat cross-legged under a tree, day after day and night after night. For a few months he felt quite peaceful; but then three different kinds of emotions welled inside him, one after the other. The first emotion was fear: he felt very frightened of death. The second was elation: he felt as a child does anticipating some treat. The third was pride: he felt himself to be spiritually superior to all other human beings. He fought against each of these emotions in turn, and defeated them.

Ashvagosha: Buddhacarita

11

The Four Truths

Gautama now knew he was on the verge of attaining his goal. He felt impelled to forgo sleep entirely, and spend a whole night meditating.

In the first quarter of the night he perceived within his mind the suffering of the world. He saw rich and powerful people forcing the poor and the weak to work hard throughout the day, and yet giving them only the most meager wages. He saw human beings forcing animals to pull plows and carts all day, and yet giving them only a few handfuls of hay at night. He saw kings going to war with one another, destroying entire towns and villages in the violence. And as Gautama observed all this misery, he himself felt miserable.

In the second quarter of the night he realized that desire is the cause of suffering. The rich oppress the poor because they desire to become richer. Humans oppress animals because they desire more than their own labor can provide. Kings go to war because they desire greater power.

In the third quarter of the night Gautama understood that suffering would cease if desire ceased. If the rich were free from desire, they would share their riches with the poor, and all would have enough. If humans were content with what their own labor can provide, they would cherish the animals in their care. If kings were willing simply to serve their people, there would be no more wars.

Gautama now said to himself: 'I have grasped three Truths.'

Vinaya Pitaka: Mahavagga

12

THE EIGHTFOLD WAY

During the final quarter of the night Gautama grasped the fourth Truth: that there is a Way leading to the cessation of suffering – and this Way has eight parts.

The first part is right vision; this consists in grasping the four Truths.

The second part is right purpose; this consists in renouncing all violence, and never deliberately harming another living being. The third part is right speech; this consists in never telling lies, never speaking harshly to other people, and never spreading false rumors about other people. The fourth part is right action; this consists in never taking what has not been freely given. The fifth part is right livelihood; this consists in working honestly, and never profiting from deceit, fraud or oppression. These parts concern morality – how people live in the world.

The sixth part is right effort; this consists in controlling the mind, to drive out all hateful and selfish thoughts. The seventh part is right vigilance; this consists in watching over the heart, to drive out hateful and selfish impulses and emotions. The eighth part is right meditation, by which inner serenity is attained. These parts concern spirituality.

It was now dawn. As he surveyed the Way within his mind, he realized that he was standing at the end of it; and he was basking in an inner light that was far brighter than the outer light of the sun. 'At last I am enlightened,' he thought. He spent the next seven days in silent meditation, enjoying the bliss of being enlightened. He arose from his meditation only to eat and drink.

Vinaya Pitaka: Mahavagga

13

THE DECISION TO TEACH OTHERS

At the end of the seven days he asked himself whether he should tell others about the Truths and the Way. 'The Truths,' he thought, are very hard to grasp. The human mind recoils from the idea that desire is the cause of suffering; most people believe that if they satisfy their desires, they will be happy. So, if I speak publicly about the Truths and the Way, most people will either be baffled, or they will become hostile. That would irritate me, and make me cross. It is better for me to remain silent.' He then resumed his meditation.

A few hours later he was suddenly filled with compassion. In his mind he looked across the world. He saw some people in whom the soul was covered by only a few specks of dust; and he saw others in whom the soul was darkened by a thick layer of dust. 'Those with the thick layer of dust,' he thought, 'would be hard to teach. But those with only a few specks of dust would be easy to teach; and as they followed the Way, those specks would be wiped away - they would be enlightened, as I am. So for their sake I must speak publicly.'

He now wondered to whom he should first speak. He thought of returning to his father; but he feared that the luxury of the royal palace, the anxieties of ruling a nation, and the grief of losing his heir, would have darkened the soul. It then occurred to him that he should go to the five men who six years earlier had asked him to be their teacher. He went to the deer park in the city of Varanasi, where they were staying.

Vinaya Pitaka: Mahavagga

14

GAUTAMA THE BUDDHA

The five men were still disgusted at Gautama's decision to eat a normal diet; so as they saw him approach, they remained seated. But when he drew closer, they noticed that his complexion was bright and glowing; and they realized at once that some momentous change had occurred within him. Without thinking, they rose to their feet, walked over to him, and knelt down in front of him, with their foreheads touching the ground.

'Let us sit together,' Gautama said, 'and I shall tell what I have learnt.' He knew that they each had only a few specks of dust covering the soul; so he spoke to them quite briefly about the Way. At once they fully understood his words. 'You are the Buddha, the enlightened one!' they exclaimed. 'You too are buddhas,' he replied, ' because you too are now enlightened.' 'You attained enlightenment through you own meditation,' they said, 'whereas we depended on your teaching.' From that moment onwards Gautama was known as the Buddha. And the five men were his first followers - the first Buddhists.

Later that day two merchants passed by; they were leading mules loaded with silks and spices that they intended to sell in the market place. They saw the Buddha and his five disciples, and asked the Buddha if he would teach them something that would inspire them. 'Let us eat first,' the Buddha replied, 'and then our minds will be strong.' The merchants took out from a bag a large number of cakes, made from rice and covered in honey. When they had all eaten, the Buddha taught the merchants about the Way; and they too became disciples.

Vinaya Pitaka: Mahavagga

15

THE BUDDHA'S COMMUNITY

'Now that we're your disciples,' the merchants said, 'should we live as you do, out in the open with no home and no possessions?' 'No,' the Buddha replied, 'people should live as their nature and destiny requires. For some the life of the monk or nun is right; and by abandoning their homes and possessions, they can devote themselves entirely to meditation and to teaching others. For others it is right to be married, to have children, to work, and to have a home. Both types of people can follow the Way in their own fashion – although it is easier for monks and nuns to reach the end, and attain full enlightenment.'

The Buddha then rose to his feet, and declared: 'This day I form a community, that will last as long as my name is remembered. It is open to anyone who wishes to follow the eightfold Way as a monk or nun. And I invite my five companions, who gave me my title, to be the first members.' He turned to the five men, and beckoned them to stand in front of him. 'If you wish to accept my invitation, raise your arms, join your hands together, and declare your commitment three times to the Way.' Each of the men in turn raised his arms, joined his hands together, and declared his commitment three times.

'I do not ask lay disciples, who continue to live in their homes, to join any kind of community. But I ask them to seek spiritual and moral guidance from monks and nuns, as and when they need it; and to provide food and clothing for monks and nuns.' The merchants agreed both to seek guidance, and, as far as their wealth allowed, to provide food and clothing.

Vinaya Pitaka: Mahavagga

16

THE MONKS' WAY OF LIFE

The Buddha then instructed the merchants to go to the market to purchase yellow robes for the five monks to wear, so they would be dressed like the Buddha himself; he also asked them to buy a razor. When the merchants returned, the five monks each put on a yellow robe. The Buddha then shaved each of their heads, so their bald heads shone in the sun; and he asked one the monks to shave his own head. 'From now onwards,' the Buddha declared, 'people will know the members of my community by their yellow robes and shaved heads.'

The Buddha said to the merchants: 'For the next few weeks I do not want you to give us food. We shall rely on the generosity of the people of the city.' He then told the merchants to return to their homes.

Every morning the Buddha and the five monks went into the city. They each stood in the main street carrying a bowl, and waited for people to put food in it. Many people were suspicious of them, and refused to give anything; so on some days their bowls remained empty. But usually a few people were struck by the brightness of their faces, and said to themselves: 'This brightness may be a sign of inner enlightenment; and in times of difficulty their advice may be helpful.' And with these thoughts they filled the bowls.

In the evenings a growing number of people came to the park where the Buddha was staying. He asked each person many questions, so that he understood fully that person's spiritual and moral needs – and only then did he offer advice.

Vinaya Pitaka: Mahavagga

17

THE RICH YOUNG MAN

The wealthiest merchant in the city had a son called Yasa. From the boy's earliest years the merchant had given him all he wanted; and when Yasa reached adulthood, the merchant built a great mansion for him; and he employed beautiful young women to entertain the young man with music and dancing.

One evening Yasa fell asleep earlier than usual; and as a result he awoke early, just as dawn was breaking. He looked around him at the women sleeping nearby. Their hair was disheveled; the make-up on their faces had turned streaky with sweat; and one, who had drunk heavily, had saliva dripping from her mouth. 'How quickly human beauty can fade away!' he thought. And a few moments later he thought: 'How quickly every pleasure fades away!'

Yasa had seen the Buddha in the city street, and had heard he was staying in the park. So he slipped out of his mansion, and ran there. He threw himself at the Buddha's feet, and exclaimed: 'Show me the happiness that never fades.' 'What has caused you to make this request?' the Buddha asked. Yasa told him about the sight of the female musicians asleep. 'Those musicians have done you a great favor,' the Buddha said with a smile; 'they have wiped away much of the dirt within you; now only a few specks remain.'

The Buddha then taught Yasa the Truths and the Way. Yasa was determined to devote his whole life to following the Way. So he asked to join the monastic community, and the Buddha received him.

Vinaya Pitaka: Mahavagga

18

THE WEALTHY FATHER

In the meantime Yasa's mother had called at his mansion, as she did each morning; and when she had found him missing, she had rushed to tell her husband, Yasa's father. He sent his servants on horseback in every direction in search of Yasa; and he himself happened to go the park.

He was astonished to see his son sitting cross-legged next to the Buddha. 'Your mother is beside herself with anxiety at your disappearance,' he exclaimed; 'go to her at once, and tell her you are safe.' Yasa turned to the Buddha, and asked for permission to go; and the Buddha ordered him to run to his mother, to relieve her anxiety.

'Why did my son come and see you?' Yasa's father asked. The Buddha replied by explaining to him the Way. At the end Yasa's father bowed before the Buddha, and said: 'By teaching that desire is the cause of suffering, and not the signpost to happiness, you overturn all conventional attitudes. I do not fully understand you, but in my heart I know that you are right. Please accept me as a disciple, so that in the fullness of time I may become enlightened.'

'Before I answer your request,' the Buddha said, 'I must ask you a question. Do you want your son to return to his mansion, and continue devoting himself to pleasure? Or would you prefer him to become a monk in my community?' Yasa's father paused, and said: 'Come today with your monks, and have your meal at my house; in the meantime I shall consider your question.' The Buddha accepted the invitation.

Vinaya Pitaka: Mahavagga

19

The first female Buddhist

At midday the Buddha led his five monks to the vast mansion, almost as large as the royal palace, in which Yasa's father lived. The Buddha sat between Yasa's father and mother; and Yasa himself, as a public display of his commitment to the Buddha, served them. 'Can you now answer my question?' the Buddha asked Yasa's father. 'I have spent the past few hours in great turmoil,' he replied, 'because I have always hoped that Yasa would take over the great business which I have created. Yet I now see clearly that wealth does not bring lasting happiness – and that he can only be happy by following your Way. Therefore I entrust him to your care.'

When she heard these words, Yasa's mother was livid. 'He is my only son,' she cried; 'he is the light of my life. I shan't allow him to leave me, and live with this strange man in a yellow robe.' Her husband begged her to listen to the Buddha's teaching. The Buddha then explained to her the Way. At the end her anger had turned to joy. 'Not only do I gladly entrust my son to you,' she cried, 'but I entrust myself as well. Let me become a nun in your community, and my husband a monk.'

Yasa's father smiled at her and said: 'A few moments ago you were angry with the Buddha and with me. Now you are saying that I should give up all my wealth for the Buddha.' That day Yasa's father distributed his wealth amongst the poor – keeping only three yellow robes, for himself, his wife and his son to wear. His wife was the first female disciple of the Buddha.

Vinaya Pitaka: Mahavagga

20

THE GROWTH OF THE COMMUNITY

When Yasa's friends heard that he had become a monk, they came to see him in the park. They were astonished to find him dressed in a yellow robe, rather than in silk studded with jewels, and sitting cross-legged on the ground, rather than on a soft cushion.

'What do you eat?' they asked. 'Whatever people give me,' he replied. 'Were do you sleep?' they asked. 'On the ground under a tree,' he replied. 'And what do you do all day?' 'I meditate,' he replied, 'and, when people come to see me, I answer their questions honestly.' 'Surely your life now is utterly miserable compared with your former life in your mansion,' they said. 'Although I enjoyed many pleasures in those days,' he replied, 'inwardly I was empty and miserable. Now I have few pleasures, but inwardly I am filled with joy.'

'Tell us about this joy,' the young men asked. 'The Buddha can speak far more eloquently than I can,' he replied. He led them to the Buddha, who was sitting nearby; and he spoke to them at length, answering all their questions. At the end half of them asked to become monks, while the rest became lay disciples. This in turn stimulated their friends to come to the park, and hear the Buddha

In this way Yasa's decision to become a monk led fifty more young men also to become monks, and others to become lay disciples. In every case the parents were initially hostile, and came to the Buddha to protest; and the Buddha spoke to them all. Some remained hostile; some became lay disciples; and a few became monks and nuns.

Vinaya Pitaka: Mahavagga

21

THE GROWTH OF THE COMMUNITY

Thus the Buddha's community grew rapidly, and soon had several hundred members.

One evening the Buddha summoned all his monks, and said: 'I want you to go to every town and village, and teach people who are ready to learn - those in whom only a few specks of dust cover the soul. You do not need to seek these people. When you arrive in a town or village, settle in some open space; and go into the main street each morning, to beg for food. Those ready to learn will notice you; and later they will come to you, and ask spiritual questions. Explain to them the four Truths and the eightfold Way. If a man wishes to become a monk, or a woman wishes to become a nun, bring that person back to me, to be received into the community.'

Soon the Buddha's monks were bringing men and women back to him, to become monks and nuns. Having spoken to them personally, to test their sincerity, he asked them to raise their arms up, clasp their hands, and declare their commitment three times to the eightfold Way. Then he arranged for lay disciples to buy them each a yellow robe, and for other monks and nuns to shave their heads.

After several months his monks complained that they were becoming weary of constantly bringing new monks and nuns back to him. The Buddha considered this complaint, and decided to give his monks authority to receive people into the community themselves. In this way the size of the community grew even faster, until there were many thousands of men and women with shaven heads and dressed in yellow.

Vinaya Pitaka: Mahavagga

22

The Fire of Desire

One day the people of a nearby town invited the Buddha to come and speak to them. On the journey the Buddha felt tired, and left the road to sit under a tree. Nearby a group of thirty young men were playing. One of the young men had brought a prostitute with him; and while the men's attention was engaged on their game, she stole all their belongings, and ran away.

When the men finished their game, and found that both the prostitute and their belongings were missing, they went off in search of her. They found the Buddha sitting under a tree, told him what had happened, and asked if he had seen the woman. 'You have put a question to me,' the Buddha said; 'but before I try to answer it, I shall put a question to you. Which is better: to search for a woman, or to search for yourself?' The young men were perplexed. 'What do you mean by searching for yourself?' they asked. The Buddha beckoned them to sit down.

'If you look inside yourself,' the Buddha said, 'you will find many fires burning. Each fire is a desire – for food, for sex, for wealth, for power, for status, and so on. You imagine that by satisfying these desires, you will extinguish the fires, and be content. In fact you are merely throwing more fuel on the flames, causing them to rage ever more fiercely. But if you starve the fires of fuel, so they go out, you will find the soul beneath. By living in accordance with the soul, you will find true happiness.'

The men forgot the prostitute; half became monks, and half lay disciples.

Vinaya Pitaka: Mahavagga

23

Another community

When the Buddha returned to the capital city, he found that another monastic community had arrived; it had two hundred and fifty monks and nuns, and was led by a man called Sangaya. Two of these monks, called Sari and Mog, met one of the Buddha's monks in the main street, begging for food. They were impressed by the brightness of the Buddhist monk's face, and asked him how he had acquired it. 'If my face is bright,' the Buddhist monk replied, 'it is because I am happy; and this is entirely due to the teachings of the Buddha.'

'I should like a bright complexion,' Sari said to Mog. 'And I should like to be happy,' replied Mog. So they went to see the Buddha; and he explained the Way that leads to enlightenment. 'We must follow that Way!' they exclaimed when he had finished. They rushed off to their fellow monks and nuns, and told them about the Buddha. 'If you decide to leave Sangaya and join the Buddha,' the monks said, 'we shall go with you.'

Sari and Mog now went to Sangaya himself, and told him about the Buddha. Sangaya enjoyed being a spiritual leader, and was frightened at the prospect of his followers deserting him. So he said to Sari and Mog: 'I invite you to share with me the leadership of this community. You can take ideas from the Buddha, and teach them to our followers. And you can also enjoy the status that spiritual leadership brings.' Sari and Mog realized that taking pleasure in status was incompatible with the Buddha's teaching; so they left Sangaya, and led all his monks and nuns to join the Buddha's community.

Vinaya Pitaka: Mahavagga

24

Opposition to the Buddha

Most of the men and women who joined the Buddha's community were young; and many came from wealthy and powerful families. One day a group of landowners and merchants came to the Buddha 'You are a thief,' their leader exclaimed; 'you have stolen our sons. We demand that you give them back – so they can inherit the wealth we have acquired.' 'Your sons may return to you whenever they wish,' the Buddha replied; 'but they have no desire for your wealth – and you yourselves would gain great happiness if you gave it to the poor.'

The men turned and left, their faces red with anger; and they began to spread false rumors about the Buddha, in order to stir the people of the city against him. When the Buddha and his monks went next morning into the city to beg for food, they faced a barrage of insults. The monks fled in terror, while the Buddha walked calmly away. When he reached the park, the Buddha said to his monks: 'Why are you frightened? The people may kill you with their swords, but the soul will remain unscathed. Besides, if you show no fear, the body will survive also.'

Each morning the Buddha led his monks into the city; and when insults were hurled at them, they walked calmly away. People were so impressed at their courage, that they concluded the wealthy landowners and merchants had lied to them. Within seven days they were as generous as ever in giving food to the monks. And on the eighth day the Buddha stood in the main square, and begged people not to turn against his rich enemies.

Vinaya Pitaka: Mahavagga

25

Awareness of the Body

On many occasions monks and nuns, as well as lay disciples, said to the Buddha: 'We understand the first five parts of the eightfold Way; but we are perplexed by the other parts – right vigilance, right effort, and right concentration. How can we practise these?' So the Buddha decided to call together all his monks and nuns, and speak to them about these parts; they would then be able to pass on his teaching to lay disciples.

Monks and nuns came from distant towns and villages, and gathered in the park. Then the Buddha spoke: 'In order to follow the last three parts of the eightfold Way, you must first become aware of your breathing. Go each day into the forest or an empty room, where you will not be disturbed; sit down with your legs crossed and your back erect; and then observe yourself breathing. As you inhale a long breath, say to yourself: "I inhale a long breath." And as you exhale a long breath, say to yourself: "I exhale a long breath." As you inhale a short breath, say to yourself: "I inhale a short breath." And as you exhale a short breath, say to yourself: "I exhale a short breath."

'Gradually you will become aware of your breathing without needing to say these words to yourself. Then extend your awareness to the different parts of the body. With each breath say to yourself: "As I breathe, I am aware of my right arm." Do that several times, and then change to another part – the left arm, the stomach, the chest, the left and right shoulders, and so on. Once you become adept at this self-awareness, you may do it as you are walking, working, eating and drinking.'

Sutta Pitaka: Maha Satipatthana Sutta

26

THE STAGES OF MEDITATION

The Buddha continued: 'Awareness of your breathing and your whole body enables you to relax; and it also makes you ready for the last three parts of the eightfold Way. Right effort means extending your self-awareness to your mind – and then exerting control. As you sit in the forest or in an empty room, observe the thoughts that pass through your mind. Say to yourself: "I am thinking this," and "I am thinking that." Then, whenever you observe a hateful or selfish thought, banish it at once.

'Right vigilance means extending your self-awareness to the heart - and then exerting control. Observe the emotions that stimulate your heart. Say to yourself: "I am feeling this," and "I am feeling that." Then, whenever you observe a hateful or selfish feeling, banish it at once. Since selfish thoughts and emotions arise from desire, right effort and vigilance suppress desire.

'Right effort and vigilance comprise the first stage of right meditation; so you are now ready to enter the second stage. Here you empty your mind of all thoughts, and your heart of all emotions. You do this by fixing your attention on a single point – either in front of you, or in the middle of your forehead. As thoughts and emotions depart, joy takes their place. In the third stage of meditation you empty yourself of joy; and its place is taken by tranquility. And in the fourth and final stage of meditation you empty yourself of tranquility, and thus become utterly serene; this state leads to nirvana, and can never be disturbed or upset.'

Sutta Pitaka: Maha Satipatthana Sutta

27

Completing the Way

When the Buddha had finished speaking about the final parts of the Way, one of the monks asked: 'Describe to us what happens when a person has completed it.'

'Those who have completed the Way,' the Buddha replied, 'are filled with light; they are enlightened. They may choose to die at once, and enter heaven; or they may decide, as I have done, to delay entering heaven, in order to enlighten others. In heaven there is no earth, no water, no fire and no air; there is no sun and no moon. There is nothing to learn in heaven, and yet everything is known. There is neither birth nor death; and there is neither pain nor pleasure. It is not bounded by space or time; heaven is infinite and eternal.'

Dusk had fallen, and it was now almost dark. The Buddha asked for an oil lamp to be lit, and placed it beside him. Insects were drawn to the flame, and many flew into it and were killed. 'These insects,' the Buddha said, 'misunderstand the flame. They imagine it offers life and happiness, but in fact it causes suffering and death. To human beings wealth, power and fame are like flames, which seem to offer life and happiness; and they rush towards them. Our purpose is to guide people away from these flames, towards the true light – that shines at the end of the Way.'

With these words the Buddha ordered the monks and nuns to meditate. Many of them spent the whole night meditating; but some eventually lay down and slept. The following day they returned to their towns and villages.

Sutta Pitaka: Udana

28

INNER GUIDANCE

At the age of eighty, when the Buddha had been teaching people the four Truths and the eightfold Way for half a century, he had the first illness of his life: there was a sharp pain in his chest, and he could hardly move. A young monk called Ananda had become his closest companion, and looked after his bodily needs. When Ananda saw the Buddha suffering, he became extremely anxious. 'Do not fret on my behalf,' the Buddha said with a smile; 'I long for my body to die, so that I can enter nirvana.'

Ananda pleaded with the Buddha to use his spiritual powers to cure his body. 'The community depends on your leadership;' Ananda said; 'we cannot exist without you.' 'On the contrary,' the Buddha replied, 'the monks and nuns, and also the lay disciples will benefit from my death. Until now I have held their hands, and guided them along the eightfold Way towards enlightenment. But once I have died, they will each have to look within themselves for guidance – and they will find it in their own hearts.'

'But no-one can teach as you teach,' Ananda persisted; 'so far fewer people will be inspired to follow the eightfold Way.' 'Since my enlightenment,' the Buddha replied, 'I have spoken to many different kinds of people: to kings and noblemen, to monks and nuns, to landowners and merchants, and to men and women who work with their hands. I have tried to use words and phrases, images and stories, which the particular listener would readily understand. Every enlightened person is able to do the same – and hence be as good a teacher as I am.'

Sutta Pitaka: Mahaparinibbana Sutta

29

Morality and Immorality

The Buddha asked Ananda to summon all the monks and nuns that were staying nearby. When they had assembled, the Buddha said: 'My body is now like a ripe fruit, ready to fall from the tree. I have spoken to you in depth about the last three parts of the eightfold Way, leading to the four stages of meditation; and as monks and nuns you spend much of you time meditating. But when you are teaching and guiding lay people, you should emphasize the first five parts of the eightfold Way, which concern morality – how they should behave in their daily lives. And do not be afraid of appealing to their self-interest.

'Tell people that there are four evil consequences of behaving immorally. First, immoral people lose energy and sense of purpose, and become listless and lethargic. Secondly, since they cannot be trusted, they are unpopular with their neighbors. Thirdly, when they find themselves in the company of moral people, they feel ashamed and confused. Fourthly, they are frightened of death, because they fear that after death they will suffer the consequences of their immoral behavior.

'And tell them that there are four good consequences of behaving morally. First, moral people have a strong sense of purpose, and so they are energetic. Secondly, since they frequently help their neighbors, they are popular. Thirdly, they are confident of themselves in company; they know that they deserve the respect of all. Fourthly, they have no fear of death, because they look forward after death to enjoying the consequences of their good behavior.'

Sutta Pitaka: Mahaparinibbana Sutta

30

THE LAST NIGHT

A few days later a local blacksmith, who was an ardent disciple, invited the Buddha to eat with him. But the food served by the blacksmith had turned bad; and that evening the Buddha had terrible pains in his stomach.

The Buddha called Ananda, and said: 'Tonight I shall die. I am anxious that the blacksmith will blame himself for my death, and will be overwhelmed with remorse. So go to him at once, and tell him how much I enjoyed his meal.' Ananda rushed to the blacksmith; and on his way he told people that the Buddha was dying. By the time Ananda returned, hundreds of people – monks, nuns and lay disciples – had gathered round the Buddha.

The Buddha asked Ananda to spread a cloak on the ground beneath a tree, so that he could lie down. The tree was in blossom; and, as the Buddha lay down, there was a gust of wind, that caused petals to fall from the branches, and cover his body.

Although his body was now very weak, his voice was still strong. After a few minutes the Buddha asked Ananda to lift his head, so he could speak to the crowd. 'When I have died,' the Buddha said, 'beware of worshipping me. There have been hundreds of thousands of buddhas in the past, and there will be hundreds of thousands more in the future; so there is nothing unique or even special about me. Simply remember my teaching. The four Truths have always been true, and always will be true; and the eightfold Way always leads to enlightenment.'

Sutta Pitaka: Mahaparinibbana Sutta

31

THE BUDDHA'S PRAYER

The Buddha's voice now grew even stronger and louder. 'I shall give you a prayer,' he exclaimed, 'which you may say at any time:

'In a world full of hatred, let us be loving.
In a world full of conflict, let us be peaceful.
In a world full of greed, let us regard nothing as our own.
In a world full of sorrow, let us be joyful.'

The Buddha now finished speaking, and Ananda gently laid his head on the ground. Within a few moments the Buddha entered the first stage of meditation, and then rapidly passed through the second stage to the third. His breathing became very slow. In the middle of the night his breathing ceased, and he entered nirvana.

Sutta Pitaka: Mahaparinibbana Sutta and Dhammapada

MONTH

3

ZEN

Introduction

ORIGINS

In about 520 CE a man called Bodhidharma traveled from India to China. He was well-versed not only in the ancient Buddhist writings, but also in a newer work, the ***Diamond Sutra***, which was said to 'cut through ignorance like a diamond'. He attempted to win over the emperor, but was disgusted by the emperor's arrogance. So he settled far away from the imperial palace, and waited for people to seek him out. In this he was successful; a large number came, and he taught them both the ***Diamond Sutra*** and his interpretation of it.

Disciples of Bodhidharma formed schools of their own; and by this means his teaching gradually spread across the entire Chinese empire. It became known as *Ch'an*, which means 'meditation'.

Buddhist ideas probably first reached Japan in the sixth century CE; but they were soon integrated within the native religion, Shintoism. It was not until the twelfth century that disciples of Bodhidharma arrived in Japan – and *Ch'an* became known as ***Zen***. As in China, schools were founded, where people could study for whatever period they wished.

Buddhist influences came to Tibet both from India and China from the eighth century onwards. The first great Tibetan teacher, Marpa, studied ***The Diamond Sutra*** in India in the tenth century; and through his disciple Milarepa Buddhism reached the entire country.

Teachings

Enlightenment, in Zen teaching, is to know without any objects of knowledge. Objects of knowledge, while they seem to be external, are, according to Zen, figments of the mind; thus they entangle the mind and disturb the soul. By learning to know without object, the mind becomes free and the soul becomes calm.

There are four main techniques for attaining enlightenment. The first is the ***koan***. This is a nonsensical phrase, an insoluble question, or an absurd situation that defeats the normal workings of the mind. The pupil is required to focus attention on the koan, so that it becomes the mind's sole object. Ultimately the paradoxical nature of the koan makes this impossible – and the mind rejects all objects.

The second technique is the ***mondo***. This is a rapid dialogue between the teacher and pupil, which aims to accelerate the process of thought beyond what the mind can handle. The teacher may conclude the mondo with a sudden act of violence or a shriek, which shocks the pupil.

The third technique is for the teacher to undertake some pointless activity or suffer some needless discomfort. Thus the mind's normal method of ascribing value and making choices is defied.

And the fourth is for the teacher to create a situation in which the inner reality of enlightenment is made externally manifest.

Expression

By its nature Zen is indifferent to the external aspects of religion – temples and shrines, rituals and festivals. Zen teachers have usually treated them with respect, as mental props on which many people depend; but as such they are objects of the mind, and so must ultimately be abandoned.

Nonetheless Zen has held many sports, especially archery and fencing, in high esteem. Through enlightenment the arrow or the blade ceases to be regarded as an object outside the mind, but becomes part of the mind itself. Thus the individual can shoot an arrow or aim a sword with the same precision as thinking a thought.

The greatest expression of Zen has been in art. As with the arrow and the blade, plants and trees, animals and birds, are regarded as parts of the mind. Thus the mind of the artist becomes the mind of that which is being portrayed; in drawing a tree, the artist becomes the tree, and the tree becomes the artist. And the person looking at a work of art is invited to enter this union. Zen drawings and paintings are astonishing in their sensitivity; and Zen sculpture is flowing and free, as if the subject of the sculpture were alive.

In all sports and arts Zen aims at wabi – which is finding unity within multiplicity, simplicity within complexity. It is a quality of mind and spirit from which the necessary technical skills flow naturally. Indeed, wabi should infuse every activity, even eating a meal or taking a stroll.

Us

Human civilization depends on reason and on the accumulation of knowledge. Thus the primary purpose of our education has been to train the intellect and the memory. Zen, however, urges us to transcend these mental abilities, and reach a higher spiritual plane.

Yet at the heart of Zen is a paradox. Zen pupils are not required to be irrational or dim-witted; on the contrary, in the koan or the mondo, they are required to push the intellect to its limit. Thus Zen does not treat education with contempt, but uses education to defy its own fruits. The resolution to the paradox is that Zen encourages us to live at two levels, the rational and the spiritual – and to move freely between the two. Thus by sharpening the faculty of reason, we are better able to rise above it; and by rising above reason, our practical skills are enhanced.

While the koan and the mondo are peculiar to Zen, the experience induced by them is in some degree common to everyone: all people have sudden flashes of insight, which break through the confines of logic. Zen urges us to take those flashes seriously.

1

Arrival in China

A thousand years after the Buddha had died, a man called Bodhidharma traveled from India to China. From his youth he had followed the Way that the Buddha had taught, and he had attained enlightenment; so he was ready to enter nirvana. But he decided, as the Buddha had done, to delay nirvana in order to teach others the Way; and he felt impelled to go to China for this purpose. The voyage took him three years.

When he arrived, he did not know what to say. So he found a cave, and spent nine years deep in meditation, with his face to the wall. At the end of that time he knew that he must visit the emperor of China. As soon as he saw Bodhidharma, the emperor knew that he possessed great spiritual wisdom; and he began to boast how religious he was, and how many temples he had built. 'Your efforts are useless,' Bodhidharma declared. The emperor was offended, and asked in a curt voice: 'So what is your religion?' 'I do not have a religion,' Bodhidharma replied.

'By what principle do you live?' the emperor asked. 'The principle of emptiness,' Bodhidharma replied. By now the emperor was feeling angry. 'Who are you?' he asked in a loud voice. 'I do not know,' Bodhidharma replied. 'Do you know anything?' the emperor asked. 'I know nothing,' Bodhidharma said – and walked away.

The emperor regretted his anger, and sent a messenger to fetch Bodhidharma back. Bodhidharma said to the messenger: 'If the emperor sent his whole army, I would not go.' Some bystanders heard these words; and news quickly spread of Bodhidharma's defiance.

Setcho: Hekiganroku

2

No self or being

It was now winter, and the land was covered with snow. Bodhidharma found a derelict house, and settled there. A few days later a young man arrived, and said to Bodhidharma: 'My mind is in turmoil. Teach me the Way that brings peace.' Bodhidharma replied: 'Wait outside.' The young man waited outside in the snow for seven days and nights. Then Bodhidharma came out, and said to the young man: 'Show me your mind.' The young man replied: 'I cannot produce it, because I do not possess it.' 'So,' declared Bodhidharma, 'I have brought it peace.' The young man understood; and Bodhidharma allowed him inside.

During the following months many men and women from all over China came to Bodhidharma, in the hope that he would bring peace to their minds. They collected wood and stone from the countryside nearby, and erected huts for themselves; and they waited for Bodhidharma to teach them. Finally, one hot summer's day, he came out of his house, sat cross-legged on the ground, and began to speak. His words were not his own; he had learnt them, and understood their meaning, many years previously in India.

'It is the task of enlightened men and women,' he began, 'to lead all living beings in the universe towards nirvana. And in the course of time innumerable beings have been led to nirvana by enlightened men and women. Yet in truth no being at all has been led to nirvana. How is this? If people have in their minds the concept of being, they are not enlightened. An enlightened man or woman has no concept of self or being, no concept of mind or person.'

Setcho: Hekiganroku, and Diamond Sutra

3

ENLIGHTENED MEN AND WOMEN

'Enlightened men and women,' Bodhidharma continued, 'are loving. Yet their love is detached. This means they love without regard to appearance – and without regard to sound, fragrance, or any other attribute. Their love is not motivated by attachment, nor does it cause attachment. Can you measure all space to the east? Can you measure all space to the south, west or north? Can you measure all space upwards or downwards? Love, which is detached, is also beyond measure.

'Enlightened men and women cannot be recognized by any physical features. This is because physical features are not real; they are delusions. If you perceive that physical things are not real, you perceive the nature of enlightenment.

'Enlightened men and women teach the truth. Some people are close to enlightenment; so when they hear the truth, they understand it. The truth is that no being, and no entity of any kind, is separate and distinct; all are one. So all sense of individuality is relinquished. Even the sense of truth, as distinct from falsehood, is relinquished.

'You may cut the flesh from every limb of an enlightened person; yet that person will not flinch, or show any response. This is because that person has no sense of self as separate and distinct.

'Enlightened men and women have thoughts which contain no images, no smells, no feelings, no objects of any kind. They do not even think about the Way; for them the Way is neither present nor absent.'

Diamond Sutra

4

Total loss

'Imagine,' continued Bodhidharma, 'that someone filled three thousand planets with treasure – with gold and silver, diamonds and pearls – and then gave that treasure to the poor. We should admire that person's goodness. Imagine that someone heard four words of true teaching, understood them, and then explained them to others. That person would merit far greater admiration.

'Imagine that there were as many rivers as there are grains of sand in the bed of one river. If someone gave to the poor seven pieces of gold for every grain of sand on the bed of all those rivers, we should admire that person's goodness. But if someone heard one word of true teaching, understood it, and explained it to someone else, that person would merit far greater admiration.

'Enlightened men and women are determined to save all living beings from darkness. Yet they know that, when all living beings have been saved, no one has been saved. This is because the concept of saving a living being assumes that living beings are separate, distinct entities. The light of truth shows that there are no distinct and separate entities. If people declare their intention to save other living beings from darkness, they show themselves not to be enlightened.

'If you become enlightened, nothing is gained; there is no profit in enlightenment. Enlightened men and women know that all things, including even virtues, are like bubbles in a stream or flashes of lightning.'

Diamond Sutra

5

FORM AND LACK OF FORM

Not long after Bodhidharma came from India, another Buddhist sage also came. His name was Avalokita. He settled in another part of China; and he too attracted numerous disciples. His teaching was short – and yet embraced all true teaching.

'Form has no form,' Avalokita taught; 'and lack of form is true form. The Way to enlightenment lacks form; that is what gives it form. It is not constructed by anyone; it does not start somewhere, and end somewhere else; it is neither rough nor smooth, neither complete nor incomplete.

'Emotion has no emotion; and lack of emotion is true emotion. The Way lacks emotion; that is what gives it emotion. Thought has no thought; and lack of thought is true thought. The Way lacks thought; that is what makes it thoughtful.

'For enlightened men and women there are no colors, sounds, smells, tastes or textures. There is neither consciousness nor unconsciousness. There is neither ignorance nor knowledge. There is neither decay nor permanence. There is neither death nor immortality. There is neither suffering nor happiness. There neither rationality nor irrationality. There is neither starting nor stopping. There is neither progress nor lack of progress.

'If you are enlightened, you are indifferent to success and failure, profit and loss. You are indifferent to honor and disgrace; you never wish to justify yourself. Nothing can upset you or please you.'

Heart Sutra

6

CHILDREN IN A BURNING MANSION

Aalokita also told two parables. This was the first: 'There was a man who was rich beyond measure. He owned hundreds of ships that sailed across the vast oceans, trading with distant nations. And he lived in a vast mansion, filled with the finest furniture and ornaments that human hands can make. But to prevent thieves from entering the mansion, it had only a single door, which was guarded.

'One day a fire broke out in the mansion, and quickly spread from room to room. The owner ran to the room where his children were playing, told them that the mansion was on fire, and urged them to leave at once. But the children could not feel the heat of the fire, so they did not listen. Then the owner told them that outside in the garden where there were lots of new toys that he had bought for them, and suggested that they go and play with them. Immediately the children rushed out of the door of the mansion into the garden. When they saw their father had deceived them about the toys, they were angry; but when they looked back, and saw the mansion engulfed in flames, they thanked him.

'In this parable the father is an enlightened teacher. There was only a single door to his mansion because there is only one Way to nirvana. The children are ordinary men and women; their refusal to listen to his truthful warnings shows that fear never induces people to follow the Way. The father deceived the children, just as enlightened teachers are compelled to give false images of nirvana. As people follow the Way, they realize that nirvana is beyond all images, beyond all words – and they give thanks for the deception.'

Lotus Sutra

7

AN HEIR TO AN ESTATE

This was the second parable that Avalokita told: 'There was a man who was rich beyond measure. He owned a vast estate stretching further than the eye could see; and he employed hundreds of men and women. He wanted his son to inherit the estate, and manage it as he did. But the son hated this prospect, and ran away. The father sent his men in all directions searching for his son, but they could not find him.

'The son worked as a laborer on other estates; and after many years he forgot where his father lived. So by mistake he returned to his father's estate, and asked the steward for work. A few days later his father recognized him cleaning out the stables. The father knew that if he revealed himself at once, his son would run away again. So he dressed in dirty clothes, smeared himself with manure, and for several weeks worked alongside his son. Only when they had struck up a firm friendship as equals, did the father reveal himself. The son burst into tears, apologized for running away, and kissed his father. A few years later the father died, and the son willingly took over the estate.'

'The father is an enlightened teacher. The son is a disciple; he runs away because the prospect of following the Way is frightening. The father works with his son, because good teachers befriend their disciples, and so ease their fears.'

As soon as disciples became enlightened, Avalokita ordered them to go elsewhere, and teach others. Before they left, he gave them copies of his own teaching and that of Bodhidharma.

Lotus Sutra

8

THE DANGER OF RELIGION

Thus enlightened teachers went to every part of China, and attracted disciples of their own. Schools were built; and each school had a large hall where the teacher passed on the words of Bodhidharma and Avalokita, and explained their meaning.

One of these teachers, called Hung, established a school in a small town in southern China. A boy called Hui lived in the town; his family was poor, and he sold firewood in the market to earn extra money. One day two disciples sat down near Hui's stall, and began to discuss the Way. Hui overheard them, and was entranced. He asked them how he too could learn the Way; and they told him about Hung. He immediately rushed home to his parents, and begged them to allow him to join Hung's school. They knew that they could not resist their son's destiny; so they agreed.

When Hui arrived at the school, he immediately went to see Hung, and asked to be taught the Way. 'Are you educated?' Hung asked. 'No,' Hui replied; 'my parents are too poor to pay for education.' 'How can you expect to be enlightened, if you are not educated?' Hung demanded. Hui hesitated, not knowing what to say. Then he blurted out: 'Education is not relevant to enlightenment.' 'You are too clever,' Hung exclaimed; 'go and work in the kitchen.'

The following morning Hung came to see Hui in the kitchen, and said: 'I have one thing to teach you. Do not become religious. If you engage in religious rituals, you will think of yourself as good – and that will prevent you from following the Way.'

Hui-neng: Sutra

9

LIVING WITH HUNTERS

Hui remained for a year in Hung's school. He worked in the kitchen, and hoped that Hung would say something more to him. But Hung never spoke to him again; so eventually Hui left, feeling very miserable.

He wandered for many weeks, not knowing where he was going, and entered a dark forest. He met a group of hunters, who set traps for wild animals; and he offered to work as the hunters' servant. They brought the animals to him, and he cooked them in a large pot over an open fire. He added wild vegetables, which he dug from the ground beneath the trees. Month by month, without telling the hunters, he used less meat and more vegetables; and this made the hunters less aggressive and calmer. They became so accustomed to the taste of vegetables, that they gradually lost their taste for meat. So finally Hui discarded meat altogether; and the hunters were now so lacking in aggression, that they could not bring themselves to kill any more animals. Instead they cleared part of the forest, and became farmers, tilling the soil to grow crops.

Hui congratulated himself that, as a result of his actions, the animals of the forest could now roam safely. Then he thought: 'Hung told me not to think of myself as good – yet, even though I have avoided religion, I am still allowing my head to swell.' So he decided to remain with the hunters, adopting their rough manners and speech, in the hope that this would cure him of all moral pride. Only after fifteen years in their company did he feel ready to continue his spiritual education.

Hui-neng Sutra

10

Appointed as Teacher

Hui traveled to Canton, where another teacher, trained by Avalokita, had recently established a school. When he arrived at the school, he found two disciples arguing. Above the school building a flag was blowing in the wind; one disciple was asserting that the motion of the flag was in the flag itself, while the other claimed it was in the wind. Hui intervened: 'Everything perceived by the senses is in the mind; so the motion of the flag, which you both perceive, is neither in the flag nor in the wind, but in your minds.'

The teacher at the monastery overheard these words, and invited Hui to have tea with him. Over tea the teacher asked Hui about many spiritual and moral matters, and was deeply impressed by the precision of Hui's replies. Then the teacher said: 'Tell me what you know about the Way, and about the soul.' I cannot tell you both about the Way and about the soul,' Hui replied. 'Why not?' the teacher asked. 'If I could tell you both about the Way and about the soul,' Hui replied, 'that would imply that the Way is separate from the soul. Yet the Way is entirely concerned with the soul.'

The teacher was delighted with Hui's answer. He put his palms together as a sign of respect, and declared: 'You are undoubtedly wiser than I am. From this day forward you must be teacher, and I shall be your most eager disciple.' Hui was astonished. 'I am not worthy to be a teacher,' he replied; 'I have no education, my speech and manners are rough, and I am not even religious.' 'In that case,' the teacher replied, 'you are even more worthy to be our teacher than I had imagined.'

Hui-neng Sutra

11

Hui's sayings

Hui taught at Canton for forty years. When he was about to die, he called together his disciples, and said: 'All my teaching has been spoken; I have never written anything down. And I have instructed my disciples never to write down what I say; their own minds remember what they need to remember, and forget the rest. Now that I am near to death, I am going to summarize my teaching; and when I have died, you must write it down.'

The disciples did as Hui instructed, and this is what they wrote down: 'Every human being is capable of enlightenment; and every enlightened person is capable of teaching others. Therefore treat every human being as a potential teacher.

'You may be able to speak about the Way with great eloquence; but eloquence is no substitute for practice. Only when you have reached the end of the Way, and become enlightened, you should talk to others about it.

'Enlightenment is the same for all people; but people are confused about it in different ways. Some confuse it with knowledge, some with religion, and some with obedience. As people follow the Way, knowledge, religion and obedience can sometimes help, and sometimes hinder; but enlightenment is far greater than all three.

'The greatest hindrance to following the Way is a solid mind – a mind that is hardened by old ideas, and thinks it has nothing to learn. The greatest help to following the Way is a liquid mind – a mind that can be shaped by new ideas, and knows it has much to learn.'

Hui-neng: Sutra

12

DRIVING A NAIL INTO THE SKY

About a century after Hui's death, a young man from northern China, called Lin, became a disciple at the school in Canton. He spent every hour of daylight studying the words of Bodhidharma, Avalokita and Hui; and through the hours of darkness he meditated. After six years he became enlightened.

He decided to return to northern China, and set up a school of his own. This proved hugely successful, and attracted hundreds of disciples. Whereas Hui's method was to give lectures, Lin pioneered a new way of teaching: he encouraged his disciples to speak themselves; and in his encounters with his disciples he was deliberately illogical, and sometimes violent. He believed that by defying normal notions of thought and action, he could prompt people's minds to leap towards enlightenment.

One morning Lin said to his disciples: 'We are here to discuss the meaning of Buddhism. Does anyone have anything to say about this?' One of the disciples began to speak; Lin immediately slapped him. Another disciple began to speak; Lin slapped him. A third disciple began to speak; Lin slapped him also. There was a long silence, during which Lin stared at the disciples, and the disciples stared at him. Then Lin asked: 'Can you drive a nail into the sky?' All the disciples wanted to say: 'No!' But none of them dared speak, for fear of being slapped. So Lin said: 'It is easier to drive a nail into the sky, than to put the meaning of Buddhism into words. And anyone who opens his mouth to explain the meaning of Buddhism, is about to say something foolish.'

Lin Chi: Record

13

Buying high and selling low

Lin said to his disciples: 'Look at this lump of flesh who is your teacher. What do you think of it?' 'You are not merely a lump of flesh,' a disciple said; 'you are a human being.' 'What makes me a human being?' Lin asked. 'Within your flesh is the soul,' the disciple replied; 'that makes you a human being.' 'Yet the soul within me and within you are one and the same,' Lin replied. The disciple said nothing. Lin said: 'When you are enlightened, you do not think of human beings as separate. You simply think: "We are human."'

Lin asked his disciples: 'One man who spends his time sitting on a mountain peak and meditating; another man who buys and sells goods in the market. Which do you admire most?' 'The man who sits on the mountain peak and meditates,' a disciple replied. 'But what if he is meditating on his own desires,' Lin asked, 'while the man in the market is free from desires.' 'Then I should admire the man in the market.' 'So do not judge by appearances,' Lin said; 'besides, the man in the market may be buying from the poor at a high price, and selling to them at a low price.'

Lin asked: 'A man wanders from one school to another, and listens to what the teacher at each school has to say; another man stays at home, and tills his land. Which do you admire most?' 'The man staying at home is most admirable,' a disciple replied, 'because, while he tills his land, he may be meditating. Besides, he can give away part of his crop to the poor.' Lin rose to his feet, walked towards the disciple, and shouted: 'You are too clever for your own good.' Then he slapped him.

Lin Chi: Record

14

Like the Buddha

One day Lin came into the dining-hall while the disciples were eating. One by one he knocked over their plates of food. None of the disciples spoke. 'Are you too cowardly to tell me how rude I am?' Lin cried. The next day Lin again came into the dining-hall, and knocked over the plates of food. With one voice the disciples said: 'You are rude.' 'How dare you speak to me like that!' Lin cried, and slapped each disciple in turn.

Lin sent his disciples with a bag of rice to the market, with instructions to sell it at the highest possible price. The disciples were successful in obtaining a high price, and returned to Lin feeling pleased with themselves. Lin took a stick, drew a beautiful picture on the ground, and said: 'Now take this picture to the market, and sell it at a high price.' The disciples stood with their mouths open, not knowing what to do. 'You're incompetent!' Lin shouted; 'I should never have entrusted that rice to you.'

A young woman arrived at the school, and asked to become a disciple. Lin ordered her to sit in his own chair, and teach the disciples. 'I am not worthy to be a teacher,' the woman replied. 'Then you are not worthy to be a disciple either,' Lin replied. The woman sat in Lin's chair, and told the other disciples all she knew. When she had finished, Lin embraced her, and declared: 'You are ready to learn.'

One morning Lin sat washing his feet in a bowl of water. When he had finished, he picked up the bowl, and threw the water over the disciples. 'Why did you do that?' the disciples asked. 'To make you ask why,' Lin replied.

Lin Chi: Record

15

HANGING BY THE TEETH

When his disciples became enlightened, Lin ordered them to start schools of their own; and their disciples in turn founded schools. So within a few decades there was a school in every town in China, and in some villages also. Many teachers became famous, with stories about them being passed from person to person.

One famous teacher was called Nansen. A disciple asked Nansen: 'Where is the Way of which people speak?' 'Everyday life is the Way,' Nansen replied. 'Can it be studied?' the disciple asked. 'If you try to study the Way,' Nansen said, 'then you are far from it.'

Another famous teacher was called Kogen. A disciple asked Kogen: 'Can you define the Way?' Kogen replied: 'The Way is like a man who falls over a cliff. As he falls, his teeth clasp the branch of a tree. The branch is too small for his hands to grasp; and there is no ledge for his feet. So he is holding his entire weight in his teeth; and were he to open his teeth, he would plunge to his death. Then another man appears, looks over the cliff, and asks: "Do you want any help?"'

Another famous teacher was called Ketsu. A very intelligent disciple asked him: 'Is it possible to define the Way?' Ketsu replied: 'Go outside at dawn on a spring day, look up at the blossoms on the trees, and listen to the birds sing.'

When a new disciple joined his school, Ketsu said: 'If you had a walking-stick, I should take it from you. If you didn't have a walking-stick, I should give one to you.' Some disciples became enlightened immediately.

Setcho: Hekignaroku, and Mumon: Mumonkan

16

A DROP IN THE OCEAN

Another famous teacher was called Rutan. One night a disciple came to Rutan's house, and began asking questions about the Way. Rutan answered each question with care and precision; but the disciple was never satisfied, and asked another question. Eventually Rutan said: 'It's getting late. Why don't you retire to bed.' The disciple opened the door of Rutan's house, and said: 'It is very dark outside.' 'Would you like a candle to light your way?' Rutan asked. The disciple nodded. Rutan lit a candle, handed it to the disciple. But as the disciple took it, Rutan blew it out. At that moment the disciple understood the answer to all his questions, and was enlightened.

The next morning this disciple, who owned many books about religion, burned them in front of the other disciples. 'The knowledge contained in these books,' he declared, 'is no more than a single drop in the ocean of enlightenment.'

Another famous teacher was called Gutei. Whenever Gutei was asked a question, he raised his right forefinger. A young disciple began to imitate this mannerism, in order to make the other disciples laugh. When Gutei heard about this, he took a knife, seized the young man, and cut off his finger. The young man shrieked with pain, and ran away. Gutei called after him, and ordered him to stop. The young man turned his head towards Gutei. Gutei raised his right forefinger. At that moment the young man was enlightened – and himself became a great teacher.

Setcho: Hekignaroku, and Mumon: Mumonkan

17

CLIMBING A POLE

Another famous teacher was called Hyak. One of Hyak's disciples was from a wealthy family, and was highly educated; this disciple treated another disciple, who was from a poor family with no education, with contempt, ordering him to do menial tasks for him. Hyak, however, knew that the poor disciple had the deeper spiritual understanding. So one day Hyak placed a vase filled with water in front of all his disciples; and he called the rich and the poor disciple to come forward. 'I want you to say what this is, without using its name,' Hyak said. The rich disciple was perplexed, and said: 'No-one can call it a wooden shoe.' The poor disciple tipped the vase over with his foot, spilling the water on the ground. 'Well done,' Hyak said to the poor disciple; 'you are right.'

Another famous teacher was called Sekso. A new disciple said to Sekso: 'I feel drawn to the Way, but I do not know what it is.' Sekso replied: 'The Way is like climbing up a pole. While you are climbing, you must use all your strength; and your movements are restricted by the pole itself. But when you reach the top, you can relax, and you can move freely.'

Another famous teacher was called Tozan. A disciple once said to him: 'In the winter I feel cold, and in the summer I feel hot – and I find both uncomfortable. How can I avoid both cold and heat?' 'Why don't you go where there is neither cold nor heat?' Tozan asked. 'Where is that?' the disciple asked. Tozan said: 'In winter expose yourself to the cold so that it kills you. And in summer expose yourself to the heat so that it kills you.'

Setcho: Hekignaroku, and Mumon: Mumonkan

18

A GRAIN OF RICE

Another famous teacher was called Seppo. A disciple said to him: 'The world is so complex that no-one can understand it.' Seppo took a grain of rice between his thumb and forefinger, and said: 'The world is as simple as a grain of rice.' Then he threw the grain of rice at the disciple, and added: 'If I throw it in front of your face, you do not see it.'

Another famous teacher was called Korin. A disciple asked him: 'What is the purpose of the Way.' Korin replied: 'To make us sit down and get tired.'

Another teacher was called Ummon. He said his disciples: 'Why have you come to me?' 'Because we wish to become enlightened,' they replied. 'And why do you wish to become enlightened?' Ummon asked. 'Because enlightenment makes people happy,' they replied. 'In that case,' Ummon asked, 'why doesn't everyone seek enlightenment?' None of the disciples could answer. So Ummon supplied the answer: 'Because enlightenment doesn't help people plough fields or chop wood.'

A disciple said to Ummon: 'When the leaves turn brown and fall, I feel sad. How can I overcome this feeling?' Ummon replied: 'Remember that within you is that which makes the sun shine, causing the leaves to turn brown, and makes the wind blow, causing them to fall.'

A disciple asked Ummon: 'What is the essence of the Way?' Ummon slapped him. The monk did not move. 'Why don't you bow?' Ummon asked. The disciple bowed, and at that moment was enlightened.

Setcho: Hekignaroku, and Mumon: Mumonkan

19

A NEW ROBE

Another famous teacher was called Joshu. A disciple once doubted whether Joshu was truly enlightened. So the disciple asked: 'Are you clear about the meaning of the Way?' 'No, I am not clear,' Joshu replied. 'If you are not clear about the meaning of the Way,' the disciple protested, 'how can you claim to be teach it?' 'I am clear that I am not clear,' Joshu replied. Many years later the disciple understood this, and was enlightened.

Another disciple said: 'The Buddha taught that there are four noble Truths. And yet surely all truth is one.' Joshu replied: 'I recently wove myself a new robe, made from hemp. It weighed four kilos.'

Another famous teacher was called Kosi. On one occasion it was raining, and Kosi asked his disciples: 'What is that noise?' A disciple answered: 'It's the noise of raindrops on the roof.' 'You are right that there are raindrops on the roof,' Kosi said; 'but the noise is in your head and mine.'

Another famous teacher was called Dashi. The emperor of China asked him to give a lecture on Buddhism. Dashi agreed, and went to the emperor's palace. In the great hall of the palace a special platform was erected opposite the emperor's throne, and seats for the noblemen were placed around the throne facing the platform. When the emperor and the nobleman had sat down, Dashi climbed the platform, and struck the reading-desk hard with his fist. Everyone was astonished. 'Have you understood?' Dashi asked. 'No,' the emperor replied. 'My lecture is over,' Dashi said, and left.

Setcho: Hekignaroku, and Mumon: Mumonkan

20

Dead or Alive

Another famous teacher was called Dogo. He once went to visit a family where the grandfather had just died, to express his sympathy; he was accompanied by a disciple called Zengen. The disciple touched the coffin, and asked Dogo: 'Is he dead or alive?' 'I shall not tell you,' Dogo replied. On their way home Zengen repeated his question. 'Hit me, if you wish,' Dogo replied, 'but I still shall not tell you.' So Zengen hit Dogo; and Dogo did not flinch. Then Dogo said: 'If you were to hit me again after I had died, I should again not flinch.' Zengen now knew the answer to his question.

Some years later Dogo died, and Zengen took his place as teacher. One day Zengen was wandering all over the school, as if he were searching for something. 'What are you looking for?' a disciple asked. 'The remains of my dead teacher,' Zengen replied. 'Even if you were to find them, what good would they do?' the disciple asked. 'The act of looking for them is excellent exercise,' Zengen replied.

Another famous teacher was called Kos. A young man arrived at his school, and asked to be a disciple. 'What is your name?' Kos asked. 'My name is Ejak,' the young man replied. 'My name is Ejak as well,' Kos declared; 'we are just the same.' The disciple understood, and laughed; he quickly became enlightened.

Another famous teacher was called Tosu. He once said: 'A rough voice and a smooth voice can express the truth equally well.' 'So can I call you a donkey?' a disciple asked. Tosu slapped him for being rude, and then embraced him for being wise.

Setcho: Hekignaroku and Mumon: Mumonkan

21

The Wicked Uncle and Aunt

About five centuries after Bodhidharma arrived in China from India, a man from Tibet called Marpa traveled to India. And whereas Bodhidharma came to teach the Way, Marpa went to learn it. He spent two decades at a school, and became enlightened; then he returned to his home. He soon gained a reputation for great wisdom, and attracted disciples from throughout that mountainous land. The greatest of these disciples – who became even greater than Marpa himself – was called Milarepa.

Milarepa's father was one of the wealthiest men in Tibet, with a large estate and a fine mansion; his mother was renowned for her beauty. At the age of six Milarepa was betrothed to a cousin called Zessay. A year later Milarepa's father caught a fatal disease. He summoned his relatives to his bedside, and declared: 'Until my son reaches adulthood, I entrust my property to my brother and his wife.'

As soon as the funeral rites were over, Milarepa's uncle and aunt moved into the mansion. They forced Milarepa and his mother to live in a small hut nearby, and to work as servants in the mansion. And they employed ten large men to protect themselves. When Milarepa reached adulthood, they claimed that his father had intended that they should keep the mansion and estate permanently.

Milarepa's mother was furious, and poisoned by hatred. She sent her son to the great magician Yung, to learn how to destroy the wicked uncle and aunt. And she gave him her own small inheritance, in order to pay Yung.

Milarepa: Life

22

THE MAGICIAN AND THE SAGE

Yung taught Milarepa his most deadly magic, and Milarepa began to cast spells. His uncle and aunt suffered two terrible misfortunes: a hailstorm destroyed all their crops; and one night soon afterwards a fire broke out in the wing of the mansion where their children were sleeping, and burnt them all to death.

Milarepa's mother was delighted to see her enemies suffer. But Milarepa was filled with remorse. When Yung saw Milarepa's reaction, he said: 'You are too good to be a magician. Go to the great sage Marpa, and learn the Way.' Milarepa had heard of neither Marpa nor the Way; and he asked Yung for directions to Marpa's house.

Milarepa walked for several days across the mountains. When he reached the region where Marpa lived, he saw a fat, ruddy-faced man plowing a field. 'Where is Marpa's house?' he asked. 'If you finish plowing this field,' the man replied, 'I shall show you.' Milarepa took the plow; and the man immediately walked away. Milarepa felt obliged to finish plowing the field. Then he followed the man.

He came to a small white house, and went inside. He was surprised to find that the man was now dressed in a yellow robe. 'I am looking for Marpa,' Milarepa said. 'I am he,' the man replied. 'I wish to follow the Way,' Milarepa said. 'I can only teach you,' Marpa said, 'if you submit yourself to me in body, as well as in mind.' Milarepa agreed.

The next day Marpa said: 'I want you to build me a tower, six stories high. When you have completed it, I shall teach you all the wisdom I learnt in India.'

Milarepa: Life

23

Towers and a Cave

So Milarepa began to build a tower, collecting large stones, and laying them one on top of the other. When it was three stories high, Marpa came, and said: 'This is the wrong site; it should be on the western crest of the mountain.' So Milarepa pulled down what he had built, and repeated his work on the western crest.

When the tower was three stories high, Marpa came, and said: 'You are building it the wrong shape. It's round, and it should be square.' So Marpa pulled down what he had built, and reconstructed it on square foundations. As soon as it was finished, he went to Marpa, and begged to be taught. 'How tall is it?' Marpa asked. 'Six stories,' Milarepa replied. 'I want it ten stories high,' Marpa declared; 'only then shall I teach you.'

Milarepa was now utterly miserable; his hands were covered in sores from lifting stones, and every joint in his body was aching. So he decided to leave; and that night he slipped away. But at dawn the next day he said to himself: 'I made a vow to submit myself to Marpa in body as well as in mind. I cannot break it.' So he turned round, and slowly trudged back.

As Milarepa reached the house, Marpa came to the door, smiled broadly, embraced him, and declared: 'My son!' During the following weeks Marpa taught Milarepa all that he knew. Then he said to Milarepa: 'You must now go and live in a cave, and meditate alone.' He directed Milarepa to a cave halfway up a steep cliff, gave him food for a year, and promised to visit him each year with more food.

Milarepa: Life

24

TWO CAVES

Milarepa remained for eleven years in the cave; and each year Marpa brought him food. At the end of that time Milarepa said to Marpa: 'Will you release me from my vow? I feel impelled to return home.' 'You are destined to become a great teacher,' Marpa replied; 'and your return home is part of your preparation. Therefore I release you.'

Milarepa walked across the mountain for several days until he reached the place of his childhood. The mansion was now a ruin, and a herdsman was sheltering in it; he told Milarepa that his uncle and aunt had been so stricken with grief at the death of their children, that they had given up farming, and now lived in a small hut. Milarepa then went to his mother's house. It too was a ruin; and a neighbor told him that his mother had died some years earlier.

He now visited the home of Zessay's parents, to inquire about her; and he found Zessay still living there. 'Why have you not married?' he asked her. 'Since you went off to learn magic,' she replied, 'no man dared to marry me, for fear that you would cast an evil spell on him.' Milarepa was filled with guilt. He did not know what to say; so he turned his back, and left.

Nearby was one of the highest mountains in Tibet. He climbed almost to the top, where he found a cave. As a penance for the harm he had caused to Zessay, and to his uncle and aunt, he vowed to remain on the mountain for the rest of his life. He ate only the nettles that grew on the mountain slopes; and gradually his skin turned green.

Milarepa: Life

25

Two unhappy souls

One day a group of hunters passed by the cave, and went inside for shelter from the cold wind. They were astonished to see inside a naked, green man, so thin that every bone was visible under his skin. He was deep in meditation, so he did not notice them. After staring at him for several minutes, they left. When they returned home, they mentioned to friends what they had seen; and soon the story of the green man on the mountain spread throughout the region.

Zessay knew in her heart that the man was Milarepa; and despite the harm he had done to her, she overflowed with love for him – and wanted to look after him. So she wrapped herself in her warmest clothes, filled a bag with food, and climbed the mountain. When she arrived, she called out: 'Milarepa.' Even though he was meditating, the familiar sound of her voice alerted him; and he came out to her. She was aghast at his appearance. 'You are no more than a skeleton!' she exclaimed. She offered him one of her tunics, but he refused. 'At least you must wear a cloth over your penis,' she said. 'I have no cause for shame,' he replied; 'I am as I have been made.'

'Are you happy?' Zessay asked. 'When I came to this cave, I was deeply troubled,' Milarepa replied; 'but now I am numb, both in mind and in body – I feel nothing.' Then he asked Zessay if she was happy. 'No,' she replied; 'I can find no peace.' With these words she opened her bag of food, and they both ate. And when they were satisfied, they embraced. Then Milarepa took Zessay to a cave nearby, where she could make her home.

Milarepa: Life

26

THE MOUNTAIN SCHOOL

That evening Milarepa passed on to Zessay all that Marpa had taught him about the Way; and then he went back to his own cave. They both spent the night meditating; and at dawn they both attained enlightenment. At midday they emerged from their caves. Milarepa's skin was no longer green, but was brown and shiny; and Zessay's complexion gleamed in the bright sunshine.

Meanwhile Zessay's parents were anxious at their daughter's failure to return. So they too climbed the mountain. When they saw Zessay, they were astounded at her appearance. 'For years your face has been darkened by sadness,' her mother exclaimed; 'but now it is bright. What has happened?' When Zessay explained, they immediately went to Milarepa, and asked him about the Way. And he repeated to them Marpa's teaching. They decided to remain on the mountain; and a few weeks later they too became enlightened.

News soon spread that Zessay and her parents had joined Milarepa on the mountain. Others began to come, some out of curiosity, and some to learn the Way. Like Marpa, Milarepa required his disciples to submit to him in body and in mind; then he told them to find a cave on the mountain, as near to the summit as possible. By learning to endure the bitter cold, his disciples gained the same benefits that he had gained from building towers. With a few years every cave on the mountain was occupied by a disciple – and then his school spread to other mountains throughout Tibet.

Milarepa: Life

27

SAVED BY TWO BAGS

Soon after Marpa brought the teaching of Bodhidharma and Avalokita to Tibet, various teachers sailed to Japan, and began to teach the Way there. Many of their disciples then became teachers; and so knowledge of the Way spread throughout the country.

The most famous Japanese teacher of the Way was called Hakuin. As a young man he attended a school, but did not understand what was taught; so he left. Then one day, on a long journey, he caught up with two men, each carrying a large bag. He said to the older man: 'Let me carry your bag for you.' The man happily handed his bag to Hakuin. After a while the younger man asked Hakuin to carry his bag as well. The travelers came to a wide estuary, and boarded a ferry. Hakuin was so exhausted from carrying the bags that he immediately fell sound asleep – and did not awake until the ferry reached the other shore. There was a foul smell, and the three men were green; there had been a violent squall that had tossed the ferry about, and made the three men vomit – whereas his exhaustion from carrying their bags had saved him. At that moment he became enlightened; and soon afterwards he founded his own school.

Each morning a woman from a nearby village brought cakes made from millet for Hakuin and his disciples. One day a nobleman arrived, and asked Hakuin to teach him. Hakuin offered him a millet cake; but the nobleman, who was accustomed to the finest food, refused. 'If you force yourself,' Hakuin said; 'you will leap along the Way.' The nobleman ate the cake and enjoyed it – and soon afterwards became enlightened.

Hakuin: Stories

28

Words on an Umbrella

A merchant, who enjoyed imposing harsh rules on his servants, forbade them from carrying umbrellas. One of his servants, a strong-willed young woman, decided to disobey this rule; she purchased an umbrella, and kept it at a friend's house, collecting it whenever she went out. Hakuin saw her carrying this umbrella one day, and asked her if he could write something on it. 'Yes please,' she replied; 'write my name.' Hakuin took out a pen, and wrote something; as she was illiterate, she could not read it. Later that day her friend told her that Hakuin had written: 'Whether it rains or pours, I always obey my master.' She was furious, and went at once to Hakuin, demanding that he buy her a new umbrella. 'I promise you,' he replied, 'that by tomorrow you will be happy with what I have written.' Hakuin then went to the merchant, and said: 'Do you have children?' 'Yes, I do,' the merchant replied. 'Remember,' said Hakuin, 'that every servant is someone's child.' The merchant abolished all his rules, and began to treat his servants well.

The daughter of a servant had a love affair with another servant, and became pregnant. When her pregnancy became obvious, the merchant was furious; and to protect her lover, she said that Hakuin was the father. So when the baby was born, the merchant handed it to Hakuin, and demanded that he care for it. Hakuin loved the baby, and carried it everywhere. One day the true father saw Hakuin with the baby, and was overcome with remorse. He told Hakuin the truth. 'So the baby has two fathers!' Hakuin replied. The man joined Hakuin's school, and they raised the child together.

Hakuin: Stories

29

Restoring a ruin

Another famous teacher In Japan was called Bankei. A man came to see him, and said that he had been born with a very short temper. 'Try as I may,' the man said, 'I cannot control it.' And he asked Bankei to cure him. 'Show me this short temper,' Bankei said, 'and then I can cure it.' 'But I don't feel angry at this moment,' the man replied; 'my temper comes out when nasty things happen.' 'In that case,' Bankei said, 'you were not born with it.'

Another famous teacher was called Zenko. He purchased an old building that was lying in ruins, with the intention to restore it and turn it into a school. But he spent all his money on the purchase, and had none left for the restoration. So he announced that on a certain date he would burn himself to death at this ruin. Meanwhile he and his disciples collected wood, and made a huge pile in the middle of the ruin. When the day arrived, crowds of people came, and his disciples charged them a fee to enter the ruin. Zenko climbed onto the pile of wood, sat on the top, and meditated. After an hour he announced: 'I have heard a voice saying it's too soon for me to leave this world; I still have much teaching to do.' He climbed off the pile, and embraced all the spectators in turn, thanking them for their kindness. Then, with the money they had paid, he restored the building.

Another famous teacher was called Seng. One of his disciples grew chrysanthemums in the garden of Seng's school, and took great pride in their beauty. A visitor one day tripped over, and squashed some blooms. The disciple flew into a rage. The next day Seng cut off all the blooms, saying: 'These have become weeds of the mind.'

Various collections

30

One hand clapping

Another famous teacher, who was also skilled in martial arts, was called Boku. One day he was crossing an estuary on a ferry. Another passenger, a man of immense size and strength, challenged Boku to a fight. 'I have practiced martial arts since childhood,' Boku replied, 'but I have vowed never to harm another person.' 'In that case,' the big man declared, 'your skills have never been tested.' 'Very well,' said Boku; 'I shall beat you without breaking my vow.' There was an island in the middle of the estuary, and Boku asked the boatman to steer towards it. 'This is the place I shall beat you,' Boku said. The big man jumped off the boat onto the island, exclaiming: 'Now I'll split your head in two.' Boku then directed the boatman to push the boat away from the island – leaving the big man stranded. The big man went red with anger. 'I have beaten you,' Boku shouted, 'without harming you. In fact, I've done you good.'

Another famous teacher was called Inzan. A young man came to see him, and asked to be enlightened. 'You will be enlightened,' Inzan replied, 'when you can hear the sound of one hand clapping.' The young man became a disciple of Inzan, and lived at his school. He meditated day and night, striving to hear the sound of one hand clapping. Sometimes he sat for hours in a tub of hot water, in the hope that it's heat would help his meditation; and sometimes he sat at the top of a snowy mountain, hoping that the cold would help. But after several years he still could not hear the sound of one hand clapping. Finally he gave up trying; and that moment he became enlightened.

Various collections

31

HAIKUS

Many Japanese teachers composed short meditations, known as haikus. The haikus composed by Basho became especially famous:

To the willow-tree, I give all the hatred and desire of my heart.

I look for the real flowers in this painful world.

I have fallen sick on my journey; but over parched earth my hopes wander on.

Grass on the field of battle is all that remains of a fallen soldier's dreams.

Don't weep, insects; lovers, even the stars, must eventually part.

Where there are humans, you'll find flies and enlightenment.

Children, do not harm the flea; it has children of it's own.

Under cherry trees there are no strangers.

Basho: Haikus

MONTH

4

TAOISM

Introduction

Origins

The Chinese term for religion, ***tsung chiao,*** means tradition of teachings. And in this sense China may be said to have three religions: Taoism, whose origins are lost in pre-history; Confucianism, which stems from the teachings of Kung Fu Tzu (latinized as Confucius) in the fifth century BCE; and Buddhism, imported from India. Despite occasional tension between these traditions, they have mostly co-existed in peace. Buddhism within China was heavily influenced by Taoism, so that in many minds there was barely a distinction between the two; and Confucianism, which is primarily concerned with morality and public life, has been seen as complementary.

The central figure of Taoism is Lao Tzu, whose book ***Tao Te Ching*** contains the core of Taoist teaching. According to popular tradition, he was an older contemporary of Kung Fu Tzu, and he served as librarian to a king who ruled in western China; he eventually became a hermit beyond the western border. But almost nothing is known for certain about him, and some even doubt his historical existence.

The two other great figures of Taoism are also shrouded in mystery. Chuang Tzu is said to have been a wandering sage in the fourth century BCE; while Lieh Tzu is said to have lived a more settled existence in the same period. Both became subjects of numerous stories and aphorisms; and the books ascribed to them are collections of these. It seems likely that there were many similar teachers in this period, whose ideas were based on ***Tao Te Ching***, and that Chuang Tzu and Lieh Tzu are composite figures.

Teachings

The most well-known concepts associated with Taoism are yin and yang. Yin is the female element in the universe, and yang the male; yin also represents being, and yang non-being. When yin and yang are awry, there is illness, misery and conflict; but when yin and yang are in harmony, there is health, joy and peace. Tao – which is best translated as the 'Way' – is the means by which yin and yang are reconciled; and a Taoist is one who tries to follow the Way.

Taoists accept all living beings, including themselves, as they are; they seek to live according to their own natures, and allow other living beings to live according to theirs. Equally they accept all events, including death, with equanimity. So they are indifferent to both honor and dishonor, praise and blame. They make no attempt to conform to moral or social standards that others have set. They do not wish to accumulate wealth, and do not regard themselves as owners of what they happen to possess. They adapt to the circumstances in which they find themselves. And above all, they cherish all living beings, but want power over none.

Although in the first millennium CE Taoism acquired the outward forms of religion, the original Taoists had no interest in temples and rituals. And although Lao Tzu is reputed to have been a great scholar, they had no interest in the acquisition of factual knowledge. On the contrary, they recognized that rituals and knowledge are frequently used to manipulate people and other beings, and so should be treated with great caution.

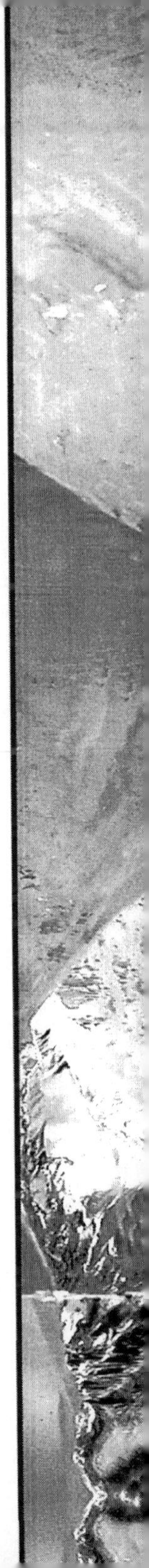

Expression

The three Taoist sages lived in a period when China was divided into separate kingdoms, which were frequently at war with one another. But after China was unified under a single emperor in 221 BCE, two books became popular which gave practical expression to Taoism; one book was devoted mainly to health and illness, while the other concerned sexuality. The apparent author was the Yellow Emperor, a mythical ruler from the ancient past; but in the popular mind he was frequently identified with Lao Tzu.

Illness occurs, according to the Yellow Emperor, when yin and yang are out of balance. If yang is too strong, the body becomes hot, the limbs feel heavy, the pulse is weak, and the mind confused. If yin is too strong, the body becomes cold, the limbs tremble, the stomach cannot digest food, and the mind is anxious. The main causes of imbalance are excessive stress, inability to control anger, an unhealthy diet, lack of regularity in eating and sleeping, and lack of exercise.

The main method of restoring balance between yin and yang, and hence curing diseases, is acupuncture. By putting needles in different parts of the body, excessive yin or yang is drained away. Another treatment is moxa, in which balls of powdered mugwort are placed on the skin and ignited.

In sexual intercourse, according to the Yellow Emperor, a man and a woman can experience perfect unity of yin and yang – but only if their moods and emotions are in harmony. If there is emotional disharmony, intercourse may cause illness.

Us

Success in life is usually judged by the amount of wealth we accumulate, and the power and status we attain; and our value to society is judged by our visible achievements. Taoism reverses those judgments. We are successful if we learn to need little and to want nothing, if we exert no power over any other living being, and if we are indifferent to status. But if we try to manipulate the natural order for the benefit of humanity, we will simply damage it to everyone's detriment.

Taoism also reverses the conventional judgments about education and morality. Success in education is usually judged by the amount of knowledge we acquire and skills we master. But Taoism teaches us the wisdom to accept ourselves as we are, and other living beings as they are – and from this acceptance all practical skills flow naturally. Morality is usually regarded as a set of rules and standards which society imposes on its members. But Taoism teaches us to study yourself, and act only in accordance with our own nature.

Thus if we successfully follow of the Way – the Tao – we shall harm no one, love everyone, achieve nothing, and be content with all things.

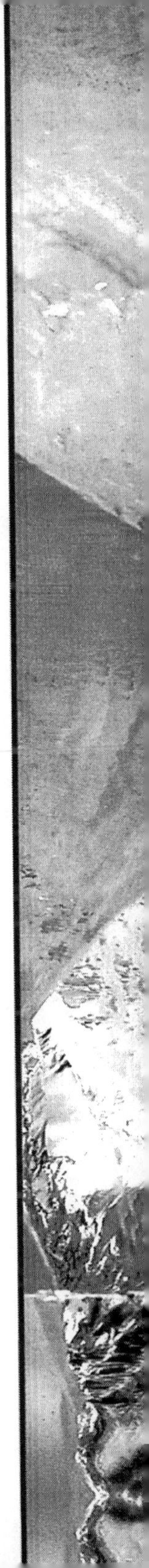

1

THE WISE LIBRARIAN

Lao Tzu was a very learned man. He was librarian at the palace of the most powerful king of China; the library contained copies of all the books that had been written in China; and Lao Tzu had read each book several times. Thus his head contained all the knowledge that anyone had ever recorded. He was also very wise. He understood how human beings can be happy and contented; and he understood how human society should be organized, to enable human beings to find happiness and contentment.

Lao Tzu gradually became famous for his knowledge and wisdom, and people came from throughout China to seek his advice. Eventually more people were coming to the palace to see this humble librarian than to see the king himself. The king, who was proud and arrogant, resented this; and as a result he refused to seek Lao Tzu's advice, either on personal or political matters.

Many of the people visiting Lao Tzu reported great misery amongst the common people. The king was constantly issuing decrees on every aspect of their daily lives: how they should look after their animals and grow their crops; how they should educate their children; how they should build their homes; and so on. And he sent soldiers to every town and village, to ensure his decrees were obeyed. These decrees were often foolish; and besides, people wanted to be free to manage their lives as they pleased.

Lao Tzu was deeply saddened. He knew that the king issued these decrees not for the benefit of the people, but because he relished the exercise of power.

Lao Tzu: Legends

2

A SHORT BOOK

Every month Lao Tzu sent a message to the king, in which he urged him to stop issuing decrees, and allow the people to live freely. But, when these messages were delivered to him, the king merely laughed, and referred to Lao Tzu as 'an old fool'.

Owing to Lao Tzu's popularity, the king did not dare dismiss him. But finally Lao Tzu himself concluded that he could no longer remain an employee of the king, or even live under the king's rule. So one morning he walked out of the palace, and continued westwards until he reached the border of China.

At the border there was a large gateway built of green stone. One of the guards asked Lao Tzu his name. When Lao Tzu answered, the guard exclaimed: 'You are the wisest man in all China! Why are you leaving?' Lao Tzu explained his reasons. 'Before you pass through this gate,' the guard said, 'you must write down all your wisdom.' The guard escorted Lao Tzu to a small house; and there Lao Tzu wrote a short book about the 'Way'. Then he passed through the green gateway, and was never seen again.

The guard gave Lao Tzu's book to a scribe, who made a several copies of it. These were sent to scribes in other parts of China, where other scribes made copies. Soon his book was being read throughout the country - and Lao Tzu was even more famous in his absence than he had been when he lived in the king's palace. The king was furious, and he issued a decree that forbade people from reading Lao Tzu's book. But even his own soldiers refused to obey.

Lao Tzu: Tao Te Ching

3

The Way

This is what Lao Tzu wrote about the Way: 'There is an entity that contains everything. It existed before the earth and the sky. It is unmoving and unchanging. It has no body and no form. It is self-sufficient; it needs nothing apart from itself. It pervades all that exists and all that happens; it is present in every object and every event. It is the mother and father of everything. We cannot know it in itself, so we call it God. Yet we know that path which leads to it, and we call this path the Way.

'The Way is broad; you can move far to the right and to the left, and still remain on it. It is so broad that every living being on earth could move along it together.

'When you walk about a town, you stop in one place, and listen to some stirring music; you stop in another place, and eat some delicious food; but eventually you become satiated. If you listen to the Way, it seems dull; if you taste the Way, it seems insipid; yet you can never get enough of it.

'If you study books and memorize facts, you learn more day by day. If you follow the Way, you do less day by day. Eventually by following the Way, you arrive at the place of inaction; in that place nothing is done, and nothing is undone.

'Wise people hear about the Way, and strive hard to follow it. Ordinary people hear about the Way, and wander off and on it. Foolish people hear about the Way, and make jokes about it. After all, if the Way were not funny, it would not be the Way.

'The Way gives life.'

Lao Tzu: Tao Te Ching

4

Yin and Yang

Lao Tzu wrote about yin and yang: 'There are two principles, created by God, that govern all that exists: yin, which is female and dark, and yang which is male and light. The female should understand the male, yet not imitate him; she should be happy to be female. The male should understand the female, yet not imitate her; he should be happy to be male. Nothing can be built on a female foundation alone, or on a male foundation alone; but if the female and the male are together and yet distinct, the whole world can be built on them.'

He wrote about wisdom and folly: 'When wise people do good, they expect no gratitude, and ask for no reward; but when foolish people do good, they demand honor, wealth and praise. Wise people are indifferent to other people's opinion of them, so they speak and act to please their own consciences; foolish people crave respect, so they bend their words and actions to please others. Wise people need little, and want less; foolish people need much, and want more. Wise people understand the unity of all people and things, and so they rejoice in diversity; foolish people want to impose unity on people and things, and so they hate diversity. Wise people cherish all humans, all animals, and all plants; foolish people exploit all living beings to satisfy their desires. Wise people lead or follow, are gentle or hard, are strong or weak, and are angry or calm, as circumstances require; foolish people pay no heed to changing circumstances, and behave as their impulses dictate.'

Lao Tzu: Tao Te Ching

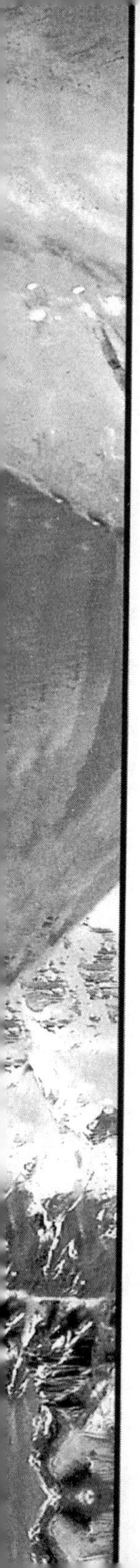

5

Paradoxes

Lao Tzu wrote about the paradoxes in the human condition: 'In order to be whole, you must be broken. In order to be straight, you must be twisted. In order to be full, you must be empty. In order to be renewed, you must be worn out. In order to gain much, you must have little. In order to understand the truth, you must be confused about facts. In order to be above suspicion, you must never justify yourself. In order to be honored, you must never seek praise. In order to win, you must never compete.'

He wrote about paradoxes in human society: 'When grand ambitions come to nothing, generosity and gentleness take their place. When scholarship is given undue respect, hypocrisy flourishes. When members of a family bicker, it is a sign of their love. When members of a society engage in heated debates about how that society should be organized, it is a sign of their patriotism.'

He wrote about goodness: 'Goodness is like water. Since water benefits everything, it competes with nothing. It even finds its way to the lowest and most filthy places.'

He wrote about inner peace: 'Accept what is, and know what endures. With that acceptance and that knowledge your mind will be at peace. Without it your mind will be in turmoil.'

He wrote about virtue: 'To have without possessing, to act without claiming credit, to lead without controlling – these are the mysterious virtues of the Way.'

Lao Tzu: Tao Te Ching

6

Freedom

Lao Tzu wrote about freedom: 'Do not strive to be holy, and forget trying to be wise; if you cast aside all ambitions towards holiness and wisdom, your relatives and friends will be greatly relieved. Do not strive to be virtuous, and forget trying to be good; if you cast aside all ambitions towards virtue and goodness, you will be filled with compassion. Do not strive for wealth, and forget trying to accumulate riches for the future; if you cast aside all ambitions towards wealth and riches, thieves and cheats will leave you alone. Do not strive to keep rules that others have made, and forget trying to live up to standards that others have set; if you cast aside all ambitions to conform, you will be free.'

He wrote about what is better and best: 'If you know how other people behave, you are intelligent; if you know yourself, you are wise. If you are content with your circumstances, you are fortunate; if you are content with yourself, you are rich. If you persevere in the face of adversity, you have determination; if you remain unmoved in the face of temptation or insults, you have courage. If you are happy to live, you are blessed; if you are happy to die, you will live as long as you want.'

He wrote about the world: 'Some people want to win the world by changing it; they always come to grief. The world is a sacred object. Nothing should be done to change it; any attempt to change it is bound to damage it. To try and possess the world, and to treat it as your own, is to destroy it.'

Lao Tzu: Tao Te Ching

7

Leadership

Lao Tzu wrote about leadership: 'The best leaders are those who are hardly known to the people they lead. The next best leaders are those who are loved and admired by their people. Below them come leaders who are feared by their people. And the worst leaders are those who are despised by their people. If leaders do not trust their people, their people will not trust them. Good leaders enable their people to look after themselves; so the sign of a good leader is that the people achieve much – and take the credit upon themselves.'

He wrote about war: 'Good rulers want their people to be prosperous, not victorious. They want their people to enjoy comfort through honest toil, not glory through the slaughter of others. Glory never lasts; it flourishes for a while, and then fades. Even the finest weapon is a tool of misery and grief; so the follower of the Way avoids all weapons. The murder of people in war should be mourned; the victors in war should be received with funeral ceremonies.'

He wrote about power: 'Great power consists in not clinging to power, and true power consists in not wanting power; when people want and cling to power, they show their weakness. The exertion of great power consists in doing nothing, and the exertion of true power consists in having nothing to do; weak people are constantly trying to achieve something. When we seek power, we lose the Way; when we lose power, we find the Way.'

Lao Tzu: Tao Te Ching

8

Three treasures

Lao Tzu wrote about hardness and softness: 'A living being is soft and tender; when it dies, it becomes hard and brittle. Look at the green leaves on the trees; then look again at the leaves after they have turned brown and fallen. Men and women with hard hearts are dead, even while they remain alive; men and women with soft and tender hearts are alive, even after they have died.'

He wrote about weakness and softness: 'Nothing in this world is as weak and soft as water. Yet nothing is so effective as water at wearing away stones, which are hard and strong. As a river runs over jagged rocks, the water remains unaltered, while the rocks become smooth. Thus weakness overcomes strength, and softness overcomes hardness.'

He wrote this about morality: 'Obedience to moral laws is the husk of the truth; it is like barren blossom that will not turn to fruit; it is ignorance masquerading as goodness. Wise people want the kernel, not the husk, the fruit and not the flower. Moral laws are rocks along the Way, which the wise push aside.'

He wrote about the three greatest treasures: 'The first treasure is compassion: if you are compassionate, you will also be brave, in order to protect those for whom you feel compassion. The second treasure is frugality: if you are frugal, you can afford to be generous, because your wealth and abilities exceed your needs. The third is modesty: if you are modest, with no desire to lead others, people will want to be led by you, because they know you will not oppress or exploit them.'

Lao Tzu: Tao Te Ching

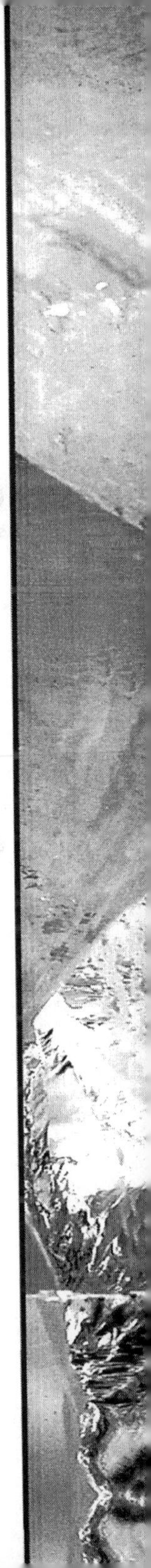

9

THE WORLD'S PATH

About two centuries after Lao Tzu left China, another great teacher appeared, called Chuang Tzu. No one knew where he had been born and raised, and he had no home; he wandered from place to place.

He gained such a reputation for wit and wisdom that the king sent two ambassadors to search for him, and ask him to become prime minister. When they eventually found him, he was fishing in a river. He declined their offer without even turning his head. So the king himself went to Chuang Tzu, and said: 'When the sun rises, there is no point in keeping torches lit. When the rain comes, there is no point in watering the ground. Now that you have appeared, there is no point in my continuing to rule. If you were to rule China, there would be perfect order; but while I continue to rule, there is disorder.'

Chuang Tzu replied: 'Your rule is not perfect, but it is satisfactory. If I were to become ruler, people would think that I wanted power, fame and wealth for myself; and as a consequence of these thoughts there would not be perfect order.' The king looked disappointed. Chuang Tzu added: 'The bird makes its nest deep in the forest, but uses only one branch. The animal drinks from the river, but takes only what it needs. The cook may not run the kitchen well, but the priest does not take his place.'

Then he offered this advice to the king: 'Let the world follow its own path, and do not try to control it. Let the world be as it wants to be, for it possesses its own virtue; any interference corrupts it.'

Chuang Tzu: Nan Hua Chen Ching

10

THE OAK TREE

Chuang Tzu was passing through a village with a companion. In the middle of the village stood a huge oak tree. The companion stopped and stared at the tree in astonishment for several minutes, but Chuang Tzu continued walking without even looking up.

The companion then ran to catch up with Chuang Tzu. 'Were you not impressed with that huge oak tree?' the companion asked. 'Yes,' Chuang Tzu replied. 'So why didn't you stand and admire it?' the companion asked. 'By ignoring it, I showed contempt for it,' Chuang Tzu replied. The companion was perplexed.

'That tree is so knotted and twisted,' continued Chuang Tzu, 'that it's completely worthless. Make boats out of it, and they'd sink. Build houses out of it, and they'd collapse. Make posts out of it, and the worms would eat them. As a result nobody has chopped it down – and it's been allowed to grow to its full height. If I had stood and admired it, people in the village might have changed their minds about it, and chopped it down.'

At that moment a weasel ran across the road. Chuang Tzu pointed to the animal, and said: 'The weasel is small and agile; it crouches in the undergrowth until it sees its prey – and then leaps out. But weasels rarely live long; they soon leap onto a trap and are killed. Now think of the yak. It's big and clumsy, and can catch nothing. But most yaks live to a great age. So learn from the yak and that oak tree in the village; if you want to enjoy a long and contented life, strive to be worthless.'

Chuang Tzu: Nan Hua Chen Ching

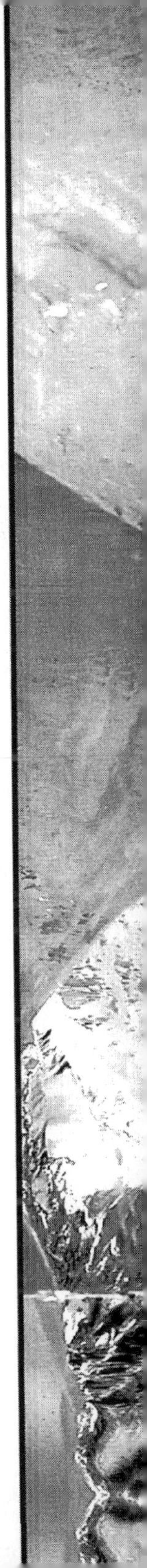

11

Reality, truth and destiny

A young man came to Chuang Tzu, and asked him to explain the Way. 'The Way is like the hub of a wheel,' Chuang Tzu replied; 'at the hub all the spokes are unified. Compare a tiny stalk with a great pillar, a leper with a beautiful woman, a comic event with a tragic event. On the Way these opposites are reconciled – the differences between them disappear.'

Then the young man asked Chuang Tzu to explain reality. 'One night a man dreamt he was a butterfly,' Chuang Tzu replied; 'in his dream he flitted from one flower to another. In the morning he awoke, and saw that he was a man. But then he wondered if he had dreamt of waking up. He asked himself: "Am I man who has dreamt he was a butterfly, or am I a butterfly who is dreaming he is a man?" On the Way dreams are reality, and reality is a dream.'

The young man asked Chuang Tzu about truth. 'Suppose you and I had an argument,' Chuang Tzu replied,' and you got the better of me. Does that prove that your view is true and mine false? I could go out and find someone who agrees with me. Does that prove that my view is true and yours false? There is no single voice that can resolve all disagreements. On the Way all things can be as they are, and can change as they wish.'

The young man asked about destiny. Chuang Tzu pointed to the man's shadow, and replied: 'Your shadow does exactly what your body does; it cannot do otherwise. But is your body controlled by another entity? And if so, what controls that other entity?'

Chuang Tzu: Nan Hua Chen Ching

12

Right and Wrong

Another young man asked Chuang Tzu about right and wrong. 'Eels live in the water; birds live in trees; and human beings live in houses. Which of these three chooses the right place to live? Humans eat grain, fruit and meat; deer eat grass; centipedes devour snakes. Which of these three chooses the right food to eat? A male monkey mates with a female monkey; a male fish enjoys the favors of a female fish; a man might be attracted to a certain woman. Is the monkey, the fish, or the man right in assessing beauty? Would you like an eel to tell you what is right and wrong – or a bird, or a deer, or a centipede, or a monkey, or a fish?'

Then the young man asked about wisdom and folly. Chuang Tzu told a story: 'A father sent his son and daughter to tend his sheep, which were grazing on a hillside; but they lost the sheep. When the father asked the boy what happened, the boy replied that he was reading – and so did not notice the sheep disappearing. When the father asked the girl what happened, the girl replied that she was playing a game – and so did not notice the sheep disappearing. They were each doing something different, but they both lost the sheep. There are many different ways of being foolish, but only one way to be wise.'

The young man looked puzzled. 'You seem to be saying that wisdom consists in doing what is right,' he said; 'but earlier you suggested that there are no standards of right and wrong.' Chuang Tzu smiled, and said: 'Wisdom consists in bringing your nature and your circumstances into harmony.'

Chuang Tzu: Nan Hua Chen Ching

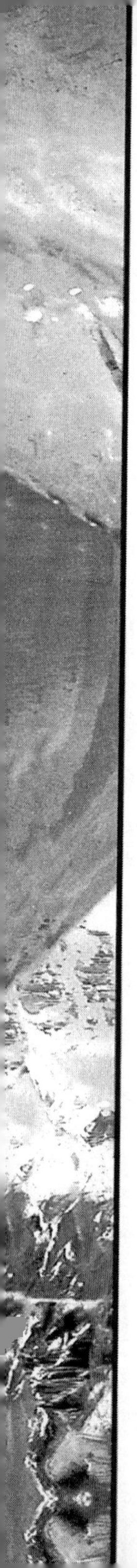

13

THE ART OF BUTCHERY

At one time Chuang Tzu worked as a butcher for a nobleman. He soon became supremely efficient at his task: every movement of his hand, every heave of his shoulder, every step of his feet, and every thrust of his knee, helped him to cut up a carcass with speed, elegance and ease.

One day the nobleman came to the shed where Chuang Tzu worked, and watched him cut up a huge bull. The nobleman was entranced by Chuang Tzu's skill, and asked him how he had acquired it. 'I follow the Way,' replied Chuang Tzu. 'But how does the Way enable you to butcher meat?' the nobleman asked. 'Most butchers are guided by what they see with their eyes,' Chuang Tzu said, 'but I am guided by what my mind understands and perceives. Thus I perceive the natural lines of the animal, and my knife follows those lines. I perceive the weak points in the animal's flesh, and my knife pierces those points. I never touch the smallest ligament or tendon, let alone any bone. An ordinary butcher has to change his knife every month, because he hacks at the meat; but the blade of my knife is as sharp as ever.' 'What do you do when you come to a difficult part of the animal?' the nobleman asked. 'I think for a few moments,' Chuang Tzu replied; 'then I gently move my knife until the flesh falls apart.'

Chuag Tzu concluded: 'Use your ears and eyes to hear and see what is within yourself; and use your heart and mind to feel and know what is outside yourself.' The next day Chuang Tzu left the nobleman.

Chuang Tzu: Nan Hua Chen Ching

14

TIGERS AND HORSES

A nobleman decided to keep tigers as pets; and he employed a team of men to train them, in the hope that the tigers would perform tricks for the entertainment of his guests. But the tigers frequently attacked the trainers, and killed them.

Chuang Tzu was grieved to hear that so many men were being killed. So he went to the nobleman, and offered to train the trainers; the nobleman accepted. Chuang Tzu said to the trainers: 'If you wish to remain alive, you must understand the tiger's nature, and adapt yourself to it. Do not give tigers living animals to eat, as this engenders in them a love of killing. Do not give them whole carcasses, as the act of tearing these apart excites them. Do not give them too much meat, as this will make them lazy; and do not give them too little meat, as this will leave them hungry, and they will bite your flesh. By this means the tigers will become gentle and obedient – which is how they wish to be.'

Another nobleman employed a man called Po to train his horses. Po branded the horses with a hot iron; he cut their hair and trimmed their hooves; he gave them too little to eat and drink, in order to make them lean; and when he rode them, he whipped them to make them gallop faster. Some of the horses died; and the others became aggressive.

Chuang Tzu heard about this, and asked the nobleman if the could replace Po; the nobleman agreed. He put the horses in a large field, where they could gallop freely, and eat as much grass as they wished. And he invited people to ride them whenever they wished. Soon the horses were healthy and docile – as they wish to be.

Chuang Tzu: Nan Hua Chen Ching

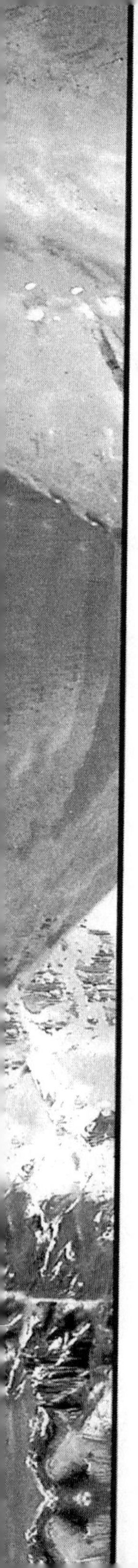

15

Two funerals

A wise old man died, and Chuang Tzu went to his funeral. At the funeral the old man's relatives and friends were weeping and wailing; and one by one they gave speeches in his honor. Finally it was Chuang Tzu's turn to speak. 'I am ashamed of you all,' he began, 'because you betray the man whom you mourn. He accepted life as it is, and death when it came; and he was indifferent to both honor and disgrace. So if you wish to be true to him, forget him – but remember his wisdom.'

An old friend of Chuang Tzu died. Chuang Tzu showed no signs of grief or distress; and many people concluded that Chuang Tzu had not really loved his friend. At the friend's funeral, Chuang Tzu rose up, and spoke: 'When my friend died, I wept. But then I looked back to the time before his birth, when he did not have a body. Then I looked forward again to the mysterious process by which he acquired a body at conception and birth. Then I reflected that at death another mysterious process has occurred. Birth, death – these are like the passing of seasons.'

The people begged him to continue. 'It is not only at birth and death that we change,' he said; 'every moment we are changing from one state to another. None of us understands the process of change, so we cannot predict the future. But when we recognize the constancy of change, our hearts are no longer troubled by it. My friend has changed from life to death; and the same time I have changed from having him as a friend to not having him as a friend. Neither he nor I have reason to be sad.'

Chuang Tzu: Nan Hua Chen Ching

16

A GOOD RULER

The old king died, and his son took his place. The new king sent an emissary to Chuang Tzu, to ask advice on being a good ruler. The emissary thought that he himself knew the answer. So when he met Chuang Tzu, he said: 'In my view a good ruler should desire to guide his people; so, with the help of advisors like me, he will frequently issue decrees on every aspect of human life. He should be as swift as an echo in moving from one part of his country to another; so, in fear that he might arrive at any time, all people will obey his decrees. And he should be as strong as an oak-tree; so, in fear of his wrath, no enemy will attack him.'

'The tiger and the leopard are hunted for their beautiful hides,' Chuang Tzu replied; 'and the monkey is kept in captivity so people can admire its agility.' The emissary was baffled by this remark, and asked Chuang Tzu to explain himself. 'The people would rise up against a king as swift as an echo; and rebels and foreign kings would combine their armies against a king as strong as an oak-tree. The good ruler is quite different.'

'So how do you describe a good ruler?' the emissary asked. Chuang Tzu replied: 'His mind is simple, so he has no opinions of his own; and he is at one with that which is beyond definition. He neither promotes one person above another, nor praises one person above another, but lets all people fulfill their natures. Thus they achieve what they want to achieve without obeying him; and they have what they want to have without depending on him. And, since he threatens no one, he has no enemies.'

Chuang Tzu: Nan Hua Chen Ching

17

A HAMMER AND CHISEL

A wealthy nobleman was sitting on a terrace outside his house and reading a book. Chuang Tzu passed by and asked him what he was reading. 'The writing of a very wise man,' the nobleman replied. 'Is he still living?' Chuang Tzu asked. 'No, he died long ago,' the nobleman said. 'Then the book is nothing but rubbish left over from the past,' Chuang Tzu declared. The nobleman was furious. 'How dare you comment on what I choose to read!' he exclaimed. 'Let me justify myself,' Chuang Tzu said; 'if I fail to convince you, then you can have me whipped.' 'Very well,' the nobleman replied.

Chuang Tzu asked the nobleman to lead him to his carpenter's workshop. The carpenter was making a piece of furniture. 'I want you to observe how the carpenter uses his hammer and chisel,' Chuang Tzu said. So the two men stood for several minutes in the workshop, and watched the carpenter.

Then Chuang Tzu spoke: 'If he were to strike the chisel too softly with his hammer, it would make a pleasant sound, but it would not cut the wood. If he were to strike too hard, he would soon become tired, and have to stop. He has learnt to strike the chisel with just the right amount of force that both cuts the wood and conserves his energy. This means that he holds the hammer both in his hand and in his mind. If you were to ask him to explain this, he would not have words; he could not even explain it to his son. The knowledge will die with him. So it is with the wisdom of the wise.'

The nobleman threw down his book, and asked Chuang Tzu to teach him the Way.

Chuang Tzu: Nan Hua Chen Ching

18

THE FIELD AND THE JAR

When he grew very old, Chuang Tzu was too weak to walk from place to place. So he found a small piece of land on the bank of a river. Each spring he cleared the land of weeds, and planted vegetables. Then he irrigated the land by dipping a jar in the river, and pouring the water on the soil; this process was so slow that it took an entire month to cover the land – and then it was time to start again.

One day a young man passed by, and saw Chuang Tzu watering his vegetables. He went up to Chuang Tzu, and said: 'There's a machine that can irrigate a large field in a day. You should get one.' 'How does is work?' Chuang Tzu asked. The young man explained its elaborate mechanism.

Chuang Tzu smiled. 'Young man,' he said, 'such a machine would frequently go wrong. In fact, all machines go wrong. And when a machine on which you depend goes wrong, your mind becomes anxious and upset. And when the mind is anxious and upset, it is impossible to follow the Way. Besides, what would I do with my time if a machine did my work for me?'

The young man looked bewildered. Chuang Tzu put his arm round the young man's shoulders, and said: 'I can see that you confuse knowledge with wisdom, and efficiency with happiness.' The young man wandered away, his face white with confusion.

The following day the young man returned, with a jar in his hand; and he offered to help Chuang Tzu irrigate his land. 'You have understood the Way,' Chuang Tzu said.

Chuang Tzu: Nan Hua Chen Ching

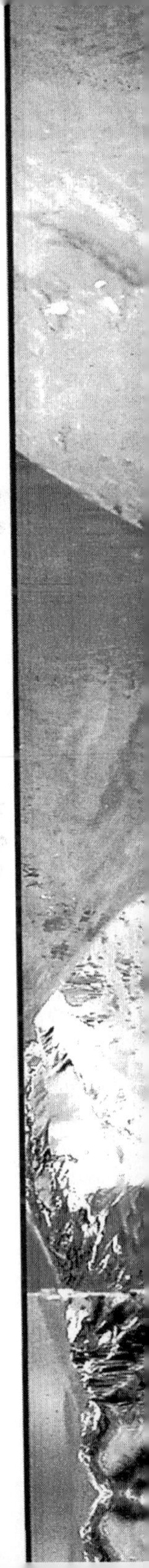

19

The Bird and the Monkeys

Soon afterwards Chuang Tzu fell ill, and he knew that he was dying. The young man cared for him; and shortly before his death, Chuang Tzu told three parables that summarized his teaching.

This was the first: 'One day a beautiful bird flew into the garden of the king's palace, and perched on one of the trees. The king saw it, and was enchanted by its appearance. He ordered his servants to capture it in a net, and put it in his ancestral temple. There the king arranged for his chefs to prepare the finest food for it, and his musicians to play their sweetest music for its entertainment. But the food made the bird sick, and the music made its head spin; so three days later it died.'

Chuang Tzu concluded: 'Let all living things be as they are. And do not try to understand why things are as they are. The more you understand the reasons for things being as they are, the more you will be tempted to change things.'

This was the second: 'A monkey trainer was handing out acorns. He said to the monkeys: "You will each get three in the morning and four in the evening." This made the monkeys furious. So the trainer said: "Very well, you will get four in the morning and three in the evening." The monkeys were delighted. There was no difference between the monkey trainer's two statements; but one provoked anger, and the other joy.'

Chuang Tzu concluded: 'Wise people are like the monkey trainer; they present the truth in such a manner that it provokes joy.'

Chuang Tzu: Nan Hua Chen Ching

20

THE FROG IN THE WELL

This was the third parable that Chuang Tzu told: 'There was a frog who lived in a well. A giant turtle, who lived in the great ocean, came to visit the well. He looked over the side, and introduced himself to the frog. The frog said: "What fun I have in this well! The stones above the water have lots of little ledges, and I can hop between them. If I become hot, I can dive into the water and have a bath. There are all kinds of little insects flying about, which I can capture in my mouth and eat. I am the complete master of my well. Come inside and share my pleasure."

'But when the turtle lifted its left foot into the well, its right knee became wedged; so it drew back, complaining that the well was too small. Then it said: "Let me tell you about my home, which is the ocean. It's so wide that no one can measure its width. It's so deep that no one can measure its depth. When the rain comes down, it never rises; when there is a drought, it never falls. It never changes, whether for an instant or forever."

'The frog was dumbfounded – and from that moment it ceased to enjoy its life in the well.'

Chuang Tzu concluded: 'Be content with what you have, and do not hanker after what others have. Be content with the knowledge you possess; but remember that your knowledge is only a fraction of all that can be known. Search for wisdom, for with wisdom you can fathom the deepest ocean, and soar above the highest star. In searching for wisdom you follow the Way.'

Chuang Tzu: Nan Hua Chen Ching

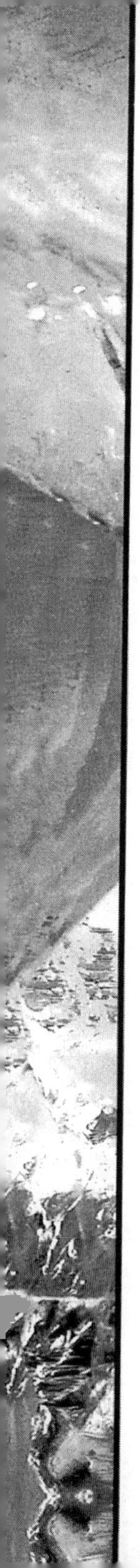

21

THE MAN IN THE FOREST

At around the time Chuang Tzu was wandering across China, a man of great wisdom called Shang lived in a hut, deep in a vast forest in the center of China. Only one man ever met Shang, and his name was Lieh Tzu.

Lieh Tzu grew up in a town on the edge of the forest. Most people in the town were frightened of the forest, which was thick and dark. But throughout his childhood Lieh Tzu had a deep desire to explore it; and when he reached the age of twenty, he decided to satisfy his desire. He walked for many days beneath the trees; at night he plucked their berries to eat; and he collected fallen leaves to make a mattress on which to sleep. He knew that he was searching, yet he had no idea for what or whom.

Finally he reached Shang's hut. He looked inside, and saw Shang sitting on a mat, perfectly still; and he realized that he had found the object of his search. 'Will you teach me the wisdom you have acquired?' Lieh Tzu asked. Shang did not reply. Lieh Tzu repeated the question several times, but Shang remained silent. He built himself a hut nearby, in the hope that one day Shang would speak to him.

Every morning he asked Shang to teach him. Finally after three years Shang nodded. Another five years passed; and by that time Lieh Tzu had lost all sense of right and wrong, good and bad. Then Shang turned to him, and smiled. A further seven years passed; by that time Lieh Tzu was indifferent as to whether Shang replied or not. Then Shang invited him to sit on the mat beside him.

Lieh Tzu: Ch'ung-hsu chih-te chen-ching

22

THE YOUNG CARPENTER

Another nine years passed. Lieh Tzu sat on the mat beside Shang from dawn until dusk each day. Eventually Lieh Tzu reached a state when his eyes had become like his ears, his ears like his nose, and his nose like his tongue; all his senses were unified – and his mind was at peace. Then Shang pushed him hard on the arm. Lieh Tzu rose up, and walked out of the forest to his town.

He built a small house on the edge of the town. When he had been living there for several months, a young man called on him, and said: 'I wish to be wise; and I believe that you possess wisdom. Will you teach me what you know?' Lieh Tzu did not reply, and the young man went away. He called nine more times, and asked the same question; and still Lieh Tzu did not reply. On the tenth visit he became angry, and called Lieh Tzu an arrogant old fool.

A year later the young man returned. 'My anger towards you has subsided,' the young man said, 'and I come again in search of wisdom.' Lieh Tzu now spoke: 'Even though you feel no anger at this moment, you still have the capacity for anger.' 'So how can I rid myself of anger altogether?' the young man asked. 'You must rid yourself of all ambition to be wise,' Lieh Tzu replied. 'How can I do that?' the young man asked.

'What is your work?' Lieh Tzu asked. 'I am a carpenter,' the young man replied. 'Then,' said Lieh Tzu, 'work as a carpenter to the best of your ability.' The young man felt disappointed; but he understood Lieh Tzu's advice – and became a superb carpenter.

Lieh Tzu: Ch'ung-hsu chih-te chen-ching

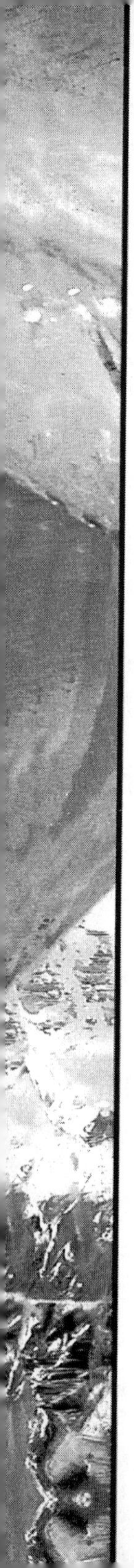

23

The Harsh Landowner

A man called Chu owned a large estate near the town where Lieh Tzu lived. Chu compelled his employees to work hard from dawn to dusk each day, and allowed them no days of rest. One of his employees, called Fu, was elderly and frail, and Chu took pleasure in making him work even harder than the rest.

One evening Fu came to visit Lieh Tzu, and complained about Chu's harsh regime. Lieh Tzu listened with compassion, and then said: 'As you lie in bed at night, imagine yourself leading a life of ease. Conjure up in your mind every kind of comfort.' Fu did as Lieh Tzu instructed. As a result his nights were pleasant; and even during the day he felt better, because a glimmer of hope shone in his heart – hope that one day his vision of ease and comfort might be realized.

Later that evening Lieh Tzu went to visit Chu, and said: 'Imagine yourself as one of your employees – such as Fu.' Then he left. Chu could not get the thought of being Fu out of his mind; he could feel Fu's aching limbs and back, and sense his despair. Night after night he could barely sleep; and during the day fear darkened his heart – fear that one day his vision might be realized.

A month passed. Lieh Tzu invited both men to his house, and asked: 'Which of you now has the better life: Fu, whose nights are pleasant, and whose days are lit by hope; or Chu, whose nights are miserable, and whose days darkened by fear?' Chu knew at once the answer; and from that day treated all his employees with kindness.

Lieh Tzu: Ch'ung-hsu chih-te chen-ching

24

The dying ruler

The local ruler was called Ching. He lived in a large and elegant mansion, which was situated in a beautiful lush valley. Ching admired Lieh Tzu, and many times he invited Lieh Tzu to stay in his mansion. For several years Lieh Tzu refused. But then Ching contracted an illness that was fatal; so Lieh Tzu decided to accept.

One morning Lieh Tzu suggested that they ride in Ching's carriage to the top of one of the hills surrounding the valley. The two men set out, accompanied by several of Ching's servants. When they reached the top, they say down on the grass, and looked down over the valley and mansion. Tears welled up in Ching's eyes. 'Why are you weeping?' Lieh Tzu asked. 'Soon I shall die,' Ching answered, 'and then I shall depart from this lovely place. If only I could stay alive for ever!' One of his servants echoed his sentiments: 'We too love this place so much that we dread death.'

Leh Tzu smiled, and said: 'Suppose that your father, grandfather, great-grandfather, and all your ancestors had remained alive. The mansion would now be packed with them and their wives, and there would be no space for you. So, instead of enjoying its luxury and splendor, you would be working in a rice-field and living in a thatched hut. You must die in order that you son, grandson and all your descendents can have their opportunity.'

In the following months, as he steadily grew weaker, Ching remembered Lieh Tzu's words, and was content to die.

Lieh Tzu: Ch'ung-hsu chih-te chen-ching

25

THE MERCHANT AND THE SCHOLAR

The wealthiest merchant in the town was called Kung, and the most learned scholar was called Chi. Kung spent every hour of the day making money, while Chi remained at home reading and thinking.

One summer both Kung and Chi fell ill. The town's physician treated them with acupuncture, but they both grew worse. Physicians from neighboring towns were called in, but their efforts also failed. Finally it occurred to both Kung and Chi that they should seek the advice of Lieh Tzu.

Lieh Tzu invited them to his house, and they were carried there on stretchers. He knew them well, but nonetheless he asked each of them many questions about his way of life. Finally he said to Kung: 'Your problem is that your ambition is greater than your energy. You are ambitious to become the wealthiest man in the region; and you are constantly straining yourself to achieve this ambition. That is why you are ill.' Then he said to Chi: 'Your problem is that your energy is greater than your ambition. You have no ambition to serve others as a scholar; so you only read and think, and never write or teach. That is why you are ill.'

'So how can I regain my health?' Kung asked. 'And how I regain mine?' Chi added. 'You must become close friends,' Lieh Tzu, 'and each must guide the other. You, Kung, must teach Chi the pleasure of hard work; and you, Chi, must teach Kung the joy of leisure.' Thus Kung became quite learned, and Chi earned handsome fees as a teacher.

Lieh Tzu: Ch'ung-hsu chih-te chen-ching

26

ARCHERY AND THE WAY

A young man called Tai came to Lieh Tzu, and said: 'I wish to follow the Way, and I also wish to learn archery. Is it possible to do both?' Lieh Tzu nodded, and replied: 'Obtain a bow and arrows, and I shall watch you shoot the arrows.' The next day Tai returned with a bow and arrows, and eagerly started to shoot. But he proved utterly inept: if he aimed at a tree, his arrow might hit a nearby hedge; if he aimed at a hedge, his arrow might fly past the nose of a nearby cow.

Lieh Tzu said to him: 'Leave your bow and arrows with me. Go to the home of the weaver, and lie under his loom. As the shuttle passes to and fro in front of your eyes, strive not to blink.' Tai did this for an entire year, and learnt to control his blinking.

He returned to Lieh Tzu, and asked: 'Am I now ready to resume archery?' 'No,' Lieh Tzu replied. 'What else must I do?' Tai asked. Lieh Tzu replied: 'You must catch a flea each day, and attach it to a hair from a yak's tail. As dusk approaches, hang the flea over a window facing west; and watch the flea with the sun behind it.' Tai did this for an entire year. Gradually, month by month, the flea seemed to grow larger, until it was as big as a cartwheel. And when he looked at other objects, they too seemed very large.

He returned to Lieh Tzu, and Lieh Tzu told him he was now ready to resume archery. Tai took his bow with great excitement; and he found he could hit the target with every arrow. When he looked at the target, he could focus his eyes on it without blinking; and it seemed so large that it filled his vision.

Lieh Tzu: Ch'ung-hsu chih-te chen-ching

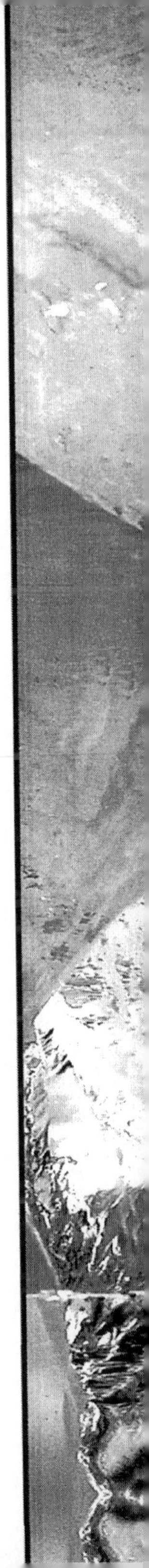

27

A DEER IN A DITCH

A woodcutter named Cheng went into the forest each day to collect firewood. One day he encountered a deer. It was paralyzed with fright; so Cheng hit it with a stick, and killed it. Then he buried it in a ditch, with the intention of returning for it later, after he had carried a load of firewood back home. But when he came back, he could not find the ditch – and he eventually concluded that he must have dreamt the whole incident.

He mentioned this to a group of friends. The next day one of this group, called Yan, went into the forest in search of the deer. He found the deer, brought it home, cut it into pieces, and sold the meat in the market-place.

When Cheng heard that Yan had found the deer and sold its meat, he was furious. He went to Yan, and demanded the money he had made; but Yan refused to hand anything to him. So they went to Lieh Tzu, and asked him to pass judgment.

When he had heard the full story, Lieh Tzu said to Cheng: 'You cannot distinguish between waking and dreaming. So you would not know whether the money was real or not.' Then he said to Yan: 'You distinguish too clearly between waking and dreaming. So you regard money as more important than it is.' Lieh Tzu concluded: 'Neither of you should have the money. Hand it to me, and I shall give it to the poor.'

Lieh Tzu now smiled. 'You must now become like brothers,' he said to them both, 'because you need one another. Let Yan help Cheng to distinguish between waking and dreaming. And let Cheng show Yan that the two are equally important.'

Lieh Tzu: Ch'ung-hsu chih-te chen-ching

28

INNKEEPERS AND GUARDS

A new king had come to the throne who was cruel and harsh, and who was levying heavy taxes on the people. Lieh Tzu decided to visit him, and set out for his palace.

When he had covered half the journey, he turned back. He met an old friend on the road, who asked him why he was returning home. 'I was alarmed,' Lieh Tzu replied. 'By what?' the friend asked. 'I stopped at ten inns,' Lieh Tzu said; 'at each inn the innkeeper served me first, and the innkeeper's wife brought me warm water to wash my hands and face. Worse still, the other guests bowed to me. That's a sign that I am not following the Way.' The friend looked baffled.

'I must be behaving as if I deserve respect and honor,' Lieh Tzu continued; 'and this shows that deep within me I must be craving these things. If I had continued my journey to the king's palace, the king might have offered me some high office; and out of desire for respect and honor, I might have accepted it.'

Lieh Tzu remained at home for a further year; then he set out again for the king's palace. The innkeepers no longer served him first, their wives no longer brought him warm water to wash his hands and face, and the other guests ignored him. Lieh Tzu was pleased.

When he arrived at the palace gates, the guards thought he was a beggar, and beat him with sticks. He smiled, and said to himself: 'Yes, I am truly following the Way.' The next day he returned to the palace gates, and deliberately behaved as he had done a year earlier. The guards bowed to him, and allowed him to enter.

Lieh Tzu: Ch'ung-hsu chih-te chen-ching

29

WAY FOR A KING

When he stood before the throne, he introduced himself as a teacher of wisdom. 'I have no interest in wisdom,' the king replied gruffly. 'Suppose that I could teach you a Way,' Lieh Tzu said, 'which would enable you to deflect any knife or sword that was aimed at you – so you could repel any attacker. Would you be interested?' 'Yes,' the king replied, 'I certainly would.'

'Suppose that I could teach you a Way,' Lieh Tzu continued, 'that would enable you to instill great fear in your people, so that no-one would dare to attack you. Would you be interested?' 'Yes,' the king replied, 'I certainly would.'

'Suppose that I could teach you a Way,' Lieh Tzu continued, 'that would enable you to instill great love in your people, so that they would all want to serve you. Would you be interested?' 'Yes,' the king replied, 'I certainly would.'

'This Way is very simple,' Lieh Tzu declared; 'it requires you to give up all attempts to rule your people, and to let them rule themselves. The people will then flourish and prosper, and they will hold you responsible for their happiness. Thus they will love you beyond measure, and be eager to serve you in any manner you wish.'

That day the king lifted the taxes he was levying, and revoked every decree he had issued. Rumors soon spread that Lieh Tzu was the cause of this change. So on his journey home every innkeeper served him first, every innkeeper's wife brought him warm water to wash his hands and face, and every other guest at every inn bowed to him.

Lieh Tzu: Ch'ung-hsu chih-te chen-ching

30

FINAL QUESTIONS

When Lieh Tzu reached the age of ninety, he knew that he would soon die. So he sent a message to everyone in the town: 'If you wish to ask me any more questions, come to me at noon tomorrow.' At noon the next day every man, woman and child of the town gathered outside his house.

'Have you any regrets?' one person asked. Lieh Tzu replied: 'As a child I never learnt to behave politely; as a man I never strove for success; and in my old age I look forward to death. So what have I to regret?'

'What pleasures have you enjoyed?' another person asked. Lieh Tzu replied: 'I have enjoyed food, because I have never wanted to eat more than my body needs. And I have enjoyed women, because I have admired the beauty of all women without wanting to possess any woman.'

'Have you been happy?' another person asked. Lieh Tzu replied: 'The causes of happiness are the same for everyone. Some people worry about being happy, so they never attain happiness. I have never worried about being happy, so I have experienced great happiness.'

'What have you learnt?' another asked. Lieh Tzu replied: 'All people understand the complexities of life; I have learnt its simplicity. All people understand the weariness of old age; I have learnt its hope. All people understand the ugliness of death; I have learnt its beauty.'

Lieh Tzu: Ch'ung-hsu chih-te chen-ching

31

From and to nowhere

Lieh Tzu sang the people of the town this song:

'When you are born, you come from nowhere; that is the Way.
When you live according to your nature, you are following the Way.
When you die, you go to nowhere; that is the Way.

Since you came with nothing, depend on nothing. Since you go with nothing, accumulate nothing. That is the Way.'

Then he went back into his house, lay down, and closed his eyes. A few moments later he was dead.

Lieh Tzu: Ch'ung-hsu chih-te chen-ching

MONTH 5

NATIVE AMERICAN

RELIGION

Introduction

Origins

In no native American language is there a term which could translate as 'religion'; but in every language there is a term for 'tradition', which embraces religion. Religion is seen as an integral aspect of the tradition that is handed down from one generation to the next. This adherence to tradition suggests that the native American religions changed very little from the time when human beings first came to north America tens of thousands of years ago, until Europeans began to arrive in significant numbers a few hundred years ago.

The native American traditions are oral, without any sacred writings in which beliefs are encapsulated and rituals prescribed. But as white settlers began to encroach their lands, several native American chiefs and preachers felt impelled to articulate their faith to the white commanders and governors – and their speeches were transcribed by white witnesses. These speeches provide the most direct insight into native American religion; and they are striking in their combination of simplicity and profundity.

By the middle of the nineteenth century a growing number of white Americans became anxious that American native traditions would soon die out; and there was an urgent effort to record native American customs, rituals, social structures, and ideas. It was soon discovered that the primary means of conveying ideas, including religious ones, was the folktale. Thus hundreds of folktales from every tribe were written down. Paradoxically these records are now being used by native Americans themselves as guides to the renewal of their culture and religion.

Teachings

The central feature of native American religion lies in the attitude to nature. All living beings – all animals and birds, insects and fish, all trees and plants – are regarded as sacred; indeed, the natural order as a whole is equated with the divine order. The majority of native American peoples live by hunting. But this is not seen as an exploitation of nature, or as an assertion of human superiority over animals; rather it is regarded as human participation in the divine order. There are many folktales that warn of the dangers of excessive hunting; and when the white settlers hunted the buffalo virtually to extinction in the late nineteenth century, there was not only alarm amongst native Americans at the loss of a vital source of food, but deep moral and spiritual outrage.

The sense of the sacred extends to the earth itself. Since humanity is one species amongst many, it cannot own any land; all land belongs to God, to be shared by all the living beings that inhabit it. At the same time people are spiritually attached to the land where they were born, and where their ancestors are buried. Thus there was further outrage at the white settlers laying exclusive claim to ranches and farms – and incomprehension at white people's willingness to abandon the land of their own birth, and seek wealth hundreds and even thousands of miles away.

Attachment to land extends beyond life into eternity. At death the body is absorbed by the soil, while the spirit continues to roam the forests and fields. And the living look to the dead for both guidance and comfort.

Expression

Just as native Americans identify the natural order with the divine order, so they identify symbols with reality. In particular, rituals are seen as effective means of attaining that which they represent. The war-dances prior to combat help to ensure victory; the ceremonies prior to hunting, in which the dancers imitate the sounds and movements of their prey, help to ensure success; and the healing ceremonies actually cure the sick.

Similarly words are understood as containing that which they express. So when a person speaks of a certain animal or tree, that animal or tree is spiritually present in the sound of its name. And when a story is told, the events of the story are being re-enacted in the life of the speaker and hearers. Thus native Americans generally use words with great care, and their speech is typically slow and ponderous.

The same fusion of symbol and reality is found in native American art. If animals and trees are painted on flattened bark, then those animals and trees become present – and the bark and the pigments are treated as sacred objects. If figures are carved onto rocks, then the figures in a spiritual sense comes to life – and the rock is treated as holy.

Time is regarded as cyclical. Each generation sees itself as repeating the life of the previous generation, without seeking to change or improve its situation – just as each year repeats the seasons of the previous year. And when the native Americans finally accepted the dominance of the white settlers, they saw this as part of the natural cycle in which each tribe and race enjoys an occasional – but passing – period of power.

Us

We have been taught to believe in progress: that each generation can and should enjoy a better life than the previous generation; and that we personally, through the course of our careers, should move from a lower position in society to a higher one. We have also been taught that progress is achieved primarily through science and technology, by which humanity achieves greater and greater mastery of nature.

The native Americans challenge us to question that faith. They teach us to regard ourselves as part of the natural order, not as masters of it. They warn us that, if we behave as masters of nature, we shall destroy it. And they tell us to look to the past for guidance as to how to live now and in the future.

They also challenge our attitude to the place in which we live. We may expect to move several times in the course of our lives, and to die a great distance from where we were born. The native Americans urge us to cherish the particular place in which we find ourselves – to regard it as gift from God – and therefore to move only with the greatest reluctance.

1

The Spirit's love

When Christian missionaries came to preach their beliefs to the Seneca, Chief Red Jacket called his people together to listen to them. When the missionaries had finished speaking, the chief rose up and replied:

Friends and brothers, it was the will of God that you should come to us, and God has given us a fine day for our meeting. God orders all things according to his will. He has taken his garment of clouds from the sky, so that the sun shines with all its brightness upon us. He has opened our eyes, so that we can see clearly. He has unstopped our ears, so that we can hear clearly; and we have heard clearly the words that you have spoken. For all this we thank God, and him alone.

Friends and brothers, you requested us to speak our minds freely. You say that you want an answer to your talk before you leave this place. It is right that you should have one, as you are far from your home, and we do not want to detain you. But first we shall look back; we shall tell you what our fathers have told us, and what white people have said to us.

Friends and brothers, listen to what we say. There was a time when our people owned this great land. They could walk freely from the place where the sun rises to the place where it sets. God gave this land to us. He created the buffalo and the deer for our food. He created the bear and the beaver to provide fur for our clothing. He caused the earth to produce corn, so we could bake bread. And he showed us how to settle disputes amongst us without shedding blood. He did all this because he loved us.

Chief Red Jacket

2

AN EVIL DAY

Friends and brothers, let me tell you of an evil day. It was the day when your forbears crossed the great waters, and arrived on this land. At first their number was small. They found friends, not enemies. They told us that they had fled from their country because their own compatriots were persecuting them for their religion. They asked only for a small amount of land where they could practice their religion freely. We took pity on them, and granted their request. We gave them corn and meat.

Friends and brothers, the white people had now found our country. The first settlers sent news back to their own land, and more arrived. Yet still we were not frightened of them; we still regarded them as friends, and they called us brothers. We gave them more land. But their number continued to increase, and eventually they wanted all our land. So wars took place; and to avoid shedding their own blood, they hired one tribe to fight against another, so many of our people were destroyed. They also gave us strong liquor, and that killed many others.

Friends and brothers, our land was once large and your land was small. Now you have become a great people, and we have scarcely enough space to spread our blankets. You have seized our country. Yet still you are not satisfied; you want to take away our religion as well, and force your own upon us.

Friends and brothers, you tell us that you are right about religion, and that we are wrong. Yet how can we know this – and how can you know this?

Chief Red Jacket

3

Differences in Religion

Friends and brothers, you say that there is only one way to serve and worship God. If there is only one religion, why do you people argue so much about it? Could this not be a sign that there are many ways to serve and worship God?

Friends and brothers, you tell us that your religion was given to your ancestors, and has been handed down from parent to child. We too have a religion that was given to our ancestors, and has been handed down from parent to child. We worship in the way that our parents taught us. In our worship we thank God for all the food and clothing he provides, and for the love that binds us one to another. We see no need to quarrel about religion.

Friends and brothers, God has made us all. But he has given different customs and skills to different nations. To your nation he has given great skill in making things, including weapons; to our nation he has given great skill in hunting. We know this to be true. Since he has made differences in these material things, may we not conclude that he wants us also to be different in religion? God does what is right. He knows what is best for his children. We are satisfied.

Friends and brothers, we have no wish to destroy your religion, or take it from you. We ask only that you do not try to destroy our religion or take it from us.

Friends and brothers, you have now heard our answer to your talk. We shall take clasp your hands in our own, and pray that God may protect you.

Chief Red Jacket

4

Common principles

As white men pushed further and further westwards toward the Mississippi river, a preacher called Tenkswataya arose from among the Shawnee. He went from tribe to tribe, proclaiming that all land is a gift from God to be shared by all, and that no tribe has a right to sell land to the white people. Then he went to see the governor of Indiana, and spoke to him:

It is now three years since I began to preach my message. Initially I was opposed by many of my own people. And when white people heard reports about my message, they became hostile towards me, and accused me of misleading my people. But my message is based on the principles of both my own religion and the white people's religion.

God is my instructor. He has told me to proclaim that he made the world, and that he made all human beings, both those with red skins and those with white. He told me to tell my people that they are wrong to sell their land, because it does not belong to them.

The red people and the white people should learn to live in unity. The white people should live according to their customs, and the red people according to theirs. The red people should not drink whisky, as it was made for the white people, who alone know how to use it. The white people and the red people should not meddle in each other's business. Then the red people would not need to use their tomahawks, and the white people would not need to use their muskets.

I now inform you that we wish to live in peace with you.

Tenkswataya

5

Common obedience

In the minds of my people God has affirmed the truth of my message. All the native tribes in this part of the world now regard land as a gift from him to be shared by all; so none will sell land to the white people. The native people were once divided, but now they are as one. They are all determined to practice what I have preached; God has spoken to them.

I am a warrior, and my mind and body have been hardened by war. You are a warrior, and your mind and body have been hardened by war. But let us cast aside our weapons; let us forget the arts of fighting. Instead let us live in peace and safety, and concentrate on caring for our children. We, the red people, will treat the life of every white person as sacred, if you, the white people, will treat the life of every red person as sacred.

Before I preached my message, my people were sad, because their actions were contrary to the will of God. But now my people are happy, because they have learned the will of God and obey it. Your people are sad, because their actions are contrary to the will of God. But if you learn the will of God and obey it, you will be happy.

God does not want you to buy land; he does not want you to treat land as your own possession. He wants you to regard land as his gift, to be shared by all. Nor does he want to ruin my people by selling them liquor.

As a sign of our friendship I now offer you our finest meat and our finest grain.

Tenkswataya

6

The Strong and the Weak

As many native people began to adopt the customs of the white people, Chief Smohalla of the Wanapam urged them to return to their traditional ways:

Once the world was all water, and God lived alone. He was lonely, and had no place to walk. So he reached down to the bottom of the water, lifted up the sand, and made land. He fashioned rocks and trees, and then he created men. At that time men had wings, and could fly anywhere they wished. But men were lonely, because they had no companions; so God created women, and told each man to marry a woman.

The men and women made nets, and went to the rivers and lakes to catch fish. At first this was their only food. But they said to God that they were bored with fish, and wanted other food as well. So God made the deer and the buffalo and other animals to provide meat. The winter came, and the men and women were cold. So God told them to take the skins of animals, and use them as clothes.

The first men and women had children; and their children had children. Gradually the number of human beings increased. Then the stronger humans began to oppress the weaker ones. They drove them from the lakes and rivers with the most plentiful fish, and from the lands with the most plentiful deer and buffalo. Then they proclaimed themselves as the owners these lakes and rivers and lands.

God was very angry. As a punishment he took away the wings from all human beings, and forced them to use their legs to move from one place to another.

Chief Smohalla

7

MOTHER EARTH

God declared that the land, the lakes and the rivers should be held in common; that they should not be marked off or divided, but that all people should be free to hunt and to fish wherever they want. God proclaimed that he himself is the father of all people, and that the earth is their mother – so all people are their children. He proclaimed that the laws of nature are his laws; and that, just as all animals and fish and plants obey those laws, so must all men and women.

Then the white people came; they divided up the land, and gave tracts of land to one another. They wrote out a piece of paper for each tract of land, on which was written the name of the owner; and they said that these pieces of paper gave the owners the right to do as they wished on the land. These white owners seized red people. They ordered them to plow the soil and grow crops, to cut the grass and make hay, and to chop down the trees and build houses.

Shall I obey those orders? Shall I plow the land to grow crops? I should rather take my knife and cut off my mother's breasts. Shall I cut the grass for hay? I should rather cut off my mother's hair. Shall I chop down trees and build houses? I should rather chop the limbs off my mother's body.

The earth is our mother – the mother of all people. The soil is her breasts, the grass is her hair, and the trees are her limbs. Let us refuse to murder our own mother. And let us protect her from all who try to rape her and destroy her beauty.

Chief Smohalla

8

THE SKY'S COMPASSION

When white people settled on the Pacific coast, Chief Seattle went to their governor, and delivered this speech:

Look up at the sky. For hundreds and thousands of years it has wept tears of compassion on my people; and to us it has always appeared changeless and eternal. But soon compassion may be useless, and it will cease to weep.

My words are like stars that never change. The white people can rely on my words as much as they rely on the return of the sun each morning, or the return of spring each winter.

The white people are many; they are like the grass that covers the vast prairie. My people are few; they resemble the scattered trees on a plain swept by storms.

You tell me that your leader, far away on the other side of this great land, sends us greetings of friendship and good will. That is kind of him, because we know that he has little need of our friendship in return.

You tell me that you wish to buy our lands, and are willing to leave us enough land to live in comfort. This appears just and even generous, for the red people no longer have the power to demand anything. It may also be wise, because we do not require much land to satisfy our needs.

There was a time when our people covered the land as waves cover the sea. But that was long ago; and the greatness of our people is now only a sad memory. I shall not dwell on our decay, nor blame the white people for hastening it.

Chief Seattle

9

An Ebbing Tide

Youth is impulsive. When young men grow angry at some real or imaginary wrong, their hearts turn black; and amongst our people they then paint their faces black. With blackened hearts and faces our young men are often violent and cruel, and our old men and women are unable to restrain them. It has always been thus; and so it was when the white people began to push our forbears westward. But let us hope that hostilities between red people and white people are finished. We have everything to lose and nothing to gain from more warfare. Young men may regard revenge as a gain, even at the loss of their own lives; but old men who stay at home, and mothers who risk losing their sons, know better.

Your leader far away sends us word that, if we obey his laws, he will protect us. He wants us to believe that his brave warriors will form a great wall, so our enemies to the north can never again frighten our women and children. He desires that we regard him as our father, and look upon ourselves as his children.

We should rather look to God for protection. But God loves your people, and hates my people. With his right hand he protects all those with white faces, and with his left hand he leads them as a father leads his infant son. But he has taken his hands away from those with red faces, and abandoned them. He makes your people grow stronger every day, and our people grow weaker; and soon your people will fill all the land. Our people are like an ebbing tide that will never return. God has ceased to love the red people; the red people are orphans who can look nowhere for help.

Chief Seattle

10

THE DEAD AND THE LIVING

To us the ashes of our ancestors are sacred, and their resting place is holy ground. Yet you wander far from the graves of your ancestors, and seem to have no regrets. Your religion was written on tablets of stone by the iron finger of God, so that you would never forget it. Our religion is the traditions of our ancestors; it is the dreams of our old men, given to them by God in the quiet hours of the night; it is the visions of our sages; and it is written on the hearts of our people.

Your dead cease to love you as soon as they have passed through the gateway of death; and they cease to love the land of their birth. Our dead never forget the beautiful land that gave them life; they continue to love its murmuring rivers, its tall mountains, its quiet valleys, and its lakes surrounded by trees. They hold their descendents in their hearts, and they often return to them, in order to offer guidance and comfort. You forget your ancestors; we always remember ours.

Day and night cannot dwell together. As the white people have approached, the red people have retreated, just as the morning mist flees before the rising sun.

Yet your proposition seems fair. I think my people will accept it, and they will retire to the reservation that you offer them. They will interpret the voice of your leader as the voice of God, and will dwell in peace.

It matters little where we pass the remainder of our days; they will not be many. We shall await our final destruction as the wounded deer awaits the hunter.

Chief Seattle

11

Waves of the Sea

After a few more moons, a few more winters, no one will be left to mourn over the graves of the great people that once moved across this land. Once they were protected by God, but now he has decided that their time is past, and he has left them. Once they were happy and contented, and lived in peace; but then they were defeated in war with the white men, and soon they will disappear forever.

Yet why should I mourn the untimely fate of my people? Tribe follows tribe, nation follows nation, and empire follows empire, like the waves of the sea. It is the order of nature, and regret is useless. The white people's time of decay may be distant, but it will surely come – for even the white people, with whom God now walks and talks as friend with friends, cannot be exempt from the common destiny of all humanity. The white and the red man will be revealed as brothers, after all; and the white and the red woman will be revealed as sisters.

We shall ponder your proposal and let you know our answer. But should we accept it, here and now I make this condition: that we must always be allowed, without hindrance or molestation, to visit the tombs of our ancestors.

For us every part of this soil is sacred; in the hearts of my people every lump of earth is holy. Every turf bears the imprint of some hunter in search of food for his family. Every hillside and valley, every plain and every forest, has been hallowed by some sad or happy event in days long past.

Chief Seattle

12

The Presence of the Dead

Go down to the shore, and look at the rocks. Now, as they swelter in the sun or bear the breaking of the waves, they seem dumb and dead. Yet in their hearts they still thrill to the memory of the events they have witnessed in the lives of my people. Look down at the dust below and around you. Now, under the weight of white people's feet, it appears as mere dirt. Yet it is mixed with the dust of our ancestors; and when our feet walk upon it, then it responds with love.

The men who died in old age and those who died in battle, the women who died as grandmothers and those who died when they were still virgins, even those who died as little children, still love this land; and when night falls, they wander across it. When the last red person has perished, and the memory of my people has become a myth amongst the white people, this land will still swarm with our invisible dead. When your children's children think they are alone in some field or forest, my people will be all around them; in this land there is no place of solitude. At night, when the streets of your towns and cities are silent and deserted, and you think they are deserted, they will throng with the men and women and children who once filled this land, and who will never cease to love it. No white man or woman, no white boy or girl will ever be alone.

Do not deal harshly with my people; do not be unjust in your actions, or callous in your manner. Be fair and kind, courteous and respectful. The dead are still powerful. Did I say 'dead'? There is no death, only a change of worlds.

Chief Seattle

13

BENEFIT TO OTHERS

When a Winnebago boy reached puberty, his father gave him these instructions:

Son, when you grow up, you should ensure that you bring some benefit to your fellow human beings. And there is one way of bringing benefit to your fellows: consume less than you produce. When you go hunting and slay an animal, share the meat with others. When you pick fruit from the trees, give at least half to others.

Remember that blessings are not obtained merely by desiring them; they are obtained only by working for them. Remember that you cannot do any work well without preparation; you must constantly train your body and mind. Remember that your body and mind are gifts from God; so pray constantly for his strength. Unless you work hard, train hard and pray hard, people will not respect you; they will mock you and treat you with contempt.

When you marry, do not make an idol of your wife; if you worship her, she cannot be your companion. And do not let her make an idol of you; of she worships you, you cannot be her companion. Do not watch over all she does, as that will make you jealous; trust her to do what is right.

Never abuse your wife. Women are sacred. If you abuse your wife and make her life miserable, you will die early. Remember the earth is the mother of all people; so if you mistreat your wife, you are mistreating the earth – and she will punish you by inflicting some terrible disease on your body.

Winnebago

14

Equality of All

When strangers come to your house, welcome them; share your food with them generously – and listen carefully to what they say, because they may be wiser than you are. When neighbors fall sick, care for them; take food to them and their families, so they have no fear of going hungry.

Remember always that this world, and all that lives in this world, belong to God, and to him alone. God has put his spirit in every cloud that passes across the sky, and in every drop that flows through the rivers. He has put his spirit in every animal that walks on land, and even the tiniest insects, and in every fish that swims in water. And he has put his spirit in every baby that is born to a human mother.

Thus human beings do not possess anything; nor are they superior to any other living creature. All are members of God's family and all are equal.

Do not die in your village; and do not let your wife die before you. There is no dignity in growing weak and dying of old age. When you feel that your limbs are losing their agility and strength, do not stop hunting, but continue to hunt as you have always done. Then one day an animal will overcome you, and kill you. That is the right way to die.

I am not saying anything of my own invention. My words to you are the same as my father's words to me, and his father's to him. These words were spoken by the first human father to the first human son; and that father heard them from God himself. Live by these words, and speak them to your own sons when they have reached the age that you are now.

Winnebago

15

Bravery in Life and Death

When the son of a Pawnee chief reached puberty, his mother spoke these words:

You must always trust in God. He made us, and through him we live.

When you grow up, be brave, and face squarely whatever danger may face you. Do not forget that I have raised you, and that I shall always support you.

Your father is a chief, but do not think of that. It does not follow that since he was a chief you will be a chief. It is not a man's family that makes him great; it is his work, his sweat, and his courage that win greatness.

When you go on the warpath, do not turn around before the battle; only come back when you have fought the battle that you intended to fight. If I should live to see you become a man, I want to see a great man.

Take pity on those who are poor. Remember that one day you may fall into poverty, and you shall depend on the pity of others.

If I were to hear that you had been killed in battle, I would not cry; I would know that you had died as a man. But if you were to die of sickness, I would truly be sorry. It is better to die in the open air, where the birds will eat your flesh and the wind blow over your bones, than to die at home and be buried in the earth.

Love your friends. If you see a friend surrounded by the enemy, do not run away. Go to him; and if you cannot save him, be killed together, and let your bones lie side by side.

Heed my words, even though I am a woman.

Pawnee

16

THE GOOD WIFE

When a young woman in the Sioux was about to marry, her mother gave her these instructions:

The home is the place from which the strength of our people flows. So as a married woman in charge of a home, you will have great importance.

Your first duty is to cook. Keep plenty of food stored. If your husband returns from hunting earlier than you expected, if he brings friends, if relatives or strangers call, or if children from other families come, always be ready to offer a meal.

Let meals be orderly and quiet. Serve strangers first; then serve each person in order of age – grandparents, parent and then children. Do not allow any of your children, or even your husband, to question the portions you put on each plate; you have sole charge of how much each person may eat.

Your second duty is to sew. In every spare moment you should be sewing hides into robes and moccasins, blankets and scarves, gloves and caps. Paint the hides in bright colors, to lift the hearts of those who wear them. When your tipi needs to be replaced, turn it into clothing for children. Let nothing good be wasted.

Do not let your husband leave the tipi in the morning without his arranging your hair and painting your face.

As a parent your hardest task does not lie in watching over your children's conduct, but in watching over your own, so that you are a good example to them.

Sioux

17

THE SUN DANCE

Every summer the Shoshone people held a sun dance, at which they danced around a pole. White observers sometimes inferred that the people were worshipping the sun or the pole. Chief Washakie of the Shoshone was offended by this inference, and so one day he explained the dance and the beliefs underlying it to a group of white visitors:

When native Americans pray, they look upwards to the sun, and exclaim: 'Our Father, who is above.' Then they may offer praise to God, express gratitude, and make requests. They are not praying to the sun; but they regard the sun's brightness as a sign of God's wisdom, and the sun's warmth as a sign of his love. When the medicine man leads them in prayer, he looks up to the sun, and exclaims: 'Our Father who is above, have mercy on your children.'

In preparation for the sun dance a large circular corral is constructed. In the center a high pole is erected. The pole must be cottonwood, since this tree can grow in land where there is no water; it represents God, because he also needs nothing. Eagle feathers are tied to the top of the pole; just as the eagle soars above the earth and can see everything, so God watches over all living beings on earth. The head of a buffalo is placed at the base of the pole; the buffalo has been given by God to his children to provide food and clothing.

The dance begins early one morning. The medicine man leads a group of young men into the corral; they dance round the pole, and pray for God's blessings. Over a period of three days all the people take their turn – even the sick, many of whom are cured.

Chief Washakie

18

A HEALING CEREMONY

The Apache tell this story of how their healing ceremony originated:

When God created the world, he planned that each family should have its own plot of land, where it could grow crops and rear animals. But after a while some families wanted more than their share, and began to seize land from other families. Soon human beings were squabbling and fighting.

This angered God; and as a punishment he introduced illness. The first illness attacked two young men. Day after day they grew weaker and weaker, until they died. Illness quickly spread, so that within a few years every family had watched at least one member grow weak and die. Everyone lived in perpetual fear of being the next victim.

Finally a wise man summoned all the people of the world to one place, and said to them: 'No one of us knows how to cure illness. So let us ask God to show us.' Then he led them in prayer. When they had finished praying, four tall men appeared, one on the north side of the crowd, one on the south, one on the east and one on the west.

The one on the north side chanted a prayer. The one on the south side beat a drum. The one on the east side lit a fire. And the one on the west side gathered herbs, and made them into various potions.

From that day on, whenever someone falls sick, four men stand round the tipi. One sings, another beats a drum, another lights a fire, and another mixes herbal potions. These potions are given to the patient – who, if God wants, is cured.

Apache

19

A FUNERAL ORATION

Amongst the Crow people, these words were spoken at a man's funeral:

You are still among us. You are still the person that you always were. You are like us in every way, without any deficiency, except that you have lost the power of action.

Where has your breath now gone – breath that until a few days ago was sending smoke up to God? Why are your lips now silent – lips that until a short time ago were expressing joy? Why are your feet now motionless – feet that until recently were swifter than the deer on the mountain? Why are your arms now useless – arms that could climb the tallest tree and draw the toughest bow? We once admired your body for the grace and agility of its movement, but now it is as still and inert as a rock.

But we shall not grieve, as if you were lost to us; we shall not mourn, as if we you no longer loved us. Your soul lives in the country of souls, in the company of all who have died before you. For a short time we shall remain here, and we shall tell our children and children's children about you; but soon we too shall journey to that country.

Prompted by the respect and affection in which we held you on earth, we now render to you this last act of kindness that is within our power. We shall not leave your body in the open air, where its flesh would be consumed by wild beasts and birds. We shall lay your body with those of your relatives who have gone before; and we shall pray that your soul will feed with theirs. We pray also that, when death comes to us, your soul will be ready to receive ours.

Crow

20

THE FIRST PEOPLE

This story is told by the Penobscot:

Originally God had no one with whom to converse, and no one to assist him; so he felt lonely and tired. One day, when the sun was high and hot, God went down to the shore, and stared at the waves. The warmth of the sun, the moistness of the sea, and the depth of God's desire combined to create a young man, who emerged from the foam. This young man became God's friend and helper. Together they created all the animals, birds and reptiles that now inhabit the earth, as well as the fish that swim in the sea; and in each living being God put his soul.

Then the young man started to feel lonely. So one day, when the sun was rising and the dew was heavy, he stared at a beautiful flower. The rays of the sun, the moistness of the dew, and the depth of the young man's desire combined to turn the flower into a young woman. 'I am love,' the young woman declared, 'and my love will nourish the soul of all living beings.'

The young man married the young women; and she conceived and bore many children. God taught the children the moral principles by which they should live, the skills that they should master, and the aspects of truth that they needed to know. Then he said to them and to their parents: 'I shall now go up into the sky. But if you pray to me, I shall always hear your words, and you shall hear my answer within your hearts.' They watched as he rose up into the sky, and they wept for several days.

Penobscot

21

THE FIRST CORN

The children grew up and had children; and these children grew up and had children. With each generation the population grew larger. They lived by hunting, but eventually the population was so large that there were not enough animals to feed them all. They went to see the first mother, the original woman, and begged her to provide more food. But she had nothing to give them; and she wept to see her descendents so thin and weak.

Her husband, the original man, saw her weeping, and asked why she was so sad. She told him the reason, and he too began to weep. 'But there is one thing that could make me stop weeping,' she said. 'What is that?' he asked. 'Kill me', she said. 'I could never do that,' he protested. 'If you do not kill me,' she said, 'I shall weep forever.'

The first man prayed to God for guidance. In his heart he heard God's reply: 'Do as she says: kill her.' Then he turned to his wife, and told her that he would kill her at noon the next day. 'When I am dead,' she said, 'order my children to take me by the hair, and drag me over the earth. Let me continue until all the flesh has been worn away, and only my bones remain.'

At noon the next day her husband killed her. Then her children took it in turns to drag her body over the earth. They continued for a whole year, and covered a vast area of land. Then they buried her bones.

A few months later they returned to the land on which they had dragged her body, and found that it was covered in corn. Thus they never again went hungry.

Penobscot

22

THE CHOICE OF DEATH

The Blackfoot tell this story:

When God created human beings, there was no death. Men and women had sexual relations, and produced children; and then the next generation produced more children – and so on. But no one ever died; so the population of the world grew larger and larger.

Eventually the population was so large that there were not enough animals in the forests to hunt, not enough fish in the lakes and rivers to catch, and not enough fertile land on which to grow corn. So the people became hungry, and grew thinner and thinner.

One day God said to the original man and woman: 'If I do nothing, the population will continue to grow until every source of food is exhausted – and then people will starve. Or I could rid people of all sexual desire, so that no more children are conceived. Or I could make people grow old and die, so that the population becomes stable, and there is enough food for everyone. Which would you prefer?'

The woman said to the man: 'I cannot bear to see my children and my children's children going hungry.' And the man said to the woman: 'Life would seem very dull if there was no sexual pleasure.' They remained silent for a time. Then the woman said to the man: 'We have led a good life, but now I am weary.' The man did not reply.

So the woman said to God: 'We prefer death.' The first man and woman looked at one another is astonishment as their skin wrinkled and their hair turned gray; then they collapsed and died. And since that time all humans have grown old and died.

Blackfoot

23

The Great Flood

The Haida tell this story:

Originally all human beings lived on a single large island. They all spoke the same language, and had the same customs and religion.

One day, when some boys were playing on a beach, a strange woman appeared out of the sea. She was dressed in a fur cape, and was very beautiful. The boys rushed up to her, and asked her who she was; but she remained silent. Then they pulled at her cape; the cape fell off, to reveal her naked body.

She lifted both arms towards the sky. Thick black clouds appeared, and rain started to fall. At first the rain was slight, but it grew heavier and heavier. The boys rushed back to their homes. The rain continued to fall through the rest of the day, through the night, through the next day and next night – and on and on.

The sea began to rise. The beaches around the island disappeared, and the sea flooded the fields behind the beaches. Then it rose up the hills. All the families quickly built rafts; so when the sea flooded their houses, they were able to float away. Eventually the sea covered the whole island.

The winds blew the rafts in every direction across the world. After a month the rain stopped, and the sea began to fall. After a further month hills and fields and beaches appeared. Each family was washed up in a different land. And over the following centuries each family developed its own language, customs and religion.

Haida

24

THE WARRIOR AND THE BABY

The Algonquian tell this story:

Glooscap was a mighty warrior. He was the tallest and broadest young man of his tribe, with the swiftest feet and the strongest arms. He could hunt any animal, and defeat in combat any young man that challenged him. Everyone treated him with deference; and as a result he became proud and arrogant.

One day an old woman said to him: 'There is one person whose respect you can never win.' 'Who's that?' Glooscap asked. 'My grandson,' the old woman said. She led him to her tipi, where a baby was sitting on ground, and sucking a piece of maple sugar.

Glooscap was unmarried, so he was ignorant as to how children are managed. But with perfect confidence he smiled at the little boy, and asked him to come to him. The baby looked glumly at him, and refused to move. Then Glooscap imitated a beautiful birdsong; but the baby paid no attention, and continued to suck the maple sugar.

Glooscap's patience snapped. At the top of his voice he ordered the baby to come to him. The baby burst into loud howls that drowned out even Glooscap's shouting. Glooscap threatened to beat the little boy if he did not obey; but the little boy howled even louder.

So Glooscap calmed down; and after several minutes the baby stopped howling. Glosscap started to sing, and gradually the little boy's face creased into a smile. Glooscap was so enthralled by the smile that he continued to sing for the rest of the day. When the sun set, the old woman said quietly: 'You have not won his respect; he has won yours.'

Algonquian

25

THE LOW SKY

The Shohomish tell this story:

People ceased to treat the other living creatures in the world with care and respect. In certain forests they hunted so greedily that eventually there were no animals left. And they took so many fish from certain lakes that the lakes became empty. God became angry. And as a punishment he caused the sky to come down towards the earth, so that people often bumped their heads against it.

The wise men of every tribe gathered together and discussed what they should do. They decided that they must try to push up the sky to its proper place with long poles. But they realized that this would only succeed if every human being in the world pushed at the same time. 'But since we speak so many different languages,' one man asked, 'how can we tell each other when to push?' They agreed that when everyone shouts 'yahoo', they would all push.

The wise men returned to their people, and told them to collect long poles with which to push up the sky. Then a few days later one tribe began to shout 'yahoo.' The neighboring tribes heard the call, and also shouted 'yahoo.' The call spread quickly round the world. So, with a huge shout, everyone poked their poles into the sky, and pushed. Slowly the sky went upwards to its proper place.

The wise men gathered again. And they agreed that no one should ever take from the world more than it naturally provides.

Snohomish

26

The Death of a Young Wife

The Serrano tell this story:

A young man married a beautiful young woman. But his mother was jealous of his love for her. So one day, when he was out hunting, she stabbed the young woman with a knife, and immediately cremated the body. By the time the young man returned, there was no more than a pile of ash.

He remained by the ash throughout the night, overwhelmed by grief. Then just before dawn he saw the figure of his wife emerging from it. She ran off towards the west and he followed her. Eventually they reached a mountain with a huge boulder lodged precariously on its summit. She turned to him, and said: 'We are now entering the world of the dead. If people have led wicked lives, the boulder hurtles down the mountain and crushes them.' They ran past the mountain, and the boulder did not move.

Soon they came to a village where all her dead relatives had settled. She introduced her husband, and pleaded with them to let him stay. Her oldest ancestor put his arm round her shoulder, and said: 'The living cannot remain among the dead; but the dead can return to the land of the living.' Then he said to the young man: 'Take her back. But remember that she is dead; so you must have no sexual relations with her.'

The young man and woman ran back to the mountain, and then into the land of the living. For three days and nights they simply enjoyed one another's company. On the fourth night they made love – and the following morning he found himself all alone.

Serrano

27

A QUEST FOR WISDOM

The Sioux tell this story:

A young man yearned to acquire great wisdom, and be respected for the profundity of his advice. So he decided to climb the highest mountain in the world, in the hope that he would meet God at the top – and that God would impart his wisdom. Throughout the winter he ate large quantities of meat and corn, and performed every kind of physical exercise, to prepare his body for the ordeal. Then on the first day of spring he set out.

As he climbed higher, the temperature dropped; and soon it was so cold at night that he could not sleep. He reached the point where the trees stop growing, and the ground was so crumbly that he had difficulty keeping his foothold. Then he reached the point where the ground was covered with snow and ice, so he was forced to crawl.

At last he reached the top of the mountain. He took a deep breath, and called out: 'God, give me wisdom!' There was no answer. He called several more times. But he only heard his own voice echoing from the other mountains nearby.

With great sadness in his heart he began to descend the mountain. About halfway down a massive boulder fell from a cliff above him, and flew towards him. He was quite oblivious of the danger; but just as the boulder was about to hit him, his foot slipped, and he fell out of the way. 'So God is looking after me,' he said to himself.

When he returned to his village, people laughed at him. At first he felt humiliated; but from his humiliation he began to learn the wisdom for which he had yearned.

Sioux

28

AN OLD WORLD

The Sioux tell this story:

There was a world before this world. But the people became evil: they killed more animals than they needed for food and hides, and they chopped down more trees that they needed for firewood and poles. So God became angry, and decided to destroy the world. First he cut a tiny sliver of skin from every kind of animal and insect, bird and fish, and put the slivers in a bag. Then he cut a sliver of skin from the best man and the best woman in the world, and put them in the bag. Finally he gathered all the clouds together, so they hovered over the land, and he ordered them to rain until all the land was flooded.

After a month even the highest mountain was covered, and every living creature was destroyed – except a single crow who flew above the water. Yet it continued to rain for another month, until all the clouds had emptied themselves completely.

In the meantime God had forgotten about the world. So the crow cried out: 'Father, I must soon rest. Give me some land.' God looked at the crow, who had turned red with exhaustion, and felt sorry for it. 'Very well,' said God, 'I shall make a new world.'

God reached into his bag, took out the otter's skin, and turned it into a complete otter. 'Dive into the water,' God said to the otter, 'and bring up some mud from the bottom.' The otter dived, and with its strong webbed feet pushed itself downwards. But eventually its feet were so tired that it could push no further. So it swam back to the surface, and said to God: 'The water is too deep for me to reach the bottom.'

Sioux

29

A NEW WORLD

God reached into his bag a second time, took out the beaver's skin, and turned it into a complete beaver. 'Dive into the water,' God said to the beaver, 'and bring up some mud from the bottom.' The beaver dived, and with its flat tail propelled itself downwards. But eventually its feet were so tired that it could push no further. So it swam back to the surface, and said to God: 'The water is too deep for me to reach the bottom.'

God reached into his bag a third time, took out the turtle's skin, and turned it into a complete turtle. 'Dive into the water,' God said to the turtle, 'and bring up some mud from the bottom.' The turtle dived. It remained under the water for so long that the otter, the beaver and the crow thought it was dead. 'There shall never again be any land,' the crow cried; 'soon I shall drop into the water with exhaustion, and drown.'

At that moment the turtle reappeared. Its feet and sides, and even the cracks between its upper and lower shell, were filled with mud. God took the mud, and spread it flat on the water to form an island. God beckoned to the crow, and the crow landed on the island, singing with joy.

Then God took out the skin of an eagle, turned it into a complete eagle, and ordered it to spread the land in order to form a great mass. The land was now completely dry, so nothing could grow. God filled the clouds with water, and ordered them to rain occasionally – just enough to make rivers flow and lakes fill.

Then he formed all the other species from the skins in his bag – including humanity.

Sioux

30

The Pole and the Beaver

The Cheyenne tell this story:

When God first created the world, there was nothing above it. So the world was utterly dark and cold. But since God wanted living beings on earth, he had to find some means of bringing light and warmth.

So he made a vast blue sheet, which he called the sky; and with his left arm he held it above the earth. On the eastern edge of the sky he lit a great fire, which he called the sun. Each day he pulled the sun across the sky to the western edge, and each night he pulled it back above the sky to the eastern edge; for this he used his right arm.

At night it was still so dark and cold that no living being could survive. So God lit a smaller fire, which he called the moon – with the intention of pulling it across the sky at night. But, since he was using both his arms already, the moon simply burned uselessly at the edge of the sky.

Then God made a great wooden pole. He put this in the center of the earth to hold up the sky. This released his right arm for the moon - and now the earth had a little warmth and light by night. Soon every kind of animal, including humanity, was flourishing on earth.

One day a beaver began to gnaw the base of the pole; the more it consumed, the bigger and stronger it became, and the faster it gnawed. God noticed the beaver; and he also noticed that many human beings do great evil. So he decided to allow the beaver to continue until the pole collapses. He will only stop the beaver if human beings stop doing evil.

Cheyenne

31

To the Master of Life

The Delaware people offer this prayer:

'Master of life, you made the sky and the earth, the trees and the grass, the lakes and the rivers, the animals and the birds and all men and women; and you watch over all that you have made. You love each one of us, and we wish to act in the way that you love, not in the way that you hate. We will not fight with one another, but we will solve our disputes amicably. We will not commit adultery, but we will be faithful to the spouse you have chosen. We will not listen to anyone who tells us to ignore you, but we will always listen to you. We will never forget our ancestors, but we will remember their good example. And we will never spoil or damage the land on which we live, but cherish it as a gift from you.'

Delaware

MONTH

6

TRADITIONAL AFRICAN

RELIGION

Introduction

Origins

Early Christian missionaries to sub-Saharan Africa enjoyed little success; and many, like David Livingstone, concluded that commercial links with Europe and America would have to precede conversion – once African people saw western prowess in technology, they would infer that western religion was also superior. In the event this approach proved highly successful, but for a far deeper reason: religion was so deeply rooted in African cultures, that only by destroying these cultures by economic and political force could a new religion flourish. Happily, however, a few of the western traders and colonists came to admire the traditional religions, and recorded the parables, myths and proverbs that had been handed down from one generation to the next; and their efforts were later augmented by the more systematic studies made by social anthropologists.

If the missionaries had taken the trouble to learn the faith of those they wished to convert, they would have found their religion was similar in many respects to that of the ancient Hebrew people described in the *Old Testament* (the Hebrew Bible). For traditional Africans, as for Hebrews, faith in God is not a matter of belief, but of absolute trust. And morality is embedded in the social and political structure of the tribe. Thus, for example, polygamous marriage systems generally ensure that every woman is married, and so is cared for and protected; rules concerning revenge are the primary means by which crime is prevented and justice upheld; and the primary role of the leader is to ensure that disputes between families and clans are peacefully resolved.

Teachings

At a conservative estimate there are 750 tribes in sub-Saharan Africa, each expressing its faith within its own structures and traditions. Yet there are many common elements.

God is typically regarded as standing at the apex of a pyramid of spiritual forces governing the world. The greatest of these forces animate the sun, the moon, the wind, and the other major natural phenomena; lesser forces may affect a particular family, forest, valley, type of animal, and so on. The forces may be invoked separately; but since their power comes entirely from God, so God determines their response. Thus these forces act as intermediaries between God and humanity.

Nonetheless God's rule is not absolute. These spiritual forces develop their own purposes and attitudes, and may even try to manipulate God; so God has to negotiate with them, cajole them, and occasionally deceive them, in order to maintain control. The relationship between God and other forces is the subject of many mythical stories; and these myths generally reflect the problems of maintaining order within families and tribes.

The fertility of both humans and domestic livestock is a major concern for most African societies; and God is seen as the source of fertility. Indeed, in a large number of African cultures God is understood as androgynous, and thus is both the father and the mother of all that is born.

At the base of the spiritual pyramid are the souls of individual creatures. Health and happiness consist in submitting the individual soul to the higher spiritual forces.

Expression

The most important religious rituals within most African cultures are those that mark the individual's passage through life. The rituals following birth are usually modest, involving only the immediate family. But at puberty the rituals are far more complex; and their main purpose is to shift the individual's sense of identity from the family to the tribe. They may involve young people being taken away from their families, and put in dormitories with their peers; and amongst their peer group they may undergo various hardships to test their capacity for the challenges of adulthood. Marriage rituals celebrate both the bond between the man and the woman, and the union of two extended families; they are thus a vital means of maintaining cohesion within the tribe. When people have died, their souls can choose to work for the welfare of their descendents and the community as a whole; so the funeral rituals are intended to ensure the continuing good will of the deceased.

The cycle of the year is also marked by rituals, of which the harvest ceremonies are usually the most important. Since ancestors have played a major part in making the crops grow, sacrifices are made to them. In some cultures these are followed by festivities when rules and customs are abandoned: sexual liberties are permitted, and chiefs and priests may be mocked and insulted. By symbolically destroying the social order, it can then be renewed.

In many African societies witches play an important role. They often live in isolation; and they are both feared for their capacity to cause death and infertility, and revered for their wisdom.

Us

We are encouraged day by day to admire the achievements of scientists, whose rational methods yield astonishing results; and by contrast the African belief in the power of rituals and witchcraft seems crude and blind. Equally we may retain some of the Christian missionaries' disgust at African morality, especially polygamous forms of marriage.

Yet we also probably feel that there are aspects of human experience beyond the reach of scientific investigation; and occasionally we may be overwhelmed by a sense of the spiritual unity of all living beings. African rituals celebrate that mystical sense, and thence both deepen and extend it. Since those rituals are so deeply rooted in their cultural context, that they cannot be transplanted elsewhere. But they, and the faith that motivates them, challenge us to make mysticism normal.

And we also probably feel that the moral confusion and uncertainty of modern western society compels us to look afresh at traditional moral systems, including those of Africa. The essence of African morality is not the sexual dominance of men over women, still less sexual freedom; rather, it is the inclusion of all people within the framework of family love. Again African morality cannot be transplanted, but in this particular way it offers a standard by which we can judge your own moral inclinations.

1

THE SUN AND THE MOON

The Bushmen tell these stories:

In the beginning the sun lay on the ground; so although it was hot and bright, its warmth and light did not spread. As a result the crops grew very slowly, and people could not see the beauty of the earth.

There was a woman who had many children. It occurred to her, that if the sun were in the sky, it would shed its warmth and light across the whole world. So she said to her children: 'Go to the sun, and wait until he has fallen asleep. Then take him by the armpits, and hurl him upwards.' The children did as she said. As the sun was rising, he awoke, and called out: 'Why are doing this?' The children shouted back: 'Because we want to enjoy you to the full.'

The sun had to flap his arms in order to stay in the sky. And eventually it became so tired that it sank beneath the earth, and fell asleep. The world was now in utter darkness, and all the people and animals cried out in fear. Their cries awoke the sun; and, since it wanted to sleep longer, it sent the moon into the sky. From that time onwards the sun and the moon have taken turns to fly above the world.

The sun regards the moon as his wife, and the moon regards the sun as her husband. They love one another dearly, but he finds her irritating. Each month he chops slices off her; but when only a single slice remains, he repents – and sticks the severed slices back onto her. Occasionally in retaliation she rises during the day, and stands in front of him.

Bushmen

2

THE ORIGIN OF WIND

There was once a man who lived alone, and never spoke to anyone. He never went anywhere, and he spent all his time playing with a ball. He used to kick the ball high into the air, aiming it between two branches of a tree; and his kicking was so accurate that invariably the ball passed through the branches without getting caught amongst the leaves. People often stood and watched him. But nobody knew his name; and no one dared start a conversation with a man of such consummate skill.

One day a boy called Nakati passed by. The man kicked the ball between the branches of a tree, and it landed at Nakati's feet. The man beckoned to Nakati to kick the ball back. Nakati did so. When Nakati went home, he asked his mother: 'How does that man know my name?' She replied: 'I don't know.' Nakati then asked: 'What is his name?' And again she replied: 'I don't know.'

The next day Nakati encountered the man for the second time. Nakati, being a boy, did not feel over-awed by him. So he asked plainly: 'What is your name?' The man felt affronted that a boy should ask such an impudent question, and refused to answer. Nakati persisted: 'You know my name, so I have a right to know yours.'

'This is my reply,' the man exclaimed. Then he fell to the ground and started kicking his legs furiously in the air. For the first time the air ceased to be still, and started blowing about. From that time onwards, whenever the anonymous man lies down, the wind blows; and whenever he stands up, the wind drops.

Bushmen

3

THE FIRST FARM

The Ganda tell this story:

Many centuries ago a man called Kintu arrived in Uganda. At that time no people lived there, and there was no food. Kintu brought with him a cow, and he lived on its milk.

One day a daughter of God, called Nambi, was walking through Uganda, and saw Kintu. She immediately fell in love with him, and asked if she could be his wife. After a few days in each other's company he fell in love with her, so he consented to her proposal. Then she said: 'We must go to my father, who is God, and ask his consent.' So Kintu and Nambi went to heaven, and asked God if they could marry.

God said to Kintu: 'What food do you eat?' Kintu replied: 'I eat no food. I live on milk from my cow.' 'That is not sufficient for my daughter,' God declared; 'nor would it be sufficient for any children you might have. Show me that you can provide my daughter, and my future grandchildren, with a proper diet.'

So Kintu left heaven, and returned to Uganda. He wandered from place to place, trying out every kind of fruit and grain that grew wild. Some tasted unpleasant, and made him ill; while others tasted pleasant, and enhanced his health. He took seeds from the healthy fruits and grains, and cultivated them himself. In this way he created the first farm in the world.

He went back to heaven, and said to God: 'I have shown that I can provide your daughter, and any children we may have, with a proper diet.'

Ganda

4

THE FIRST DECEPTION

Nambi had two brothers. One of them, called Kaikuzi, was angry at the prospect of her marriage, and said to God: 'Nambi, like me, is divine, whereas Kintu is human. Divine beings are quite different from human beings, and therefore should not marry.' 'Very well,' God replied, 'you must demonstate this difference. Set Kintu a test, which a divine being would pass, but which, in your opinion, a mere human being would fail.'

Kaikuzi led Kintu to a hut, and locked him in. He then cooked a vast meal of meat and vegetables, which was large enough to feed a hundred people. He took the food to Kintu, and said: 'If you wish to marry Nambi, you must eat all this food, leaving nothing over. I shall return tomorrow, to see if you have succeeded.'

Kintu knew that he could not eat all the food, and wondered what to do. Then he said to himself: 'Divine beings can do many things that human beings cannot do. But human beings have one capacity which divine beings lack: deceit.' He took all the bones out of the meat, and used them to dig a large hole in the floor of the hut. He put the food in the hole, and pushed back the earth, treading it down firmly.

The next day Kaikuzi returned, and was astonished to find that the food had gone. Since he was divine, it never occurred to him that Kintu had deceived him; he assumed without question that Kintu had eaten the food. So he went back to God, and said: 'Kintu has proved himself worthy to marry my sister.'

God summoned Nambi; he also summoned his other son, called Death.

Ganda

5

THE ARRIVAL OF DEATH

Death said to Nambi: 'For your own sake you should not be allowed to marry a human being. You will not be content on earth, because it does not have the comforts and luxuries of heaven.' Without a moment's hesitation Nambi replied: 'Love is more important to me than any comfort or luxury.' God said to Nambi: 'You should consider Death's warning seriously. If you go to live on earth with Kintu, you will deprive yourself for ever of the luxuries of heaven.' Nambi repeated: 'Love is more important to me than any comfort or luxury.'

So God gave Nambi permission to marry Kintu, and Nambi and Kintu returned to Uganda. They lived happily for many years, and had many children. Then one day Nambi said to herself: 'When I lived in heaven, I had a soft pillow on which to rest my head; whereas here on earth I must rest my head on a stone. Now that I am growing old, I should again like to rest my head on a pillow. I shall go back to heaven, and take a pillow. I shall slip in and out of heaven so quickly that no one will notice me. And, since they have many pillows, they will not miss the one which I take.'

She did not tell Kintu of her plan, for fear that he would disapprove. One morning, when he had gone to work in the fields, she left their house, and hurried to heaven. She saw a pillow, and seized it. But as she was leaving, Death noticed her. He called out to her, and she ran back to earth as fast as her legs would carry her. Death followed her. So when Kintu returned home in the evening, he found Death at his house.

Ganda

6

THE PURSUIT OF DEATH

With tears pouring down her cheeks Nambi explained to Kintu what she had done. 'And where is the pillow that you took?' Kintu asked. Nambi looked under her arm, and found that the pillow had dissolved into dust.

Death said to Kintu: 'I order you to send one of your daughters to be my cook.' 'I have no obligation to obey you,' Kintu replied. 'If you do not obey me,' Death said, 'I shall kill your eldest daughter.' Kintu did not understand what Death meant, because no living being had yet died; so he continued to defy him. Death went away. But a short time later the eldest daughter of Kintu and Nambi fell ill, and died – followed one by one their other children. Eventually only their youngest son and youngest daughter remained.

Kintu and Nambi went to heaven, and pleaded with God to restrain Death. 'Death entered the world because you led him there,' God said to Nambi. She admitted her folly, and God took pity on her. 'I shall send Kaikuzi to the world,' God declared, 'to try and bring Death back to heaven.

Kintu and Nambi returned to earth, accompanied by Kaikuzi. When they reached their house, Death was standing at the entrance. Kaikuzi embraced Death warmly, and invited him back to heaven. 'First I must kill Nambi's youngest son and daughter,' Death replied. Kaikuzi seized him; but Death struck him on the face, and ran away.

Kaikuzi chased Death – and has been chasing him ever since. Death is too cunning to be caught; but by constantly pursuing him, Kaikuzi reduces the number he can attack.

Ganda

7

One death or many

Kintu was the first king of the Baganda people, and ruled thousands of years ago. One of his successors was renowned for his pride and arrogance. He regarded most of his people with contempt, and would frequently say: 'If my subjects were strong and brave, the Baganda would be the most powerful tribe in the world. But they are lazy and cowardly, so the Baganda is just one people among many.'

One day he summoned his most skilled blacksmith, called Waluka, and said: 'I have an important task for you. I want you to construct out of iron the perfect man. He must be stronger and braver than any man on earth. When you have completed this task, I shall order every blacksmith to copy this iron man many times - and these iron men will replace my present subjects. Thus I shall rule the most powerful people on earth.'

Waluka replied: 'It is true that I am widely admired as the most skilled blacksmith in the tribe. But this task is beyond me. How is it possible to make a man out of iron?' The king said: 'You must find a method. If you fail, I shall execute you.'

Waluka went away feeling utterly miserable. He said to himself: 'If I succeed in this task, I shall live, but the rest of the people will be slaughtered by the iron men. If I fail in this task, I shall die, but the rest of the people will live. Never has a king placed a man in such a cruel dilemma.'

Waluka traveled from village to village, seeking advice from wise men as to what he should do.

Ganda

8

One people among many

Waluka finally came to a village of the very edge of Kintu's kingdom, where he met the oldest man of the entire Baganda people. He explained to the oldest man his dilemma, and the oldest man replied: 'Since the king has asked you to do something impossible, you must ask him to do something impossible. You must go to the king, and say that, if he truly wants this extraordinary artefact, he must supply the materials. Tell him that you need a thousand loads of charcoal made from human hair in order to create the fire, and a thousand pots of human tears in order to slake the fire.'

Waluka thanked the oldest man for his advice, and went immediately to the king. 'Your majesty,' he said, 'I have now studied deeply how to forge a man out of iron. I conclude that a special fire is required, using a thousand loads of charcoal made from human hair; and this fire must be slaked with a thousand pots of human tears.' The king ordered that the head of every person in the tribe be shaved, and the hair made into charcoal. He ordered every person to become sad, and weep into a pot for a month – and by threatening to kill their children if they failed, he ensured their sadness. But the hair was sufficient for only one load of charcoal, and the tears only filled ten pots.

The king summoned Waluka, and confessed that he could not provide the necessary materials for an iron man. Waluka smiled, and said: 'Therefore you must be content for the Baganda to remain one people among many.' From that day the king lost his pride and arrogance, and treated his people with respect.

Ganda

9

The origin of war

The Masai tell these stories:

God gave to every tribe a different type of cattle, each with distinct coloring. One tribe had black cattle; another had cattle that were black and white; another had brown cattle; another had cattle that were brown and white – and so one. The tribes were content with the cattle that God had given. No tribe tried to steal the cattle of another tribe, because the distinct coloring of the stolen cattle would make the crime easy to detect.

God ordered each tribe to build fences around their fields. But with each generation the men became lazier, and they allowed the fences to rot. So one morning the cattle of every tribe escaped, and they gathered in the forest. The bulls were captivated by the beauty of the different types of cow, and had intercourse with as many cows as they could manage in the course of the day.

In the evening the men of the various tribes found the cattle in the forest. They separated the cattle according to their coloring, and the men of each tribe took back their own type. However, when the cows gave birth, the calves were no longer distinct. So soon the cattle of one tribe were no different from the cattle of another.

It was not long before the men of each tribe started stealing the cattle belonging to other tribes, in the hope of becoming rich. As a result wars broke out between the tribes, in which many young men were killed. Warfare has been continuing ever since that time, and the finest men of every generation are slaughtered.

Masai

10

A BITTER HEART

A woman grew very bitter because she had no children. She had prayed to God many times for children, but her prayers had never been answered.

One day an old man called at her house. 'Are you sure you want children?' he asked. 'Of course I do,' she replied curtly. 'If children came, would you cease to be bitter?' he asked. 'Of course I would,' she replied. 'Very well,' he said. A few weeks later she found she was pregnant. And over the next three years she had three children.

At first she loved her children. But then she grew weary of looking after them. She became bitter at having to spend her time cooking their meals and making their clothes; and their incessant noise made her head ache. Finally, when her head was especially sore, she lost her temper. 'You are not my children,' she cried; 'an old man forced me to have you.'

The children burst into tears. They rushed out of the house, and to the house of their father's parents. She ran after them, and she begged them to come home; but they refused. She now burst into tears.

The following day the old man called again at her house, and found her still weeping. 'God knew that you lacked the temperament to raise children,' the old man said; 'that is why he never answered your prayers. But he saw that your bitterness was poisoning your heart; and that is why he finally relented. Now you must accept yourself as you are, and be content.' With these words her bitterness drained away.

Masai

11

Food from the head

The Ashanti tell this story:

There was a terrible famine. The rains had failed, and all the crops had dried up. Only the river was still running, so there was enough water for people to drink. But without food people were growing thinner and thinner, and would soon die.

A young man and his wife decided to leave their home, and go in search of food. They walked for many days, until they came to a lake. Standing in the middle of the lake was a group of angels. They had taken off their heads, and were using their skulls to scoop water from the lake.

'Why are you doing this?' the young man asked. 'Like you, we are hungry,' the angels replied; 'when the lake is empty, all the fish will be lying on the bed, and we shall eat them.' 'Surely you could use buckets to scoop the water, instead of your own heads.' The young man said. 'God has given a head to all living beings,' the angels said; 'and they should use their heads in order to feed themselves.'

The young man stared in amazement at the angels. Meanwhile his wife looked at the banks of the lake, where the angels were pouring the water. 'There are wonderful plants growing round the lake,' she said. Then she used her head. A few moments later she exclaimed: 'I know how we can feed ourselves!'

She ran back to their home, followed by her bewildered husband; and she started digging channels from the river to their fields to irrigate their crops.

Ashanti

12

The presence of God

The Ashanti tell these proverbs:

In every nation and tribe, and amongst all the living beings that inhabit the world, the same God is present. He is present even amongst your enemies.

You cannot avoid, or be cheated of, the destiny that God has assigned to you. If someone tries to kill you, but God wants you to live, you will escape death. If God fills your cup with wine, but someone spills it, God will fill it again.

The spirits of the dead know what they learnt on earth, and like what they liked on earth. Their knowledge and their preferences cannot be altered.

The advice of a wise person, ripe with experience, is more valuable than any rituals.

There is no special place or time in which to see God or speak to him. Look for God and pray to him everywhere and always.

Dying takes many forms, but death has only one form. When death comes to visit you, do not point to someone else, and say: 'Take that person instead.' Embrace death as a friend.

If the rich and the poor were true friends, there would be no poverty. But when you fall into poverty, do not become angry or resentful towards the rich; enjoy your bowl of maize as if it were an entire roasted sheep.

People have faith in gold; that is why it has value. If people stopped believing in gold, it would be as worthless as stone.

Ashanti

13

WOMEN AND WEALTH

Amongst the Chagga this is advice given by an old man to his grandson:

My grandson, you may think that men are clever and women are ignorant. You see men hunting and felling trees, and you say to yourself: 'It takes intelligence to throw a spear and wield an axe.' You see women chatting with one another or playing with their children, and you say to yourself: 'Any fool can do that.' But there is more to be learnt in conversation than in stalking animals; and more wisdom is required to raise children than to chop wood. So when you are married, never try to exploit your wife; she will respond by manipulating your emotions and actions. On the contrary, always treat her with respect, and consult her before every decision. When you have daughters, do not try to beat them in argument; they will soon turn your arguments against you. On the contrary, encourage them to think deeply and speak wittily.

My grandson, you may wish to become rich, and to acquire a vast herd of cattle. Your wealth would soon swell your head. You would say to yourself: 'God has blessed me with wealth, because I am wise and virtuous.' And you would look upon others, even the elders of your tribe, with contempt. They would sense your contempt, and resent you. But wealth can be lost as easily as it can be gained; a disease might attack your cattle, and they might all die. Not only would you be cast into poverty, but also you would feel utterly humiliated. And, remembering your former arrogance, no one would come to your aid. So be content with sufficient wealth to feed yourself and your family, and desire nothing more.

Chagga

14

War and Peace

My grandson, you may think there is glory to be gained in war. In my life I have watched many times as rival chiefs gathered their warriors and marched into battle. I have heard the screams of agony as spears penetrated flesh, and seen many young men cut down. I have attended celebrations of victory, and have witnessed the desolation of defeat. What purpose have these wars served? No purpose. What good has come from so much death and injury? No good. So keep out of wars. Do not be deceived by talk of the honor to be won by fighting; and do not allow any disagreement to lead to violence. The true hero is the one who averts war; aspire to such heroism.

My grandson, let your spear be honesty; this will always bring you victory. Do not tell lies against those you dislike; if your antagonism is justified, the truth will be far more dangerous to them. Do not seek power through false promises; if people know that you will keep your promises, they will want your leadership.

My grandson, let your shield be discretion; this will always protect you. Do not pass on information that you have been told in confidence; if people feel able to trust you with their secrets, they will never turn against you. Do not speak ill of people behind their backs; the victim of your slander will be told your words, and become a bitter enemy. Do not exaggerate your own successes or the failures of others; if you deprecate yourself, but appreciate others, everyone will like you.

Always use words with care, and you will bring contentment to yourself and to others.

Chagga

15

AT A MOTHER'S DEATH

Amongst the Ekoi the eldest son speaks these words at the death of his mother:

Dear mother, you have died and left us alone. A big black cloud of loneliness hangs over us.

Today my brothers, my sisters and I have lost the one who gave us advice. Gone from our midst is the one whose words were always true and wise. She was the eye that saw life's traps before we fell into them. She was the ear that heard life's dangers before we fell victim to them. Now we are blind and deaf.

Today my brothers, my sisters and I have lost the one who gave us comfort. Gone from our midst is the one whose embrace was always warm and gentle. She was the heart of love that beat for us. She was the soul of generosity that upheld us. Now we are numb and helpless.

Goodbye, dear mother. At this moment you will be embracing your parents, who are our grandparents. Tell them that we remember them with love. You will be embracing your brothers and sisters - our uncles and aunts - who have already died. Tell them that we remember them with love. With so many relatives around you, we know that you will be happy.

Do not forget us. In your happiness do not ignore our sadness. In your comfort, do not forget our grief. In the perfect health that you will now enjoy, do not forget the sicknesses that befall us. Pray to God that he will comfort us.

Ekoi

16

THE WARRIOR, THE WRESTLER AND THE PRIEST

The Hausa tell this story:

Three men were on a journey. The first man was a warrior; the second was a wrestler; and the third was a priest. Their route required them to cross three rivers. Each of these rivers had fords where in normal conditions people could wade across. But soon after the men had set out, heavy rains had fallen, so the rivers were swollen.

When they reached the first river, the warrior said: 'I shall show how a swollen river should be crossed.' 'Very well,' the wrestler and the priest replied. The warrior tied one end of a rope to his spear, and the other end to a tree. He hurled the spear to the other bank, where it landed firmly in the soil. Then he used the rope to pull himself through the water; and the other two men followed him.

When they reached the second river, the wrestler declared: 'I shall now show you how a swollen river should be crossed.' 'Very well,' the warrior and the priest replied. The wrestler took the priest by an arm and a leg, and threw him across the river. Then he took the warrior by an arm and a leg, and threw him across the river also. Finally he jumped across the river himself.

When they reached the third river, the priest smiled at the warrior and the wrestler. Then he knelt down and prayed. As he was praying, the depth of the water fell to its usual level. The priest rose to his feet, and led the men across the ford. As soon as they had reached the other side, the river rose again.

Hausa

17

TRUE WEALTH

The Hausa tell these proverbs:

Wealth does not consist in jewels or precious metals. It consists in rain falling from the sky onto the parched earth.

When the moon is small, the stars are bright.

Terror is the worst emotion you feel in the wilds. Shame is the worst emotion you feel at home.

For cutting meat, God has given us the axe; for cooking meat, God has given us fire. God provides for every need.

Even if you spent a year trying to drain a river, you would not succeed. A river flows if God decrees it should flow.

Do not desist from doing what you know is right, just because some powerful people oppose you.

If you refuse to live with anyone who has slandered you, then you shall live alone.

If you condemn people on the word of others, you yourself will be condemned unjustly.

If you are naturally gifted at some activity, you will enjoy becoming an expert in it.

Earthly pleasures may bring happiness, but only God can bring contentment.

God's blessing goes before every person; but those who are evil, follow God's blessing in vain.

Hausa

18

True security

The hovels of the poor can never burn down, because they are built of mud.

Righteousness does not require its own home; it can settle wherever it is welcomed. But evil is just the same.

There is no evil in God; he makes the rains fall even on the gardens of the wicked.

When a blind man hears his mother being beaten, he cannot defend her. But he shouts out: 'Take me and beat me instead!'

If an evil person forces you to act against your conscience, keep the name of God constantly on your lips.

Say to those who hate you: 'God is more powerful than you are.'

If God wants an illness to be cured, the medicines of the physician will succeed. If God does not want an illness to be cured, the medicines of the physician will fail.

You own nothing; everything you possess belongs to God. You have nothing; everything you receive is a gift from God.

It is easy to marry; it is far harder to be a good spouse.

If the ear can hear God's word, the soul may be set free. But if the ear is deaf to God's word, the soul will remain in chains.

God gives water to grass growing on rocks, as well as to wheat growing in soil.

Fools may be free, but they make themselves slaves to foolish ideas.

The bee has both sweetness and a sting; there are two sides to every question.

Hausa

19

TRUE PRAYER

Some say that, if food and drink were always plentiful, everyone would worship God; people would be filled not only with the food and drink itself, but with gratitude to God for providing it. Yet if food and drink were always plentiful, people would forget God; their needs would be satisfied, so they would feel no urge to pray to God. Besides, they would imagine that their work alone had yielded such abundance.

Others say that, if food and drink were always scarce, everyone would worship God; people would be so hungry and thirsty, that they would be constantly begging God for mercy. Yet if food and drink were always scarce, people would ignore God; they would be totally absorbed in their own needs, so they would have no energy to devote to prayer. Besides, they would imagine that God is incapable of improving their lot.

Uncertainty is the best stimulus to prayer. That is why God sometimes provides a good harvest, and sometimes a bad one. That is why the rivers sometimes flow with clear, pure water, and are sometimes reduced to a trickle of mud.

When you pray, do not say to God that you deserve his blessings; you cannot make claims on him. When you pray, do not invoke the good works of your forefathers; God judges people on their own merits, not on the merits of those who went before. When you pray to, ask God to make good your mistakes and purify your intentions. When you pray, listen to God; he speaks to your conscience, and your conscience tells you what is right.

Hausa

20

Hints and images

You must know that the truth can never be described fully, and can only be conveyed through hints and images. A person cannot buy the truth; even a hundred thousand cowries would not be sufficient. Those who accumulate wealth, in the hope of buying the truth, will be sorely disappointed.

You must know that this world is like a room where the yarn is in place for weaving; the warp has been pulled taut, and the weft is ready. If you start to weave, then a beautiful cloth will gradually appear.

You must know that this world is like a market place. People wander round, making bargains. Some purchase righteous acts in exchange for evil ones, while others purchase evil acts in exchange for righteous ones. If you try to look at what everyone else is doing, you will quickly become confused. Instead concentrate on what you are doing, to ensure that you make good bargains.

You must know that you cannot hold onto life in this world. You may try to grip life with both hands, using all your strength. But at the moment of God's choosing, life will slip from your grasp. So do not waste your energy in gripping this life; use your energy in preparing for the next life.

You must know that this world is full of fools. They have been told that, if they do good and reject evil, they will attain happiness; and they can see the proof on the lives of good people. Yet they persist in doing evil and rejecting goodness.

Hausa

21

In time of famine

Among the Kamba this lament is sung by men to their wives in times of famine:

Calm yourself, dear wife. Calm yourself, and stop weeping. We have wept enough over the poverty that has befallen us. We have wept enough over the crops that dried up in the fields, and yielded no harvest. We have wept enough over the livestock that withered and died for lack of water and food. We have wept enough over the thirst that scratches our throats and the hunger that gnaws at our bellies. We have wept enough over the child which you carry under your heart, and who will never be born. Now is the time to stop weeping, and to prepare calmly for death.

Dear wife, I love you more dearly than I love my own sister, who was born of the same parents as I was. I love you more dearly than I love my own mother, who bore me and nursed me. I love you more dearly than I love my own flesh. I love you more than I love life itself.

We shall die together. We shall lie down together in God's arms, and he will take us together to the place of eternity. We shall not be separated. We shall be even closer in death than we have been in life. Is this not a comfort? If this calamity had not struck, one of us would have died before the other, and we should have been forced apart. But now even in death God unites us.

Dear wife, stop weeping, and give thanks to God. Thank him for our love, and thank him for our mutual joy.

Kamba

22

Two spears and one elephant

The Mbundu tell these stories:

Kinungu and Ngundu had been friends since childhood; and now they were adults, they frequently went hunting together. But Ngundu resented Kinungu's greater skill.

One day Kinungu killed an elephant with his spear. Ngundu saw the elephant fall, and immediately threw his own spear at the elephant. Kinungu shouted: 'This elephant is mine; I killed it.' Ngundu shouted back: 'No, the elephant is mine; I killed it.' The two men quarreled violently. Then Ngundu said: 'Let us go to the chief, and allow him to judge between us.' Kinungu agreed. Ngundu hoped that the chief would divide the elephant between them.

When each man had put his case, the chief said: 'It is hard to judge between you, because there were no witnesses. Tonight I shall ask my wife's advice. Return in the morning, and I shall give you my verdict.' The chief spoke to his wife, and she advised him to send two servants, one to spy on Kiningu, and the other to spy on Ngundu.

In the morning the servant spying on Ngundu reported: 'Ngundu spent last night drinking and laughing with his friends. Then he went to sleep in his hut.' The servant spying on Kinungu reported: 'Kinungu went to the elephant, and lay down beside it. He spent all night weeping.'

The chief then summoned the two men, and declared: 'Kinungu killed the elephant, and it belongs to him. Ngundu is a liar and a thief - and I order him to be flogged.'

Mbundu

23

One insult for another

Each evening an old man sat with his son-in-law under the stars, and they reflected on the events of the day. The old man was bald, and the son-in-law was blind in one eye. One evening, after a pleasant conversation, the old man said: 'The night has grown very dark, so it is time to sleep. Yet there is no darkness like the darkness of a blind eye.' With these words the old man went to his hut. The son-in-law remained outside, burning with anger. He said to himself: 'How dare my father-in-law refer to my blind eye! It is an insult.'

The following evening, after the two men had chatted about the day's events, the son-in-law said: 'The moon has risen, so it is time to sleep. Yet not even the moon shines as brightly as a bald pate.' With these words the young man went to his hut. The old man remained outside, burning with anger. He said to himself: 'How dare my son-in-law refer to my baldness. It is an insult.'

The following evening, instead of sitting under the stars, the old man went to the village chief, and complained about his son-in-law. The chief then went to the younger man. 'Why did you insult your father-in-law?' he asked. 'I insulted him because he insulted me,' the young man replied.

The chief called the two men together. He said to the younger man: 'You were wrong to return evil for evil.' He said to the older man: 'You were wrong to complain about another's evil, before apologizing for your own.' When they heard this judgement, the two men embraced.

Mbundu

24

Respect and Dignity

The headman of a particular village died, and the elders met to decide who should replace him. One elder said: 'We do not want a strong leader who will dominate us, telling us what to do and how to behave.' Another elder said: 'We want a leader who has dignity.' So they wondered who possessed great dignity, and had no authority. Eventually they decided that a large dog should become their chief.

They chose the largest dog in the village, and organized a grand ceremony at which to install him as their head. Colored mats were spread in the center of the village, and a large chair was put in the center. To the sound of a drum and a marimba the dog was led to the chair. For a few moments the dog sat on the chair, and gazed around him. Everyone was impressed at his dignity, and congratulated the elders on choosing him.

Then a group of young women appeared, carrying a large tray of roast fowl. When the dog saw the roast fowl, greed took hold of him. He leapt from the chair, grabbed a roast fowl, and ran into the forest to eat it. The people gasped in horror.

The oldest woman in the village walked to the chair, and stood beside it. Then she said to the people: 'Dignity without strength is a sham. Choose a leader who possesses strength of heart and mind - and confer dignity upon that leader by your own attitude.'

The people immediately chose the old woman, who without doubt possessed the greatest strength of heart and mind of anyone in the village. And by treating her with respect, they conferred dignity upon her.

Mbundu

25

Strength and Intelligence

The Mensa tell this story:

The world was originally dominated by a race of giants called roms. They owned all the cattle, and each rom drank the milk of one cow and the flesh of half a cow each day. Humans lived in poverty, eating only wild berries and roots.

One day a man said to himself: 'Although roms are stronger than human beings, human beings are more intelligent. So we should use our intelligence to defeat them.' He went to a rom, and said: 'You are strong and wealthy, whereas I am only weak and poor. I should be honored if you would allow me to work as your servant – with no reward except the knowledge that I was pleasing you.' The rom's breast swelled with pride at these words, and accepted the man's offer.

The man tended the rom's cattle, so the rom had no work to do. Out of boredom the rom began to drink large amounts of beer; and gradually his body became fat and his mind feeble. Whenever the man saw the rom, he bowed low and uttered some flattering remark. In the meantime, from every three calves that were born into the rom's herd, the man took two to his own home, where his sons cared for them. Thus the man's herd grew to twice the size of the rom's.

When other men observed this man's success, they imitated him. Soon every rom had a human servant; and every rom was becoming fat and feeble, while every human was becoming rich.

Mensa

26

Death by a blessing

God observed what was happening, and was pleased to see that intelligence was proving more powerful than strength. When all the roms had become drunkards, he decided that the time had come for them to perish.

So he gathered the roms together, and said: 'You have proved yourselves unworthy to dominate earth. I shall now destroy you, and make humanity the dominant species. Do you wish to perish by a blessing or by a curse?' The roms discussed the matter, and then replied: 'We wish to perish by a blessing.'

Very well,' said God, 'I shall answer the prayer which you have persistently offered' The roms were perplexed, and asked God what he meant. 'You have persistently prayed for male children and female calves,' God replied; 'from this moment onwards all your children will be male, and all your calves female.'

In the next generation the male roms had no one to marry, and the cows had no bulls with whom to mate. So the roms had to watch their herds gradually disappear – and then watch their own extinction. When only one rom remained, he was so lonely that he dug a deep hole, and buried himself.

When humans saw the fate of the roms, they made a vow never to ask God for male children and female calves, but to accept with gratitude whatever sex of child or animal that God gives. And the wiser humans decided never to pray to God for anything in particular, but to regard every event as a blessing.

Mensa

27

THE SACRED CORNCOB

The Togo people tell these stories:

God was sad that human beings ignored his commands. So he appointed a very clever man called Anansi as his chief minister, and said to him: 'I want you to turn men and women into my servants.' 'I cannot turn every man and woman into a servant at once,' Anansi replied; 'but if you give me a corncob, I shall bring you a hundred servants.' So God gave Anansi a corncob, and Anansi set out.

He arrived at a village at dusk, and said to the headman: 'I am on my way to your chief; and I am carrying a sacred corncob, which is a gift from God. Could you show me a place where it can be kept safely overnight?' The headman put it under the roof of his house. During the night, when everyone was asleep, Anansi took the corncob from the roof, and threw it to the birds. And when it could not be found in the morning, Anansi made a terrible fuss. In recompense the headman gave Anansi a beautiful fowl.

At dusk he arrived at another village. He said to the headman that the fowl was a gift from God to the chief, and asked for it to be kept safely overnight. It was put in a cage with other fowl. At night he killed it, smeared some of its blood and feathers on the doorpost of the headman's house, and threw the corpse aside. In the morning the people concluded that the headman had killed the fowl in some sacrilegious sacrifice; and they begged Anansi to show them how to avert God's wrath. Anansi said that a gift of ten sheep would placate God; and the people eagerly gave him their best animals.

Togo

28

God's servants

Anansi went to the cemetery outside the town where the chief lived, and sat down under a tree. A few hours later a party arrived carrying the corpse of a young man, and buried it. When the people had left, Anansi dug up the corpse, washed it, and carried it into the town, driving the ten sheep in front.

He walked straight to the chief's house, and gave him the ten sheep as a sign of good will. Then he said: 'I am God's chief minister, and I am carrying God's son, who has fallen asleep with exhaustion. He wishes to honor you for your virtue; but in the meantime I should like a hut in which to lay him down.' The chief's chest swelled with pride, and he ordered a hut to be prepared. Then Anansi added: 'I think it would be appropriate for your eldest son to bring him food in the morning.'

The next morning the chief's eldest son brought food to the hut. He gently shook the body that was lying on the bed, and said: 'Your breakfast is here.' And, when the body did not awake, he shook more vigorously. Then he realized that the body was dead, and ran out of the hut, screaming with terror. Anansi pretended to be shocked, and accused the chief's son of murdering God's son. The chief's son protested his innocence, but Anansi declared: 'There can be no other explanation.'

The chief and the people begged Anansi to tell them how they could recompense God for the loss of his son. 'Choose the hundred strongest young men in your tribe,' Anansi said, 'and give them to God as his servants.' The people readily agreed.

Togo

29

God's two sons

When Anansi told God how he had acquired a hundred servants, it jolted God into wondering whether he should have some genuine sons. Anansi supported the idea. So he took a wife, who bore him two sons, called Bia and Tano. Bia grew up with smooth, hairless skin, and liked wearing magnificent robes; while Tano was rough and hairy, and wore simple clothes.

When Bia and Tano attained manhood, God decided to present each of them with an area of the world, which they should rule on his behalf. He ordered Anansi, his chief minister, to arrange a ceremony at which this presentation would be made. Then he said to Anansi: 'Bia has been an obedient and helpful boy; so I shall give him a very fertile area near the river, where many people and animals lived. Tano has been rebellious and wicked; so I shall give him give him a barren, deserted area on the edge of the world.'

A friend of Tano, called Akua, overheard God discussing his intentions with Anansi, and told Tano of them. So on the day of the ceremony Tano sent Akua to Bia's hut, to tie up Bia , and so prevent him from coming. In the meantime Tano disguised himself as Bia: he shaved himself closely, and put on a magnificent robe. He then went to God's palace.

God was deceived by Tano's disguise. He blessed Tano, and declared that Tano would rule the fertile area near the river.

Togo

30

A GOOD DECEPTION

God then asked where Tano was. Tano, imitating Bia's voice, replied: 'That rebellious and wicked young man has not bothered to come.' God erupted with anger, and shouted: 'Let him go to the barren land on the edge of the world, and never return.' Tano smiled – and God interpreted his smile as satisfaction that justice was being done to his brother.

Eventually Akua untied Bia, and Bia rushed to God's palace. God was confused, and said to Tano: 'Since you are Bia, who is this person disguised as you?' Tano took off the magnicent robe he was wearing, and revealed himself.

God turned to Bia, and said: 'It is too late. I have already blessed Tano, and presented him with the fertile area near the river. I cannot rescind my blessing or go back on my word. So you must become ruler of the barren area on the western edge of the world.' Bia burst into tears, and cried out to God: 'The obedience I showed to you over so many years, and the help I gave you, have been wasted. I made myself miserable for nothing. I should have been rebellious and wicked like Tano - and enjoyed myself.'

Tano and Bia went to their respective lands. Tano proved a good ruler. He was just and fair, punishing wickedness and rewarding virtue; and he worked hard for his people's welfare. So his people grew to respect and love him. But Bia proved a bad ruler. He was capricious and cruel, punishing severely those whom he disliked, and rewarding those whom he liked; and he was lazy, doing nothing to help his people. So his people grew to despise and hate him. And God, as he observed the behavior of his two sons, was grateful that Tano had deceived him.

Togo

31

FOR BLESSING

The Ga offer this prayer for blessing:

Let happiness come. If we dig a well, may it be at a spot where water is buried. If we draw water to drink, may it be clean; and if we draw water to wash our bodies, may it be cool. May our village be blessed. May those speaking with God's voice be blessed. May our men be potent and our women fertile. May misfortunes jump over us. May our journeys be safe, and our returns joyful.

The Wapokomo offer this prayer for blessing:

O God, give us peace, give us tranquility, and let good fortune come upon us. Give us rain when we plant our crops, and sunshine when we harvest them. Give healing to the young when they fall sick; and give a painless death to the old.

Ga and Wapokom

MONTH

7

ZOROASTRIANISM

Introduction

Origins

During the second millennium BCE Aryan tribes moved southwards from the steppes of central Asia. Some went into India, and their religion developed into Hinduism. Others went to Afghanistan, and to the region around the southern shores of the Caspian Sea, which came to be called Iran – the land of the Aryans. Around 1200 BCE Zarathustra was born in eastern Iran; and his teachings formed the basis of a religion that dominated Iran for two millennia, and had profound influence on other faiths.

As a boy Zarathustra visited the sages of the time to imbibe their wisdom; but by the age of fifteen he had learnt all they had to teach, and was still dissatisfied. So for the next fifteen years he devoted himself to meditation. He had a series of revelations, which he interpreted as coming from 'the wise Lord' ***(Ahura Mazda)***; and at the age of thirty he began to preach, telling people what he had seen and heard. The Aryan tribes were governed at that time by local rulers, who were advised by priests. The priests near Zarathustra's home regarded his message as a threat to their status, and they urged the rulers to silence him. Eventually, at the age of forty-two, in fear of his life, Zarathustra, accompanied by a handful of disciples, emigrated eastwards to Balkh; there he succeeded in converting the ruler, called Vishtasp – who then dismissed all his priests.

Zarathustra settled in Balkh, and married a woman called Hvovi, who became his first female disciple; one of their daughters married Vishtasp's chief minister. At the age of seventy-seven Zarathustra was murdered, possibly by one of Vishtasp's former priests.

TEACHINGS

Zarathustra encapsulated his teachings in a series of hymns ***(gathas)***. These were passed orally from one generation to the next, and were not finally written down until the sixth century CE. His message is simple. God – Ahura Mazda – created the world; and at the moment of creation he also had two offspring, the spirit of goodness, and the spirit of evil. The spirit of goodness is associated with truth, love and justice; while the spirit of evil is associated with deceit, hatred and oppression. The two spirits enter every human being, and fight for influence; and human beings are free to choose between them. If they choose to act as the spirit of goodness urges, they may suffer various misfortunes, but will enjoy inner peace. If they choose to act as the spirit of evil dictates, they may enjoy wealth and power, but will always feel anxious and fearful.

After his death Zarathustra's religion gradually spread westwards into Iran. It became the official religion of the first Persian Empire under Cyrus the Great; and its priests ***(Magi)*** became famous for their wisdom. In the Magis' teaching the ultimate supremacy of God seems to have been forgotten, and the world was seen simply as the battlefield of the two spirits. The body came to be seen as the place where the evil spirit resided, stirring up desires; while the soul was regarded as the place where the god spirit dwelt. To show their contempt for the body, the magi insisted that corpses should not be buried, but placed on the top of high towers, where vultures could come and eat the flesh.

EXPRESSION

In the fifth century BCE the Greek historian Herodotus described the religion of the Magi; and Plato, who was certainly aware of it, developed a philosophy of body and soul with close similarities. The Greeks referred to the founder as Zoroaster, the name by which he is still most widely known.

Zarathustra's teaching also had a profound, but rather different, influence on Judaism. In early Jewish writings evil is not regarded as a distinct force, but simply as disobedience to God. But during their exile in Babylon Jews came into contact with the Magian ideas; and thereafter Satan, as the spirit of evil, played a major role in Jewish thought. They reasserted, however, the ultimate supremacy of God; so Satan is regarded as a servant of God, whose primary role is to test people's faith.

The Magi appear in Luke's Gospel as visitors to the infant Jesus Christ, led to him by their astrological knowledge. Zarathustra and the Magis were held in high regard by the early Christians; and Justin included them among those pagans who had apprehended part of the truth. Magian ideas were most eagerly adopted by the Gnostic groups within Christianity, who inflicted severe torture on their bodies in order to liberate their souls.

Within Zoroastrianism itself, however, there was a movement back towards Zarathustra's original ideas. This was led by a teacher called Manuskihar and an anonymous sage. After the Muslim conquest of Iran a group of Zoroastrians fled to India, where they continued to practice this simple faith.

Us

The modern mind finds it hard to grasp the notion of distinct forces of good and evil; it does not fit the conception of the world fostered by science. Yet Zarathustra's teaching accords with our actual experience. At times all of us feel strongly drawn towards some wicked and hateful action, and we can even be persuaded that the wicked action is right. At other times we have a strong urge to do what is right and loving, and nothing can deter us. Most frequently we find ourselves engaged in an inner tussle between conscience and desire.

Like most religious teachers, Zarathustra took for granted the distinction between right and wrong. To philosophers this distinction is a matter for debate, and some assert that moral judgments are determined by cultural circumstances. But again Zarathustra's teaching accords with our actual experience. The human conscience in every culture seems to affirm similar moral principles; and these principles present themselves to us as self-evidently true. Moreover, we do not need the promise of heaven and the threat of hell to affirm the value of behaving well. As Zarathustra and his disciples taught, a disturbed conscience brings misery, while a peaceful conscience brings contentment.

1

Zarathustra's boyhood

Soon after Zarathustra's birth, a wise old man called Barzinkaroos came to Zarathustra's father, and said: 'Your son is destined to become a great spiritual leader. Will you honor me by allowing me to educate him.' Zarathustra's father agreed. As soon as Zarathustra could speak, Barzinkaroos began to teach him what he knew; and by the age of seven Zarathustra had absorbed it all.

Zarathustra began to speak quite openly against the local priests and magicians, saying that their rituals and spells were useless. The priests and magicians became frightened that people would listen to him. One day, when Zarathustra was in bed with some minor illness, the chief priest came to him with a bottle of brightly colored liquid. 'Drink this, dear child,' the chief priest said; 'it will destroy your illness at once.' Zarathustra suspected that the liquid was poison. 'It would destroy my illness by destroying me!' he exclaimed. Then he seized the bottle, and threw it to the ground. The chief priest ran away, shaking with fear.

Soon afterwards Zarathustra's father, who was a wealthy farmer, held a banquet for the priests and magicians. After the meal he rose up, and spoke of the benefits that the priests and magicians brought to people. Then Zarathustra interrupted his father, saying that the priests and magicians merely exploited people's ignorance. Zarathustra possessed such authority that his father stopped speaking, and sat down. And the priests and magicians did not dare defend themselves.

Dabistan

2

Zarathustra's Call

Zarathustra visited every wise man and woman in the region, and listened to their insights; but none satisfied him. So at the age of fifteen he went to live in a cave, and set himself the task of discovering the truth through inner reflection and meditation. He meditated for many hours each day for fifteen years. Then, when he reached the age of thirty, God appeared to him. God was so bright that Zarathustra could only look at his shadow. 'What do you most desire in this world?' God asked. 'Wise Lord,' Zarathustra answered, ' I have no desire other than the desire to please you. My heart wants nothing other than I should be righteous in your sight.'

'Ask me a question,' God said. 'In what does righteousness consist?' Zarathustra asked. God replied: 'Righteousness consists in loving all men, women and children, all animals and birds, all insects and fish, and all trees and plants.' 'In what does wickedness consist?' Zarathustra asked. God replied: 'Wickedness consists in being cruel to other living beings.'

Then God said: 'I created all living beings and all that exists. I also created two spirits, the spirit of goodness and the spirit of evil. The spirit of goodness shows people the way of righteousness; the spirit of evil shows them the way of wickedness – but pretends that it is the way of righteousness. Everyone must choose between these two ways. I appoint you as my prophet; your task is to expose the deceit of the spirit of evil, and to encourage people to choose the way of righteousness.'

Dabistan

3

Support and opposition

Zarathustra now left his cave, and he went from place to place teaching people what God had taught him; and he told them to reject the rituals of the priests and the spells of the magicians. Everywhere he was hailed as a prophet, and treated with the greatest respect, and people stopped supporting the priests and magicians. The priests and magicians went to the king, and told him that Zarathustra wanted to be king himself, and would soon be urging people to rebel. So the king ordered his soldiers to kill Zarathustra. But one of the king's advisers supported Zarathustra, and sent a messenger warning him of the king's order. So Zarathustra fled the region, accompanied by a small group of disciples.

Zarathustra eventually arrived at the court of the great king Vishtasp. Priests and magicians surrounded the king, who loved to discuss spiritual matters with them. Vishtasp ordered Zarathustra to explain his beliefs; and Zarathustra recounted what God had told him. The king was so impressed that he invited Zarathustra to become his chief priest.

The priests and magicians were furious, and they begged the king to allow them to argue against Zarathustra. 'You can prepare your arguments tonight,' the king said, 'and tomorrow morning you can put them to him.' So the priests and magicians spent the entire night awake, trying to invent arguments that would show Zarathustra to be a fraud. The following morning they expounded these arguments at great length, and concluded: 'Zarathustra has never encountered God; he is a liar and a hypocrite.'

Dabistan

4

FALSE ACCUSATION

Zarathustra refuted the arguments of the priests and magicians one by one, and the king clapped his hands with delight. The sages begged for another opportunity to argue against Zarathustra, and the king agreed. So they spent another night preparing arguments, and again concluded that Zarathustra was a liar and hypocrite. But again Zarathustra refuted their arguments, and Vishtasp clapped with delight.

That night the priests and magicians wondered how they might rid themselves of Zarathustra. They feared that if they murdered him, the king might suspect their guilt and punish them. So they made a plan to turn the king against him. The following morning, when Zarathustra was with the king, they put into his room various items associated with black magic: a bottle of blood, a bundle of horse hair, a cat's head, a dog's head, and some human bones. Then they went to the king, and accused Zarathustra of being a black magician. Zarathustra pleaded his innocence. 'Very well,' the chief sage said, 'let his room be searched, to see if there is evidence of black magic.' So Vishtasp sent a group of soldiers to Zarathustra's room, and they returned with the items that had been placed there. The king was furious, and ordered Zarathustra to be locked in a dungeon, and fed only on dry bread.

Zarathustra devoted his time to meditation, and trusted in God to liberate him. A week later Vishtasp's favorite horse, a black charger fell ill. The priests and magicians prepared various potions to cure the horse, but none worked.

Dabistan

5

THE KING'S DECLARATION

Finally in desperation Vishtasp decided to summon Zarathustra, in the hope that he could cure his black charger. Zarathustra had learnt from his first teacher Barzinkaroos a recipe for horse medicine; so he made the medicine and gave it to the horse. The horse immediately recovered, and the king was overjoyed.

'What do you want as reward?' the king asked. 'I want only one thing,' Zarathustra replied; 'I want you to declare publicly that I am a prophet of God, the wise Lord.' The king was troubled, because he knew that such a declaration would again antagonize the priests and magicians. 'I shall think about your request for a day,' the king replied, 'and tomorrow I shall decide whether to grant it.' The following day the king said to Zarathustra: 'I need a miracle to prove that you are a prophet of God.' 'Your majesty,' Zarathustra answered, 'every event is a miracle. The sun rises in the morning because God makes it rise, and sets in the evening because God makes it set. Plants produce blossom at God's order, and animals give birth when God decides. I can do nothing greater than what you see every day.' 'Very well,' the king said, 'give me some other proof.'

To his own surprise Zarathustra began to recite a series of poems. The words were so sublime and beautiful that God had manifestly inspired them. The king composed a message, which was conveyed to every town and village in his kingdom: 'Zarathustra is a prophet of God, the wise Lord, and I authorize him to preach throughout the land.' He then dismissed the priests and magicians from his service.

Dabistan

6

Questions to God

These are the poems that Zarathustra spoke in front of Vishtasp, and which he recited in every town and village in Vishtasp's kingdom. Some are addressed to God as prayers, and some are instructions from God.

Answer me honestly, O God. Can you, whose power and knowledge are infinite, treat me as a friend? Do you take pleasure in my worship, and do my righteous acts give you joy? And do that pleasure and joy prompt you to look upon me with love?

Answer me honestly, O God. Will people be rewarded for the righteous actions they perform, and will they be punished for their wicked actions? Will you balance good and evil actions on scales, and determine a fair recompense?

Answer me honestly, O God. What will happen to those who do not pay for work that has been done for them? What will happen do those who break their promises? Will they suffer for their dishonesty in this world?

Answer me honestly, O God. Why do wicked people frequently prosper? Why do people who are notorious for stealing cattle, and those who deal in stolen cattle, enjoy every comfort the world can provide, while honest men and women endure poverty?

Answer me honestly, O God. If a good man captures an evil man in the act of stealing his cattle, should the good man punish the evil man, or should he try to convert him to righteousness? And if the good man succeeds in converting the evil man, should he forgive the evil man's crime?

Zarathustra: Gathas

7

More questions to God

Answer me honestly, O God. Do religious rituals bring benefit those who conduct them? Do sacrifices on altars, and processions around temples, win your favor? Are you impressed by the actions of priests and their assistants?

Answer me honestly, O God. Who will protect the weak and the poor? Who will prevent the weak from being oppressed by the strong, and the poor being exploited by the rich? Who will uphold freedom and justice?

Answer me honestly, O God. Who will protect your prophets when they speak? Who will guard them from the wrath of those they rebuke? How will they escape the fury of those whose wickedness they expose?

Answer me honestly, O God. Will you overthrow those kings and princes who treat their subjects cruelly? Will you torture the hearts and minds of rulers who torture the bodies of innocent people? Will you bring to justice those who deny justice to others?

Answer me honestly, O God. When people pray to you, will you answer their prayers? When people meditate upon you, will you bring peace to their hearts and tranquility to their minds? When people worship you, will you unite them to yourself?

Answer me honestly, O God. If I, whom you have appointed as your prophet, am pleased with particular people, will you also smile upon them? If I praise people for their righteous acts, will you bless them? If I rebuke people for their wicked acts, will you stir their consciences? Will you support me in the work that you have given me to do?

Zarathustra: Gathas

8

THE ONLY MIRACLE

Your fire, O God, purifies the righteous and destroys the wicked. Your fire refines the hearts and minds of those who exalt you, so that no malicious emotions or corrupt thoughts remain.

What glory belongs to you! What love you have for all living beings! My only desire is to unite myself with you; and for this purpose I renounce every emotion that is contrary to your nature, and every thought that is contrary to your will.

What majesty is your! What power and wisdom you possess. May you use that power to destroy all that is evil in my nature; and use that wisdom to replace evil with good.

Perform this miracle, the only miracle that I desire: remake me in your image. Then I shall have no greater joy and pleasure than offering you praise and worship.

There are many evil people who pray to evil gods. When you come near to them, they shrink, as an animal shrinks from the hunter. But good people pray to you, the righteous God. When you come near to them, they open their arms, as a bride opens her arms for the bridegroom.

Honesty and integrity are the food of the righteous, while lies and deceit are the food of the wicked. Courtesy and humility are the drink of the righteous, while pride and arrogance are the drink of the wicked.

What is your word, O God? What deeds do you want me to perform, and what words do you want me to speak? Your word is my only command.

Zarathustra: Gathas

9

God's warning to prophets

In every nation and in every generation there has been someone who has said to you: 'Let me be your prophet, O God. Let me proclaim your message to those who love you; let me oppose those who hate you.'

You have always replied: 'I accept your offer, because your faith in me is sincere. But I warn you that my opponents are fierce and strong. Their devotion to the spirit of evil is as strong as your devotion to the spirit of goodness. Their minds are as twisted as yours is straight. When you urge people to be righteous, they will urge people to be wicked with equal eloquence. In the purity of your heart, you want people to raise people to the realm of joy; and in the corruption of their hearts, they want to cheat people of every kind of pleasure, and plunge them into the realm of misery.'

The prophet, on hearing this reply, has said: 'I am as fierce as your opponents. They shall not win a single follower without a struggle. For every word that they speak in favor of wickedness, I shall speak countless words in favor of righteousness. So when people choose between good and evil, they will know fully the consequences of their choice.'

In this generation and in this nation I am asking to be your prophet and proclaim your message. Despite your warning, I am not afraid. Wherever I proclaim your message, I shall encounter enemies. In every town and village, I shall find that the men with wealth and power are hostile; and without constraint they will use their wealth and power against me. But when I cry to you for help, you will come to my rescue.

Zarathustra: Gathas

10

The Human Conscience

How can I know that you are who you are, O God? How can I know that you created the spirit of goodness? How can I know that the spirit of goodness will guide us to act righteously? How can I know that righteous actions will bring eternal joy?

I know who you are because I recognize you; as soon as I saw you, I knew that you are God. I know that you created the spirit of goodness because you alone are the source of goodness. I know that the spirit of goodness will guide me to act righteously because it has given me a conscience; I can hear my conscience within the silence of my mind, and it tells me what is right and wrong. I know that righteous actions bring joy because there is joy in acting righteously.

Who am I? I am Zarathustra, a true enemy of the spirit of evil, and a true friend of the spirit of goodness. To whom do I belong? I belong to you, who created the spirit of goodness at the beginning of time. I fight for the spirit of goodness with all my might, and I worship you with all my heart and mind.

How can I show you to others, that they too may recognize you? How can I teach them that you created the spirit of goodness? How can I help them to hear their consciences, through which the spirit of goodness speaks? How can I show them that righteous actions bring joy?

You alone, O God, can give me words that will evoke you, that will enable people to hear their consciences, and that will prompt them to follow their consciences.

Zarathustra: Gathas

11

THREE SORTS OF PEOPLE

There are three sorts of people. There are those who are devoted to righteousness, although they occasionally do evil. There are those who are devoted to wickedness, and occasionally do good. And there are those who are devoted to neither righteousness nor wickedness, and sometimes do good and sometimes do evil. You, O God, will judge each type of person justly, according to the laws of good and evil that you have laid down.

There are three kinds of influence that people wield over others. There is good influence, by which righteous people influence others to submit to your will. There is bad influence, by which wicked people influence others to defy your will. And there is deadly influence, by which people without devotion influence others to be indifferent to your will.

As a member of a family I try to exert a good influence on other members: where there is discord, I strive to bring peace. As a prophet I try to exert a good influence on all people: where there is ignorance of God's will, I strive to bring knowledge.

I try to make myself heard amongst farmers and herdsmen, that they may harvest their crops and milk their animals in a spirit of gratitude. I try to make myself heard among the priests, that they may perform rituals in a spirit of devotion.

If I ever utter words that are wrong, may God correct my tongue. If my thoughts are ever confused, may he clarify my mind. If my actions are ever harmful, may he constrain my limbs. If my emotions ever love anything he hates, may he purify my heart.

Zarathustra: Gathas

12

God as rider

What help can you expect from anyone? Who can you trust to protect your cattle? Only God, the righteous master, can help you; only God, the almighty king, can guard your possessions. So worship him with words of praise and with emotions of love; and think about him constantly with your finest thoughts.

God's hand can lead you to the realm of bliss, and his voice can guide your steps towards that realm. His smile of blessing is all that you should desire.

Swear allegiance to his will, and promise that you will always obey his commands. Speak only the words that he puts into your mouth, and promise that your tongue will always move as he requires.

Be like a horse, with God as your rider. When he presses the spurs of grace into your flesh, gallop with all speed.

Approach him with outstretched arms. Exalt him with songs of praise. With all your mind listen to him, and with all your body obey him. He will make your words wise and gentle, and your actions effective and benign.

The deeds that you will do, and those that you have already done, offer to him. The words that you will say, and those that you have already said, bring to him. The things that are precious to your eyes, lay down as gifts to him.

He alone can refresh your body, heart and mind, when they are weary. He alone can restore you to life when death overtakes you.

Zarathustra: Gathas

13

THE TRIUMPH OF GOOD OVER EVIL

People ask whether good will really overcome evil? They ask whether righteous people will triumph, and wicked people be vanquished? They ask whether generosity will be rewarded, and cruelty punished? Prophets in every generation and nation have foretold this. People wonder whether they have been speaking words that God has given them, or whether their own imaginations have guided their tongues?

I too am a prophet; and God has told me directly that good will overcome evil. He has informed me that, when the time is right, the world will be saved from wickedness, and righteousness will prevail. May generous people be assured by this knowledge, and may cruel people be prompted to repent and change their ways.

Yet this salvation is already present. The wicked are already disturbed by their consciences, which are restless and uneasy; their sleep is shallow. And the righteous are comforted by their consciences, which are serene and calm; their sleep is deep.

So listen to your conscience – let your conscience direct your thoughts, transform your desires, and guide your actions. And if you rule over others, let your conscience show you how to govern your people with justice, mercy and compassion.

Dig up the roots of anger, and chop down the tree of violence. And in their place sow the seeds of gentleness, and shelter under the tree of peace.

God has appointed prophets like me to speak to every generation and nation, and proclaim his victory.

Zarathustra: Gathas

14

THE OPPRESSION OF ANIMALS

The oxen complain to God: 'For what purpose did you create us. For whose benefit do we exist? We are forced to act as my human master demands, hauling carts and pulling ploughs. I want you to be my master, and I want to graze in peace on your pastures.'

God speaks to the spirit of goodness, who was God's agent in the creation of the world: 'Is there anyone who can protect the oxen from human oppression and tyranny? Can you provide the oxen with pasture where she can graze in safety?'

The spirit of goodness replied: 'There is no one who can protect the oxen. All other creatures would oppress the oxen even more severely than humans do. Besides, of all creatures, the human being is the most powerful, because in the human being physical strength is combined with high intelligence. So if I put the oxen under the charge of any other creature, the human would take it back.'

God said: 'Why did you not guarantee the oxen's freedom when the world was created?' The spirit of goodness replied: 'When the world was created, my work was constantly opposed by the spirit of evil. Thus from the outset some aspects of the world have been good, and some have been evil. I fashioned the ox, who is good; but the spirit of evil taught humans to oppress the ox, which is evil.'

God told the oxen what the spirit of goodness had said. The oxen replied: 'You, O God, are supremely powerful. Change human hearts, so that they no longer take pleasure in oppressing us and set us free.' God replied: 'In the fullness of time I shall do so.'

Zarathustra: Gathas

15

Two spirits

I will speak, brother and sisters; listen to what I say. Whether you have come from near or far, my words apply to you, because God is the same throughout the world – and my words come from him. False teachers oppose me; but they are motivated by jealousy and ambition, not by devotion to the truth.

Let me tell you of two spirits. There is the spirit of goodness, who is benign, and seeks to nurture and sustain all that God has created. And there is the spirit of evil, who is malign, and seeks to deface and destroy all that God has created. The spirit of goodness and the spirit of evil can never agree; their thoughts and inclinations are utterly opposed.

Let me tell you of how you can receive the spirit of goodness, and reject the spirit of evil. Seek to lead a righteous life; suppress all corrupt thoughts and emotions; and strive to obey the will of God in all that you do.

Let me tell you how you can know the will of God. Listen to the words of those whom God has appointed as his prophets. You can distinguish true prophets from false prophets by the quality of their lives: a true prophet is generous, humble and honest, while a false prophet is mean, arrogant and deceitful.

Let me tell you of the justice of God. At present the wicked prosper while the righteous suffer. But a time will come when God will make the righteous prosper and the wicked suffer. The joy of the righteous will be so great that even death will not be able to extinguish it; their joy will be eternal.

Zarathustra: Gathas

16

Loyal servants of God

I will speak, brothers and sisters; listen to what I say. I shall tell you how to serve God: how you should praise him; how you should meditate upon him; and how you should act in order to win his favor.

Clear your minds, and compare my words with the words of false prophets. You will find that the spirit of goodness guides my words, while the spirit of evil guides theirs. And look carefully at our lives. Are they righteous, or am I? Are they wicked, or am I?

From the beginning of time the two spirits, the spirit of goodness and the spirit of evil, have been active in the world. The good spirit has been promoting joy, and the evil spirit has been promoting misery. The good spirit has been guiding people to act righteously; while the evil spirit has been guiding people to act wickedly. Both the good and the evil spirit know that righteousness brings joy, while wickedness brings misery.

If you wish to serve God, open your heart and mind to the spirit of goodness, and reject the spirit of evil. Meditate on goodness, and suppress all evil thoughts. Pray to God with all devotion that good may defeat evil; and praise God for every triumph of good over evil. Above all, when you are choosing how to act, listen only to the spirit of goodness; and if you hear the promptings of the spirit of evil, deafen yourself at once.

A time will come when the victory of good over evil will be complete. The spirit of evil will be destroyed forever, and the spirit of goodness will reign supreme throughout the world. With every person that becomes a loyal servant of God, that time comes closer.

Zarathustra: Gathas

17

Two ways

Evil people, whose hearts have been corrupted by wicked desires, scoff at God's laws. But good people, who are faithful to God find joy in obeying everything that he commands.

God gives you a choice: you may follow the way of evil, or you may follow the way of goodness. And he has appointed me to make plain this choice, so that you can distinguish clearly between the way of evil and the way of goodness. I cannot persuade you to follow the way of goodness, if you wish to follow the way of evil; but I can deprive you of the excuse of ignorance.

To follow the way of goodness is not a matter of being good; it is a matter of being wise. If you are wise, you will understand that the way of goodness leads to eternal joy. To follow the way of evil is not a matter of being evil; it is a matter of being foolish. If you are foolish, you will refuse to understand that the way of goodness leads to eternal misery.

God is the beginning of goodness and the end of goodness. At the beginning of the world, he created the spirit of goodness; and at the end of the world he will embrace all those whose lives have been guided by that spirit. He is the father of goodness; and if people follow the way of goodness, they become his children.

The spirit of goodness inserts in every mind a conscience, which cannot be ignored. When people are wicked, the conscience is disturbed; and when they are righteous, it is peaceful.

Zarathustra: Gathas

18

The Purpose of Righteous Action

A disciple asked the great teacher Manuskihar: 'What makes human beings different from all the other living beings on earth?' Manuskihar replied: 'Human beings are different because they are able to judge between good and evil. The capacity for judgment arises from the wisdom that human beings possess. And its consequence is that human beings can choose how they act. Thus human beings sometimes choose to act righteously, and sometimes choose to act wickedly.'

A disciple asked the great teacher Manuskihar: 'For what purpose should people act righteously?' Manuskihar replied: 'People should act righteously because God has designed the world in such a way that righteousness brings happiness. Let people meditate on the connection between righteousness and the world around them; they will discern that to act righteously is to act in harmony with the world. Let them also meditate on the connection between harmony with the world and human happiness; they will discern that acting in harmony with the world will lead to harmony within the mind and heart, which is the source of happiness.'

A disciple asked the great teacher Manuskihar: 'Can evil people become good people?' Manuskihar replied: 'If people act wickedly, the spirit of evil clasps their hearts and minds; and if people act righteously, the spirit of goodness clasps their hearts and minds. Thus if evil people decide to reject wicked actions and choose righteous actions, the clasp of the spirit of evil weakens, and the clasp of the spirit of goodness strengthens.'

Dadistan-i Dinik

19

THE BATTLE BETWEEN GOOD AND EVIL

A disciple asked the great teacher Manuskihar: 'What happens to people that act wickedly, and what happens to people that act righteously?' Manuskihar replied: 'People acting wickedly suffer disturbance in their hearts and minds; they feel anxious and fearful, and their rest is troubled. People acting righteously enjoy tranquil hearts and minds; they feel calm and serene, and their rest is peaceful. By observing a person's state of heart and mind, you can judge whether that person is in the grip of the spirit of evil or the spirit of goodness.'

A disciple asked the great teacher Manuskihar: 'Why does misfortune befall good people more often than evil people?' Manuskihar replied: 'There are two reasons for this. The first is that evil people devote great effort to protecting themselves from misfortune, while good people devote great effort to protecting others from misfortune. The second is that the spirit of evil protects evil people from misfortune, in order to deceive others into thinking that evil people are blessed by God; but the spirit of goodness allows good people to suffer misfortune, as this strengthens their hearts and minds.'

A disciple asked the great teacher Manuskihar: 'What is the ultimate purpose of human existence?' Manuskihar replied: 'The ultimate purpose of human existence is to enable the sprit of goodness to triumph over the spirit of evil. Every human heart is a battlefield on which the two spirits fight. And the outcome of each battle contributes to the final outcome of the war.'

Dadistan-i Dinik

20

Consequences of Actions

A disciple asked the great teacher Manuskihar: 'Can one person commit a righteous act on behalf of another person? Can living people act righteously on behalf of dead people?' Manuskihar replied: 'Each individual is free to choose between good and evil; so people are responsible only for their own deeds. If a man leads a wicked life, his relatives cannot reduce his wickedness by acting righteously on his behalf. And when a wicked man dies, nothing can spare him from the eternal consequences of his wickedness.'

A disciple asked the great teacher Manuskihar: 'Should a person be held responsible for the consequences of an action, or simply for the action itself?' Manuskihar replied: 'An action is defined by its consequences: an evil action is one that has evil consequences, and a good action is one that has good consequences. But a person is not always able to foresee all the consequences of an action. Thus a person is responsible for those consequences that can be foreseen.'

A disciple asked the great teacher Manuskihar: 'Do righteous actions eradicate wicked actions.' Manuskihar replied: 'The consequences of righteous actions nullify those of wicked actions. So righteous actions eradicate wicked ones.'

A disciple asked the great teacher Manuskihar: 'When will the world end?' Manuskihar replied: 'The world will end when the spirit of goodness has finally triumphed over the spirit of evil. In a state of perfect goodness righteous actions can have no consequences; so time will cease.'

Dadistan-i Dinik

21

The Body and the Conscience

There was once a sage, who through many years of meditation had learnt to communicate fully with the spirit of goodness.

The sage asked the spirit of goodness: 'How is it possible to attain bodily comfort without injuring the conscience? And how is it possible to follow the conscience without sacrificing bodily comfort?' The spirit of goodness replied: 'Do not slander others, because slander always brings slander in return. Do not envy the possessions of others, because envy deceives you into wanting more than your body needs. Do not indulge in anger, because anger prevents you from working efficiently. Do not be anxious, because anxiety prevents you from enjoying the fruits of your work. Do not allow lustful thoughts to fill your mind, because lust prevents you from enjoying legitimate pleasure. Do not strive for power over others, because power creates enemies; regard yourself as the equal of all, and all people as your equal.

'Choose your spouse on the basis of character, not beauty or wealth; remember that your spouse will remain your companion long after beauty has faded and wealth has lost its charm. Treat all animals and birds with respect; remember that all living beings need one another. When you have more than you need, give the surplus to others; then, when you have less than you need, others will give their surplus to you. Avoid unnecessary disputes; and when a dispute cannot be avoided, act fairly and honestly, striving for a just outcome.'

Dina-i Mainog-i Khirad

22

THE ART OF HAPPINESS

The sage asked the spirit of goodness: 'How is it possible to be happy?' The spirit of goodness replied: 'If you wish to be happy, do not pursue happiness; by pursuing happiness, you will lose it. Do not confuse happiness with pleasure; when the dazzling sun of pleasure shines, there is always a black cloud coming over the horizon, which will soon block it out. Do not try to arrange the world for your own benefit, as this will merely weary your heart and mind; allow the world to be as it is. Do not confuse happiness with the ownership of great wealth; as you grow old, wealth will lose its charm. Do not confuse happiness with power; as you grow old, power will inevitably slip from your grasp. Do not confuse happiness with the respect of others; the attitude of others towards you makes no difference to your true self. Do not confuse happiness with being well-connected to people who are admired by others; put your trust in your own abilities and achievements. And do not confuse happiness with survival; eventually you must die.'

The sage asked the spirit of goodness: 'Which is most important, generosity, honesty, gratitude, wisdom, vigilance or contentment?' The spirit of goodness replied: 'For the good of your heart, generosity is most important. For the good of your mind, honesty is most important. For the good of your relationship with God, gratitude is most important. For the good of your behavior wisdom is most important. For the good of vanquishing the spirit of evil vigilance is most important. And for the good of your own body contentment is most important.'

Dina-i Mainog-i Khirad

23

Happy and Unhappy Lands

The sage asked the spirit of goodness: 'What type of action is best and most praiseworthy?' The spirit of goodness replied: 'The best and most praiseworthy type of action is being kind to your children; the second best is being kind to your spouse; the third best is being kind to your parents; the fourth best is being kind to your other relatives; the fifth best is being kind to your friends; the sixth best is being kind to anyone and everyone; the seventh best is praying to God and meditating on him; and the eighth best, which merits very little praise, is performing rituals in God's honor. God is truly honored when people do good to one another.'

The sage asked the spirit of goodness: 'What makes a land happy?' The spirit of goodness replied: 'A land is happy where people speak the truth; where they are gentle and courteous to one another; where they are kind to their sheep and cattle; where they care for the earth which provides them with food; where they worship God; and where they respond to misfortune with equanimity, and good fortune with gratitude.'

The sage asked the spirit of goodness: 'What makes a land unhappy?' The spirit of goodness replied: 'A land is unhappy where people speak falsely when it suits them; where innocent people are punished and guilty people go free; where people worship idols in place of God; where widows and orphans are allowed to starve; where people take pleasure in gaining wealth by dishonest means; and where they respond to misfortune with anger, and good fortune with arrogance.'

Dina-i Mainog-i Khirad

24

GOOD AND EVIL IN THE WORLD

The sage asked the spirit of goodness: 'Why is there both good and evil in the world. Why do some people act righteously, while others are persistently wicked? Why is there both happiness and misery in the world?' The spirit of goodness replied: 'There is goodness in the world because I live in all men and women, and prompt them to act righteously. There is evil in the world because the spirit of evil lives in all men and women, and prompts them to act wickedly. Insofar as people listen to my promptings, there is happiness; insofar as they listen to the promptings of the spirit of evil, there is misery.'

The sage asked the spirit of goodness: 'Can there ever be peace between you and the spirit of evil?' The spirit of goodness replied: 'There can never be peace. The reason is that the spirit of evil causes dishonesty, anger, malice and enmity, while I cause honesty, serenity, kindness and friendship. The spirit of evil can never change, and nor can I. Yet every man and woman is capable of change; if people have been listening only to the spirit of evil, they may start to listen to me instead. Thus all people at every moment have a choice: they must choose between the spirit of evil and me; and their actions will reveal the choice they have made.'

The sage asked the spirit of goodness: 'Is it possible to be wise without being righteous? And is it possible to be foolish without being wicked?' The spirit of goodness replied: 'If people are wise, they decide to act righteously. If people are foolish, they decide to act wickedly.'

Dina-i Mainog-i Khirad

25

True pleasure

The sage asked the spirit of goodness: 'How do people make choices between good and evil?' The spirit of goodness replied: 'When the world was created, human beings saw clearly that righteous actions cause happiness, while wicked actions cause misery; so they always chose to act righteously. But then the spirit of evil entered their hearts and minds, and tried to persuade them that righteous actions cause misery and wicked actions cause happiness. God ordered me also to enter their hearts and minds, and try to persuade them of the truth. Since that time the spirit of evil and I have been conducting a debate in every mind and heart. In some minds and hearts I win; in others the spirit of evil wins; but in most minds and hearts each of us sometimes wins and sometimes loses.'

The sage asked the spirit of goodness: 'How can a person be free from fear? How can a person win a high reputation? How can a person enjoy life? How can a person be prosperous? What things bring true pleasure?' The spirit of goodness replied: 'Only faith in God can bring freedom from fear; through faith in God a person gains the courage to face every danger and meet every challenge. The best way to win a high reputation is to be a good parent, raising children that are virtuous and generous. A loving marriage is the greatest source of joy; it can turn even the worst misfortune into a blessing. A person may become prosperous by honest work or by dishonest dealing; but honest work is its own reward, regardless of the wealth it engenders. Faith in God, virtuous children, a loving marriage, and honest work – these things bring true pleasure.'

Dina-i Mainog-i Khirad

26

Wealth and Death

The sage asked the spirit of goodness: 'Is poverty better than wealth, or is wealth better than poverty?' The spirit of goodness replied: 'Poverty through honesty is better than wealth through fraud and exploitation. If wealth is gained through fraud and exploitation, it does not belong to its owner, nor does the owner deserve it; so the owner feels constantly anxious and guilty. Only wealth gained through honest work can bring pleasure – but only if that wealth is shared with others.'

The sage asked the spirit of goodness: 'Can honest work alone bring wealth?' The spirit of goodness replied: 'Honest work will only bring wealth if it is destined to do so; otherwise honest work will yield meager fruits.'

The sage asked the spirit of goodness: 'What is good government?' The sprit of goodness replied: 'Good government is where people rule themselves. Each family and each village should rule its own affairs, punishing wickedness and rewarding righteousness. Good government also respects ancient customs.'

The sage asked the spirit of goodness: 'Why are some people frightened of death, while others face death with eq ıanimity?' The spirit of goodness replied: 'If people seek happiness through possession of material things, they are frightened of death, because death will separate them from those things. But if people seek happiness through love and friendship, they face death with equanimity, because they know that love and friendship transcend death.'

Dina-i Mainog-i Khirad

27

DESTINY AND PROVIDENCE

The sage asked the spirit of goodness: 'Is it possible for people to gain such wisdom and knowledge that they can change their destinies?' The spirit of goodness replied: 'Wisdom and knowledge enable people to understand their destinies, not to change them. But wickedness and righteousness determine whether a person's life is joyful or miserable. Foolish and ignorant people, who act wickedly, bring misery upon themselves; while wise and knowledgeable people, who act righteously, bring joy upon themselves.'

The sage asked the spirit of goodness: 'What, then, is meant by destiny?' The spirit of goodness replied: 'There is a distinction between destiny and providence. Destiny is that which is ordained from the beginning. Providence is that which occurs as a consequence of righteous or wicked actions.'

The sage asked the spirit of goodness: 'Who is truly rich, and who is truly poor?' The spirit of goodness replied: 'Truly rich people are those who accept and embrace their destinies; these people may be rich or poor in material wealth. Truly poor people are those who resent and rebel against their destinies; these people may be poor or rich in material wealth.'

The sage asked the spirit of goodness: 'Which is worse: to have blind eyes or a blind mind?' The spirit of goodness replied: 'A person with blind eyes, whose mind can see the truth clearly, possesses the sight that matters. A person with a blind mind, whose eyes are sharp and clear, can see nothing that matters.'

Dina-i Mainog-i Khirad

28

THE PERFECT PERSON

The sage asked the spirit of goodness: 'Which is worse: to be ill-tempered or ill-informed?' The spirit of goodness replied: 'Ill-tempered people cause discomfort to themselves, but do not harm others, because other people merely laugh at them. Ill-informed people exploit and oppress others, without realizing the damage they are doing to themselves.'

The sage asked the spirit of goodness: 'Is it better to have been righteous all one's life, or first to have been wicked and then to have become righteous?' The spirit of goodness replied: 'If people have been righteous all their lives, then they are inwardly serene and content. But if people convert from wickedness to righteousness, they know the joy of repenting and being forgiven by God – and that is the greatest joy in the world.'

The sage asked the spirit of goodness: 'What are the worst sins that people can commit?' The spirit of goodness replied: 'There are three terrible sins. The first is to oppress and exploit those under your authority. The second is not to help your relatives in times of sickness. And the third is to betray the trust of your friends.'

The sage asked the spirit of wisdom: 'What are the signs of the perfect person.' The spirit of goodness replied: 'The are four signs of perfection. The first is only to be angry when anger would have good consequences. The second is only to enjoy pleasures that are healthy. The third is always to speak the truth with courtesy. And the fourth is to be secretive in doing good.'

Dina-i Mainog-i Khirad

29

The first eight gates

The spirit of goodness then said to the sage: If you wish to reach God, you must walk through a series of gates, one by one.

The first gate is vigilance. Watch over your thoughts and feelings, words and actions. Suppress all that is wicked; and regard even a trifling fault as a great sin.

The second gate is the avoidance of despair. Even when you suffer the most terrible misfortunes, renew your trust in God's mercy.

The third gate is generosity. Give at least one tenth of your wealth to the poor and sick; and if you can afford more, give more.

The fourth gate is respect for your parents. Never bring disgrace on your family's name, but speak and act in ways that your parents can approve.

The fifth gate is care for pregnant mothers. A pregnant woman carries the future in her womb, and should be protected from all danger.

The sixth gate is to have benign intentions at all times. When you wake in the morning, plan the good works you can do during the day.

The seventh gate is repentance. When you lie down at night, reflect on how far your actions fell short of your plans; and promise to make amends on the following day.

The eighth gate is to find good spouses for your children. As your own experience tells you, a harmonious marriage is vital for happiness; so a good spouse is the greatest gift you can bestow on a son or daughter.

Dabistan

30

THE LAST EIGHT GATES

The ninth gate is care for animals. Look after your sheep and cattle with kindness; and never be wantonly cruel to any living being. Remember that God created every animal and bird, insect and fish; and he loves them all with equal devotion.

The tenth gate is hospitality. When strangers come to your home, give them the best meat and bread in your larder.

The eleventh gate is gratitude. Regard even the smallest good fortune as a priceless gift from God; and even when misfortune befalls you, offer thanks to him – because God alone can turn curses into blessings.

The twelfth gate is fasting. True fasting consists in resisting the temptation to sin. So the purpose of abstaining from food is to strengthen your will.

The thirteenth gate is to keep promises. When you have given your word to another person, you must never break it.

The fourteenth gate is to avoid the company of habitual sinners. Do not be so arrogant as to imagine yourself immune to bad influences.

The fifteenth gate is courage at the death of a child. If you grieve unduly over a child that has gone, you will be a poor parent to those that survive.

The sixteenth gate is instruction of children. You should instruct your children in the truth as far as your own understanding allows; and where your own understanding is limited, obtain other teachers.

Dabistan

31

Two lights

The sage asked the spirit of goodness: 'Who will lead me through these gates to God?' The spirit of goodness replied: 'I shall lead you. You will find me by looking within yourself; I am the beam of light that shines in every heart and mind. But beware! The spirit of evil also shines in every heart and mind; and if you follow that light, you will go away from God.'

'How can I distinguish between your light and the other light?' asked the sage. 'You must pray to God,' the spirit of goodness replied. Then the spirit of goodness gave the prayer that should be recited by all who are seeking God:

O God, when I look on the light of evil – the light of ignorance and folly, cruelty and hatred – fill me with fear. And when I look on the light of goodness – the light of knowledge and wisdom, kindness and love, fill me with hope. In you, and in you alone, I put my trust.

Dabistan

MONTH

8

JUDAISM

Introduction

ORIGINS

Almost the only source of information about the origins of the Jewish people is the ***Torah***, the first five books of the Jewish scriptures. This asserts that a man called Abraham, perhaps in the c18 BCE, emigrated from Mesopotamia (modern Iraq) to Canaan (modern Israel). He and his descendents settled peacefully among the local people, but continued to obtain wives from Mesopotamia, so they remained distinct. One of Abraham's descendents, a handsome and intelligent man called Joseph, became governor of Egypt; he shrewdly amassed grain during a series of good harvests, and then sold it, at great profit to his master the Pharaoh, during a famine. The Jewish people followed him to Egypt in search of food, and settled there. But a later Pharaoh enslaved them.

The pivotal moment in Jewish history and religion was the escape from slavery, led by Moses, around 1300 BCE. As the Jewish people moved back towards Canaan, through the Sinai desert, Moses promulgated the ten commandments, which he claimed were dictated by God. He also laid down a series of complex laws covering every aspect of social and economic life, prescribing various religious rituals; and he appointed judges to uphold them. These commandments and laws form the heart of Judaism.

The Jews were now sufficiently large in number to drive out the local people, and occupy the entire land. For almost three centuries they survived as a political entity; but then they split into two kingdoms, and in 587 BCE they were absorbed into the Babylonian empire – and lived under foreign rule for the next two and a half millennia.

TEACHINGS

The ten commandments are stark and simple: they assert that there is a single God, and they state the basic moral principles to which he demands adherence. The social and economic laws are designed for an agrarian, tribal community; and Jews have argued over whether and how these are applicable to other circumstances. But the ten commandments are universal in their application, and their meaning is beyond dispute.

The escape from slavery became for Jews a powerful symbol of God's power, and they regarded themselves as entirely dependent on his blessing and protection. Thus when their crops failed or they were defeated in battle, they saw this as divine punishment for breaking the commandments. This belief led to the emergence of a second element in Jewish religious teaching: prophecy. The role of the prophet was to show the link between present actions and future events – with God's response to those actions as the crucial factor. The prophet described the disasters that would result from sin, and the peace and joy that would follow repentance. Although the prophetic voice was audible at earlier times, it grew steadily louder, and more powerful in its poetic imagery, after the division into two kingdoms.

Foreign domination stimulated a third element in Jewish teaching: wisdom. The Jewish sage was worldly and witty, as well as devout. He tried to show how the commandments of Moses could be combined with human insight and intelligence, in order to attain some degree of personal serenity. Aphorisms, paradoxes and jokes were the sage's favorite tools, and quiet reflection his means of honing them.

Expression

After Babylonian domination came Persian, Macedonian, Egyptian, Syrian and Roman rule. Despite their political subjugation many Jews became successful merchants and traders; and small communities of Jews formed in the cities and towns of Europe and north Africa. These communities grew rapidly after a rebellion in 70 CE, which the Romans brutally crushed, forcing large numbers to flee.

Far from weakening their religion, the dispersal of the Jews strengthened it. And, as in the years following the arrival of Abraham in Canaan, the primary source of its strength was the integrity of the family. Jews only married other Jews; and the family was – and remains – the center of religious devotion. Thus on the eve of the day of rest (the ***Sabbath***) the father leads the family in an act of worship, in which he both praises his wife and blesses his children; and at midday on the Sabbath the family eats a special meal together. Moreover, the rites of passage, marking the crucial moments in the life of the family, are given particular prominence amongst Jews. The most elaborate of these is the wedding, which takes place under a special canopy symbolizing the new family home.

Judaism was, and remains, numerically small; but it has spawned the two largest religions of the world, Christianity and, less directly, Islam. Although the modern state of Israel, through which Jews have regained political independence, is a fruit of Christian persecution and a source of Muslim grievance, these two religions could not exist without the teachings of Abraham, Moses and the prophets.

Us

For most people today morality is relative. Thus we are inclined to judge the morality of an action by its consequences; if the consequences are benign, then we regard the action as moral. This view allows moral standards to change according to circumstances, since the same action may have benign consequences in one situation, and malign consequences in another. For Judaism by contrast morality is absolute and unchangeable. According to the ten commandments, it is always wrong to steal, lie, commit adultery, blaspheme, and so on; there are no circumstances in which these actions can be justified.

Similarly for most people today religion is personal. Thus, if there are differences in religious beliefs within our family or amongst our close friends, this causes us no concern. For Judaism by contrast religion is communal; family and social life are rooted in ancient rituals and convictions. Jewish experience over three millennia testifies that bonds between husband and wife, and between parents and children, are immeasurably strengthened by common faith. The implication for others is that, in choosing a partner, spiritual compatibility should be a vital consideration.

1

ABRAHAM'S OBEDIENCE

Abraham was living in Haran in Mesopotamia. After his father's death he heard a voice, which said: 'I am God. I order you to leave your country, your relatives and your home, and travel westwards until you reach a land that I shall give you. I make this covenant with you: if you obey me, I shall give you many descendents, who will become a great nation; I shall bless those who bless you; and through you I shall bless all the nations of the earth.'

Abraham obeyed God, taking his wife Sarah, his servants and all his possessions. Eventually he reached a land near the shore of the Mediterranean Sea. 'This is your land,' God said to him. So Abraham stopped, and he and his wife settled there.

Although his wife was old, and had borne no children, she now became pregnant; and she had a son, whom they named Isaac. When Isaac had grown into a boy, God decided to test Abraham. 'Take your son to a mountain that I shall show you,' God said, 'and offer him as a sacrifice to me.' Early next morning Abraham set out with Isaac, and God guided him to a certain mountain. When they reached the top, Abraham gathered wood and prepared a fire. He tied Isaac up, and lifted him on top of the wood. Then he took out his knife.

But, as Abraham held the knife above his son, an angel of God called from the sky: 'Do not hurt him; let him free. Now you have shown that you love God even above your own son – and that you honor and obey God in all things.' So Abraham untied Isaac, and they returned home.

Genesis

2

Moses' anger

As God had promised, Abraham had many descendents, and they became a nation known as Israel – which means 'God fights.' During a severe famine they emigrated to Egypt in search of food, and there they continued to grow in number. Eventually the ruler of Egypt, the Pharaoh, became anxious that in time of war they might join the enemy. So he enslaved them, and forced them to build new cities for his people. But their number continued to grow; so he ordered his people to kill every boy born to the Israelites.

One Israelite mother hid her baby son for three months. But she knew that the boy would soon be found. So she made a basket from bulrushes, covered it with tar, placed the baby inside, and put it amongst the reeds at the edge of the river Nile, praying that God would care for him. The Pharaoh's daughter came down to the river to bathe, and found the baby boy. She took him into her arms, and was filled with love for him. The baby's sister ran up to the Pharaoh's daughter, and offered to find someone to nurse him. 'Please do,' the Pharaoh's daughter replied; 'I shall pay you.' So the girl took the baby back to his own mother.

When the boy grew older, his sister took him to the Pharaoh's daughter, who adopted him as her own son, naming him Moses. As soon as he had grown up, Moses went to visit his own people, and was appalled at their suffering. One day he saw an Egyptian slave-master kill an Israelite; and in his anger Moses killed the Egyptian. The Pharaoh soon heard of Moses' action, and Moses fled to the desert of Sinai.

Exodus

3

ESCAPE FROM SLAVERY

God led Moses to the mountain in the middle of the desert. There he saw flames from a bush, but the bush did not burn. Then he heard a voice: 'Moses! Moses!' 'Here I am,' Moses replied. 'I am God,' the voice said, 'and I have seen the misery of your people. I am appointing you to lead them out of slavery, and back to their own country.' 'Suppose that I go to my people,' Moses said, 'and declare that you have sent me as their leader. They will ask me your name. What shall I reply?' 'I am who I am,' God replied.

'I have never been eloquent,' Moses protested; 'I am slow and hesitant in speech. Appoint someone else.' But God became angry with Moses, and Moses submitted to him.

Moses went to the Pharaoh, and demanded in God's name that he release the Israelite people. The Pharaoh refused. Then a series of disasters befell Egypt: there were plagues of frogs, gnats, flies and locusts; the river Nile turned poisonous, and its fish died; hail destroyed the crops; and there was an epidemic of boils. During each disaster Moses returned to the Pharaoh, and the Pharaoh relented; but as soon as the disaster was over, the Pharaoh hardened. Finally in despair the Pharaoh ordered Moses to lead his people out of the country – and begged Moses to bless him.

So Moses led the Israelites through the desert towards the Red Sea. As soon as they had left, the Pharaoh again hardened, and he ordered his army to chase them. When the Israelites saw the Pharaoh's army, they turned against Moses. 'It would have been better to have remained as slaves,' they cried,' than to perish here.'

Exodus

4

THE TEN COMMANDMENTS

Moses begged his people to trust in God to save them. When they arrived at the Red Sea, a strong east wind began to blow, which drove the sea back; so they were able to walk across safely. But when the Egyptian army tried to cross, the wheels of its chariots stuck in the mud; then the wind fell, the waters returned, and every soldier was drowned.

Moses and his people continued to the Sinai mountain, where they camped. Disputes began to break out between families, and Moses had to spend all his time resolving them. So he divided the people into groups, and appointed wise and capable men to act as judges.

God now summoned Moses to the top of the mountain. There he gave Moses two stone tablets, on which were inscribed ten commandments: 'Worship no one except me. Do not worship objects made by humans. Do not misuse my name. Work for six days, and then rest on the seventh. Respect your parents. Do not murder. Do not commit adultery. Do not steal. Do not slander others. And do not envy other people's possessions.' God then summarized these commandments: 'Love me with all your heart, and love your neighbor as yourself.'

Moses carried the tablets down the mountain, and read the ten commandments to the people; and he ordered the judges to enforce obedience to them. A box was then made for the tablets; and Moses ordered the people to continue towards the land that God had promised to their ancestor Abraham.

Exodus

5

Appointment of a King

By now Moses was old, and he knew that he would never enter the promised land. So as the land became visible on the horizon, he appointed his successor, a young man called Joshua; then he died. The Israelites mourned him for thirty days. Then Joshua ordered them to make weapons; and he led them onwards, driving out all the people that were currently living in the land.

For two hundred years the Israelites lived freely, appointing judges to settle disputes and enforce the commandments. One of these judges, called Samuel, possessed exceptional wisdom; and each year he traveled throughout the land, offering advice, and resolving the most difficult disputes.

When Samuel was very old, a group of prominent Israelites came to him, and said: 'We want a king to rule over us, and so be like other nations.' 'A king will turn some of your sons into soldiers,' Samuel replied, 'and he will order your other sons to make weapons, so your fields will be left unplowed. He will compel your daughters to make perfumes for him and cook for his table. He will take your best vineyards and olive-groves, and give them to his officials; and he will levy taxes on all your crops.' But the Israelites were insistent. 'A king will lead us into battle,' they declared, 'and make us glorious.'

So Samuel appointed a strong, handsome young man called Saul as king. Just as Samuel had predicted, Saul formed a great army, and went to war against the neighboring nations.

Samuel

6

Piety and Justice

Saul was followed by David, who built Jerusalem as the capital city; and David was followed by his son Solomon, who built a great temple in Jerusalem. Saul, David and Solomon were all men of courage, and they worshipped God; at times they displayed great wisdom, but at other times they were arrogant, stubborn and selfish. After the death of Solomon two rival kings divided the promised land; and during the next three centuries many of the kings in both kingdoms were cruel and oppressive, ignoring God's commandments.

During this period many prophets arose, who spoke to the leaders and people in words inspired by God. For a time the northern kingdom enjoyed great prosperity, and the wealthy merchants were extremely pious; and it was then that the prophet Amos spoke:

You hate those who challenge injustice, and despise those who speak the truth. You trample on the poor, forcing them to hand over half their harvest; and with your stolen wealth you build yourselves mansions of stone. When you sit as judges in court, you take bribes from the guilty, so the innocent are punished.

God says: 'I hate your religious festivals, and I loathe your solemn acts of worship. You bring me offerings of meat and grain, but I refuse to accept them. You sacrifice your finest animals to me, but I turn away in disgust. You sing hymns to me, and you pluck harps in my honor, but I close my ears. Replace piety with justice; let justice flow like a river that never runs dry.'

Amos

7

UNFAITHFUL TO GOD

Soon after Amos had spoken, the prophet Hosea appeared. Hosea was married to a woman called Gomer who was unfaithful to him. He compared his own predicament to that of God in relation to Israel, that God was like a husband and Israel like an unfaithful wife:

You are married to God, Israel, but you chase after the false gods of wealth and power and privilege. You hold elaborate religious festivals, where you drink wine and make love to your gods; and you believe that your gods have blessed your vines. But God will strip you naked in front of your lovers, and humiliate you. He will turn your vineyards into deserts, and your festivals into funerals. Then, when you have sunk into the deepest despair, he will try to win you back with words of love – and you will love him as you did long ago, when you were his young bride.

When that time comes, he will make a covenant with the wild beasts and the poisonous snakes and insects, so they will no longer harm you. He will abolish all weapons of war, all bows and swords, and you will live in peace and safety.

God says: 'Israel, I shall be your devoted husband; I shall be true and faithful, constant in compassion and mercy; I shall love you until the end of time. I shall belong to you, and you will belong to me; you will acknowledge me as your only lord. I shall answer all your requests. When you were unfaithful, you turned your beauty into ugliness; but our mutual love will make you lovely again.'

Hosea

8

A HOLY KING

About half a century after Amos and Hosea spoke in the northern kingdom, the Assyrian empire, which was rapidly expanding, threatened to overwhelm the southern kingdom. The first prophet called Isaiah believed that the source of his people's weakness lay in their disobedience to God. But he looked forward to a time when a man of holiness and wisdom would rule them:

We are walking in darkness, but a new light will dawn. God will break the yoke that burdens us; he will shatter the rod of our oppressors. To us a child will be born, a son will be given; and the government of our land will be on his shoulders. He will be called wonderful counselor, everlasting father, prince of peace. His kingdom will always be at peace, and it will spread across the world; and he will govern until the end of time. His power will be founded on justice and righteousness.

We are like a tree that has been cut down; but just as new branches sprout from a stump, so a new king will arise from amongst us.

The spirit of God will rest upon him – the spirit of wisdom and understanding, of discernment and power. He will know God's will, and take delight in obeying it. He will not judge by what he sees with his eyes, or decide by what he hears with his ears. He will judge the needy with righteousness, and he will defend the poor from oppression. His words will be like lightning striking the earth; with the breath from his mouth he will destroy all wickedness. Justice will be his belt, and integrity the sash around his waist.

First Isaiah

9

THE WAY OF HOLINESS

At that time the wolf will live with the lamb; the leopard will lie down with the goat; calves and lion cubs will walk together, and a little child will lead them. The cow will feed with the bear, and their young will rest together; the lion will eat straw like the ox. The infant will play near the hole of the snake; the baby will put its hand in the viper's nest. Under the holy king no creature will harm or destroy another creature.

As the seas are full of water, so the earth will be full of the knowledge of God. The desert will be glad, and flowers will bloom in the wilderness; the desert will sing and shout for joy. Everyone will see the splendor of God.

The eyes of the blind will be opened, and the ears of the deaf unstopped. The lame will leap like deer, and the tongues of the dumb will shout for joy. Streams will flow through the desert, and the burning sand will become a lake; springs will burst through the parched ground. In the haunts where jackals once lay, grass and reeds and papyrus will grow.

A highway will be there; it will be called the way of holiness. No sinners will travel on that road; and good people will not stray from it. No lions will prowl on it; no ferocious beasts will cross it. Only those whom God has saved, those whose hearts are filled with love, will walk home along it. They will enter Jerusalem with songs on their lips; everlasting joy will crown their heads. Gladness and pleasure will overtake them, and sorrow and grief will flee away.

First Isaiah

10

Swords into Plows

Soon after Isaiah spoke in the southern kingdom, the prophet Micah also spoke. He looked forward to the reign of a holy king:

He will rule his people with strength that comes from God; and God will confer on him his own authority. His people will live in safety, because all the nations of the earth will acknowledge his greatness. He will bring peace.

He will settle disputes between nations, between great powers near and far. They will hammer their swords into plows, and their spears into pruning hooks. Nations will never again go to war, nor will they train in the arts of war. All people will live in peace, among their own vineyards and fig trees, with nothing to fear. God almighty has promised this. Each nation will worship and obey God in its own fashion.

So how should we in Israel worship God? Should we bring him our finest calves, only a year old, and burn them on the altar? Would the Lord be pleased if we were to offer thousands of sheep, or countless streams of olive oil? Should we give our first-born sons to pay for our sins? No! God has told us what he requires of us: that we act justly, love mercy, and walk humbly at his side.

When the holy king rules over us, nations of the world will come to our land. Israel will be like a mountain towering above the mountains of the world; it will be like a temple, more glorious than all the temples of the world. People will say to one another: 'Let us go to Israel, and learn the way of God.'

Micah

11

New covenant

The prophet Jeremiah witnessed the destruction of Jerusalem by the Babylonians, who deported most of the population. Jerusalem foretold the restoration of the people to their land, when God would make a new covenant with them:

God says: 'People of Israel, I shall make you well again; I shall heal your wounds. I shall restore you to your land, and cherish every family. Jerusalem and its temple will be rebuilt. You will sing my praises, and shout for joy. I shall add to your numbers, and they will never be decreased; I shall bring you honor, and you will never be disgraced. Your ruler will come from among you; I shall draw him close to me, and he will devote himself to doing my will. You will be my people, and I shall be your God.

'People of Israel, I have always loved you, and I continue to love you. Once again I shall show my love. Once again you will take up your tambourines, and dance with joy. Once again you will plant vineyards on the hills, and drink the fruit of your labor.

'The time is coming when I shall make a new covenant with my people. It will not be like the old covenant that I made with their ancestors, when I took them by the hand and led them out of Egypt. Although I was like a husband to them, they broke that covenant. This is the covenant that I shall make with my people: I shall put my law in their minds, and write it on their hearts. I shall be their God, and they will be my people. They will not have to teach one another to know me, because all will know me, from the least to the greatest. I shall forgive their sins, and forget their wickedness.'

Jeremiah

12

VALLEY OF DRY BONES

The prophet Ezekiel lived in exile in Babylon. His prophecies came in the form of visions, and he had a vision of Israel coming back to life:

The spirit of God took me to a valley, where the ground was covered with bones. He led me all round the valley, and I saw a vast number of bones, all of which were very dry. He said to me: 'Mortal man, can these bones come back to life?' 'You alone can answer that.' I replied. 'Speak to these bones,' he ordered, 'and command them to listen. Tell them that I shall bring them back to life. Then they will know that I am God.'

So I spoke as the Lord had ordered me. While I was speaking, I heard a rattling sound, and the bones began to join together. As I watched, I saw sinews and muscles attaching themselves to the bones, and then skin covering them. But there was no breath in the bodies.

Then God said to me: 'Mortal man, speak to the wind. Tell the wind that God commands it to come from every direction, and enter these bodies, so they may come back to life.' So I spoke as the Lord had ordered me. Breath entered the bodies; and they came back to life, and stood up. They were like a huge army.

God said to me: 'Mortal man, the people of Israel are like the bones in the valley. They say that their bones are dried up - that all hope is gone, and that their hearts are in despair. I shall put breath in them, restore to life, and let them live in their own land. Then they will know that I am the Lord.'

Ezekiel

13

Good news

The Israelites were eventually allowed to return to Jerusalem. The second prophet called Isaiah assured them of God's love:

The spirit of God is upon me. He has chosen me to preach good news to the poor, to heal the broken-hearted, and to proclaim freedom for captives. He has sent me to comfort all who are sad: I shall crown them with joy, in place of ashes; I shall anoint them with the oil of gladness, in place of grief; I shall dress them in a tunic of praise, in place of despair. They will be called oaks of righteousness, planted by God to reveal his splendor.

My people, you will be called priests of God. Your shame and disgrace are now ended. God says: 'I love justice, and I hate oppression and crime. I shall be faithful to my people; I shall reward them by making an everlasting covenant with them. They will be famous among the nations, and their offspring will be admired throughout the world.'

No longer will people call you Forsaken, or your land Deserted Wife. Your new name will be God's Delight; your land will be called Happily Married. God smiles on you with joy, and he will be like a husband to your land. As a young man takes a virgin for his wife, God - who made you - will take you as his own; as a groom rejoices in his bride, God will rejoice in you.

People of Jerusalem, go out of the city, and build a road on which all may come to you. Prepare a highway, and clear it of stones. Raise a banner that can be seen from afar. You are God's holy people.

Second Isaiah

14

The vanity of all

Although the city and its temple were rebuilt, Jerusalem remained under foreign control. The strident prophetic voice fell silent, and was replaced by the reflective voice of the sage. One of the great sages, whose name is unknown, was famous for his skepticism:

Vanity, vanity, all is vanity! What do people gain from all their labor - from toiling under the sun? Generations come and go, but the world remains the same forever. The sun rises and the sun sets; then it hurries back to where it rises. The wind blows to the south, and then turns to the north; round and round it goes, and back again. All rivers flow into the sea; yet the sea is never full. The water returns to where the rivers begin, and then flows again.

Our eyes can never see enough to be satisfied; our ears can never hear enough. What has happened, will happen again; what has been done, will be done again. There is nothing new under the sun. People say: 'Look! Here is something new.' But it was here already; it was here before our time. No one remembers the days of old; and no one in the future will remember today.

People live for a while, and then they die. The dead are completely forgotten; their loves, their hates and their passions die with them. They will never again play any part in the affairs of this world.

So enjoy life for the days God has given you. Eat, and be happy; drink, and be merry. Take pleasure in the company of the woman you love.

Ecclesiastes

15

A TIME FOR EVERYTHING

When I was young, I undertook great projects. I built myself houses, and established vineyards. I laid out gardens and parks, planting all kind of fruit trees in them; and I dug ponds to irrigate them. I bred sheep and cattle, and I amassed silver and gold. I employed male and female singers to entertain me, and acquired a large harem to give me pleasure.

Yet when I surveyed all that my hands had done, all that my toil had achieved, I knew that it was vanity - like chasing the wind. So I regretted having worked so hard.

I realized that the same fate awaits us all – that I must suffer the same fate as the man who fails in all he does. And I realized another thing. The race is not always won by the swift. The battle is not always won by the strong. Food does not always go to the wise. Wealth does not always accrue to the brilliant. Fortune does not always smile on the able. All are vulnerable to time and chance.

There is a time for everything, and a season for every activity under the sky: a time to be born, and a time to die; a time to plant, and a time to uproot; a time to kill, and a time to heal; a time to pull down, and a time to build up; a time to weep, and a time to laugh; a time to mourn, and a time to dance; a time to scatter stones, and a time to gather them; a time to kiss, and a time to refrain from kissing; a time to search, and a time to give up; a time to keep, and a time to throw away; a time to tear, and a time to mend; a time to keep silent, and a time to speak; a time to love, and a time to hate; a time for war, and a time for peace.

Ecclesiastes

16

A MASTERPIECE OF WISDOM

Another great sage, called Jesus Ben Sirach, praised God's wisdom:

There is only one being that lives forever: God, who fashioned the universe through his wisdom. No man or woman can know or relate the full story of his works. No one trace his marvels to their source, or measure the greatness of his power. As the sun in its brilliance looks down on all things, the glory of God fills his creation.

God fathoms the heart of every man, woman and child; he knows the deepest secrets. He possesses all knowledge, and observes all events. He remembers the past, and foresees the future; he penetrates the deepest mysteries. No thought escapes his notice, and no word escapes his hearing.

This world is a masterpiece of God's wisdom; even the smallest spark from a fire has been designed with the utmost skill. Nothing can be added to his wisdom, and nothing can be taken away; no advice can add to the store of his understanding. He brought his wisdom into being before time began, and it will exist after time is complete.

If you were to honor God with every breath you breathe, he would still be far above your praise. If you were to summon all your strength to declare his greatness, your words would still fall short. Has anyone seen him? Can anyone describe him? Can anyone praise him as he truly is? You see only a small part of his works; there are even greater glories beyond your gaze.

God loves all that he has made; so drink from the cup of his love.

Jesus Ben Sirach

17

The pursuit of wisdom

Happy are those who fix their minds upon wisdom, and think about her constantly. Happy are those who contemplate her ways and ponder her secrets.

Stalk her like a hunter stalking his prey; lie in wait beside her path. Peer through the windows of her room, and listen to her through the keyhole. Set up your tent beside her house, and drive the tent pegs into her wall. To see her, to listen to her, and to dwell beside – these are the greatest honors that anyone can enjoy. Wisdom is like a great tree: put your children beneath her branches, and let them grow up in her shade.

If you worship God, you will be wisdom's most devoted lover; she will come to you as a young bride comes to her bridegroom. If you obey God's commands, wisdom will be yours; she will care for you as a mother cares for her only son. For food she will give you the bread of knowledge, and for drink she will give you the water of insight. When you stumble, she will lift you; and when you are weary, she will hold you up.

Wisdom is like a garland around your neck, with flowers of serenity and health. It gives the mind discernment and the hands skill; it makes the heart glad and the body strong. With wisdom life is happy and death peaceful.

Do not slacken in your pursuit of wisdom; and do not approach her without sincerity. Be true to yourself at all times, and never try to give a false impression of yourself. Wisdom knows both your darkest secrets and your brightest thoughts – and she never ceases to love you.

Jesus Ben Sirach

18

Wisdom and Pleasure

The sage Hillel was the leading member of a group of religious teachers, called Pharisees, who urged people to pursue wisdom and knowledge rather than wealth and power:

Do you wish to know the law of God? Love peace, and cherish one another.

If you do not win the respect of others, you will lose their respect. If you do not increase your knowledge, it will diminish. If you refuse to learn, your mind will grow in ignorance. If you use your abilities solely for your own benefit, you will commit spiritual suicide.

Do not keep aloof from the common people. Do not be confident of your own wisdom and goodness. Do not condemn another person, till you have been in the same place as that person and reacted differently. Do not say that you will delay your studies until tomorrow, because tomorrow never comes.

Fools do not fear sin. Self-doubters, who lack belief in their own intelligence, cannot learn. Ill-tempered people cannot teach. People preoccupied with the affairs of the world cannot acquire wisdom.

The fatter you are, the more food you will provide for the worms. The richer you are, the more worries you have. The more concubines you have, the more you are assailed by sexual desire. And the more slaves you own, the more you will be robbed. Yet the more you obey God's laws, the more fully you will love. The more you study, the wiser you will grow. The more advice you receive, the more enlightened you will become. And the more good you do, the more peace you will enjoy.

Hillel

19

KNOWLEDGE AND ACTION

The land of Israel was eventually absorbed into the Roman empire. The people rose up in rebellion, and the Romans razed Jerusalem to the ground. The Jews – as the descendents of Abraham were now called – dispersed across Europe and Asia, forming numerous small communities. The communities appointed rabbis to guide and advise them; and the rabbis' teachings, and stories about them, were collected in several great books:

Rabbi Simeon said: 'I grew up among wise people, and have heard many wise words. But I have found nothing better than silence. It is more important to act than to speak. Saying too much encourages sin.'

Rabbi Akiba said: 'Sarcasm leads to enmity; tradition protects knowledge; hard work preserves wealth; and silence enhances wisdom.'

Rabbi Gamaliel said: 'It is good to have a useful occupation, as well as to study religious books. The combination of work and study leaves you no time or inclination to sin.'

Rabbi Eliezar said: 'Let your friend's honor be as dear to you as your own. Be slow to anger, but quick to repent. Warm yourself at the fire of wise minds; but beware of those on fire with religious passion, as you will be scorched.'

Rabbi Hanina said: 'If your deeds are greater than your knowledge, then your knowledge is effective. If your knowledge is greater than your deeds, then your knowledge is futile.'

Mishna

20

HUMILITY AND WISDOM

Rabbi Hananyah said: 'When two people sit together, and discuss spiritual matters, then the spirit of God rests upon them.'

Rabbi Zoma said: 'Who are wise? Those who can learn from everyone. Who are strong? Those who can control their passions. Who are wealthy? Those who are satisfied with their lot. Who deserve respect? Those who respect all people.'

Rabbi Azai said: 'Despise no one, and treat no place with contempt. All people and all places have their moment.'

Rabbi Levitas: 'Be humble, for the destiny of all people is to be eaten by worms.'

Rabbi Jonathan said: 'When the poor follow God's way, they earn great spiritual wealth, and hence enjoy great happiness. When the rich abandon God's way, they make themselves spiritually poor, and hence suffer great misery.'

Rabbi Meir said: 'Be less busy with business, and more busy with wisdom. If you start to neglect wisdom, you will find more and more reasons for neglecting it.'

Rabbi Samuel said: 'Do not rejoice when your enemy falls; do not be glad when your enemy stumbles.'

Rabbi Judah said: 'What is the right faith for you to follow? The faith that seems right in your own sight, and causes you to speak and act in a righteous fashion.'

Rabbi Ben said: 'Do not try to be great, and do not look for honor. Do not crave to sit at the tables of kings; your table is better than theirs, and so is your crown.'

Mishna

21

The bracelet and the tree

The queen lost a gold bracelet. The chief minister issued a proclamation, which was read out in every town and village: 'If anyone returns the queen's bracelet within a month, that person will receive a reward. But if anyone is found in possession of the bracelet after a month, that person will be executed.' The following day Rabbi Samuel happened to find the bracelet; it was lying on a road where the queen had traveled in her carriage. But the rabbi did not return it at once. Instead he waited until a month had passed. Then he went to the palace, and told the queen that he had found the bracelet a month ago. 'Did you not hear the proclamation?' the queen asked. 'Yes,' Rabbi Samuel answered. 'Then why did you not return the bracelet immediately?' the queen asked. Rabbi Samuel answered: 'If I had returned it immediately, people would have said that I feared you. I return it now because I fear God.' With those words he handed the queen her bracelet.

Rabbi Honi, when he was very old, moved to a small house with a small garden in the front. He decided to plant a carob tree in the middle of the garden. He dug a hole, and put a sapling into it. As he was pushing the earth over the sapling's roots, a man passed by, and asked: 'When do expect that carob tree to bear fruit?' 'In seventy years,' the rabbi replied. The man laughed, and said: 'Do you expect to live a further seventy years, and see the fruit of your labor?' The rabbi replied: 'When I was a child, I lived in a house surrounded by beautiful trees. They had been planted by people who had lived in the house before me. So I plant this tree for those who will live in this house after me.'

Gemara

22

THE MAN IN THE BROTHEL

During a period of drought Rabbi Abba had a dream in which he saw a certain man, called Pentekaka, praying for rain - and the prayer was answered. When the rabbi awoke the next morning, he thought at first that the dream was meaningless. Then he found himself wondering what kind of man Pentekaka was. 'Perhaps he is the kind of man to whom God would listen,' he thought. So he decided to visit Pentekaka.

In the course of their conversation Rabbi Abba asked Pentekaka: 'What is your occupation?' 'I am a sinner,' Pentekaka replied. 'What sins do you commit?' the rabbi asked. Pentekaka replied: 'I commit five sins daily. I go to the local brothel, and have intercourse with a prostitute. I decorate the walls of the brothel with pretty paper. I wash the prostitutes' clothes. I entertain the prostitutes by singing and dancing for them. And I beat the drum at their nightly orgies.'

'Have you ever done a good deed?' the rabbi asked. The man answered: 'Once, while I was decorating the brothel, I saw a woman weeping behind one of the pillars. I asked her the reason for her tears, and she told me that her husband was in prison. In order to raise the money for his ransom, she had decided to become a prostitute – so she had come to the brothel. I immediately pawned my bed and its cover, and gave her the money; and it was just enough to redeem her husband.'

The rabbi declared: 'Your prayers will be answered. I beg you to pray for rain.' Pentekaka did so, and rain began to fall.

Gemara

23

The Scholar and the Clowns

Rabbi Nahman was renowned for the breadth of his knowledge and the depth of his understanding. In the hope of increasing his knowledge and understanding, he frequently attended lectures at the college where young rabbis were trained; and he always sat near the back of the lecture hall. The lecturers were embarrassed by his presence, since they knew that his knowledge was greater than theirs; and they felt badly that he sat near the back. So one day a lecturer came to him, and said: 'I beg you to sit at the front, in the place of greatest honor?' Rabbi Nahman replied: 'The place cannot honor the person; the person confers honor on the place. Mount Sinai did not confer honor on Moses; but Moses conferred honor on Mount Sinai.'

Rabbi Elazar was walking through a market place. A man came up to him, and asked: 'Is there anyone in this market place who is counted as superior to yourself?' The rabbi, who knew everyone present, replied: 'Many are my equal, but none is superior to me.' At that moment two young men appeared; they were dressed in robes with every color of the rainbow, and each wore a pointed hat with a small bell on top. The rabbi asked them: 'What is your occupation?' The young men replied: 'We are clowns. When we see people who are sad, we try to cheer them up; when we see people quarrelling, we try to make peace between them.' The rabbi said to the first man: 'My answer to your question was wrong. These two young men are certainly superior to me. I merely inform people's minds and hearts, but they lift them.'

Gemara

24

THE FARMER AND THE BEGGAR

A farmer purchased a field for a low price because it was covered in stones. He removed the stones by throwing them on the lane nearby. Rabbi Meir saw what he was doing, and said: 'That which belongs to all, belongs to each.' But the farmer just laughed. A few years later, while the farmer was plowing the field, a wealthy merchant offered to buy it for a large bag of gold. The farmer eagerly agreed, and ran off clutching the gold. He stumbled on one of the stones that he had dumped on the lane, and fell to the ground, breaking a leg and an arm on other stones. As he fell, the bag flew from his hand, and the gold coins were scattered over a wide area. A short time later a group of beggars passed by, saw the gold coins, picked them up, and ran away. Then Rabbi Meir passed by, and saw the farmer lying on the ground. He picked him up, and carried him to a physician. As the physician was setting the broken bones, the rabbi said: 'These injuries were the only way that God could teach you.'

Two rabbis, Johan and Simeon, were on their way to the public baths, when they encountered a man dressed in rags, begging for money. The rabbis said they would help him on their return. But when they returned, they found him lying dead. They felt utterly ashamed of themselves, and decided to make amends by burying his body. As they prepared his body, they found a bag of silver coins. At first they were angry with him for begging. Then they said: 'His dishonesty is no excuse for our lack of charity.' So they completed the preparation, and buried him according to the ancient rites.

Gemara

25

Creatures of God

Rabbi Hanina said: 'Humanity is a single species fashioned by God; he stamps every person with the same die. Yet each human being is different. Therefore every human being has a right to say: "For my sake the world was created." Equally if someone destroys a single life, that person is guilty of having destroyed the entire world; and if someone rescues a single life, that person has the merit of rescuing the entire world.'

Rabbi Joseph said: 'I am a creature of God, and my neighbor is also a creature of God. My work is in the city, and his is in the countryside. I rise early for my work, and he too rises early for his work. Just as he could not excel in my work, I could not excel in his. Perhaps his work is more valuable than mine, and perhaps my work is more valuable than his. But we have both learnt that the value of your work does not matter, so long as your heart is directed to heaven.'

Rabbi Joshua said: 'When someone is angry, speak softly and gently, in order to turn away anger, and bring peace. Anger comes to those who want the world to conform to their own desires; peace comes to those who want the world to conform to God's desires.'

Rabbi Hiyya said: 'Some people pray at great length, calculating that God is more likely to hear a long prayer than a short one. But long prayers merely bring pain to the heart. When you are addressing God, your words should always be few.'

Rabbi Meir said: 'The highest wisdom is kindness.'

Gemara

26

SHREWD JUDGMENT

Rabbi Ammi was about to die. His nephew Jonathan came to see him, and found him weeping bitterly. 'Uncle,' Jonathan exclaimed, 'you have no reason to weep. Is there any part of God's law that you have not practiced? Is there any part of God's law that you have not taught to others? I can think of none. You are acknowledged as the wisest man in the land. Surely you of all people have nothing to fear from death.' 'You are right,' the old rabbi replied, 'that I have practiced and taught every part of God's law. But several times I was asked to serve as a judge; and each time I refused, because I preferred to devote my time to religious affairs. Yet a single shrewd judgment, that brings peace to those in conflict, is worth a lifetime of religion. I weep because I wasted the wisdom that God gave me.' And with tears pouring down his cheeks the rabbi died.

Some years later Jonathan was asked to become a judge, and agreed; and he became renowned for finding amicable solutions to bitter disputes. For example, one day two men came to him. The first man said: 'I bought a house from this man. While I was repairing it, I found a large casket filled with gold hidden under the floor. Since the house is now mine, the casket is also mine.' The second man said: 'When I sold the house to this man, I knew nothing of the casket of gold coins. If I had known about it, I should have kept it. Therefore the casket belongs to me.' 'Do you have a son?' Jonathan asked the first man. 'Yes,' the man replied. 'Do you have a daughter?' Jonathan asked the second man. 'Yes,' the man replied. 'Let the son and the daughter marry,' Jonathan suggested, 'and let them keep the casket of gold coins as the dowry.'

Midrash

27

POTS, FLAX, WATER AND WINE

Rabbi Simon said: 'The potter does not test cracked pots; he knows that if he were to tap them once, they would break. But he tests the good pots, because he knows that, no matter how many times he taps them, they do not break. Similarly, God does not test the wicked, but only tests the righteous.'

He also said: 'The flax dealer, who knows that his flax is good, pounds it, because his pounding improves it; the more he beats it, the more it glistens. But when he knows that his flax is bad, he does not dare pound it, because it would split. Similarly, God is tough with the righteous, but not with the wicked.'

Rabbi Akiba said: 'Just as water is free to all people, the law of God is free to all people. Just as water is beyond price, so is the law of God beyond price. Just as water brings life to the world, so the law of God brings life to the world. Just as water washes away dirt, so the law of God washes away evil.'

He also said: 'Just as wine cannot be kept in precious vessels of gold and silver, but only in cheap earthenware vessels, so the law of God can only be kept by those who are humble. And like wine, the law of God warms the heart.'

Rabbi Shetah said: 'If you pour hot water into an old goblet, the goblet will burst. If you in put cold water, the goblet will crack. So you mix hot water with cold. If God were to show only mercy to people, then sin would multiply. If God were to show only justice to people, then no one would survive. So God mixes justice with mercy.'

Midrash

28

True value

Rabbi Judah who was renowned for his wisdom was on board a ship with several merchants. The merchants each had valuable merchandise in the ship's hold. 'What merchandise have you got?' the merchants asked the rabbi. 'The best merchandise in the world.' Judah answered. The merchants went to the ship's hold to look at his merchandise; but, when they found nothing, they laughed at him. A few days later a storm arose, and the ship was blown onto rocks, destroying all its cargo. But the merchants and the rabbi swam ashore, and they walked to the nearby town. The merchants had nothing, and were forced to beg for food. The rabbi preached each evening in the market place, attracting a large crowd; and they offered him money as a sign of their appreciation. He took only as much as he needed. But the merchants now understood what he had meant – that he possessed the most valuable merchandise in the world.

A wealthy old man died. After the funeral, the local lawyer opened the old man's will. It stipulated that his son should inherit all his wealth – but only when the son had become a fool. The lawyer was perplexed, and went to Rabbi Jacob for advice. When he arrived at the rabbi's house, he was astonished to see the rabbi on his hands and knees, with a reed in his mouth. 'What on earth are you doing?' the lawyer asked. 'I am playing with my young son,' the rabbi said – and then rose to his feet. The lawyer showed Rabbi Jacob the old man's will, and asked what it meant. The rabbi laughed, and said: 'The son can only inherit his father's wealth when he has married and had a child – because as soon as a man becomes a father, he plays like a fool.'

Midrash

29

Contentment amidst noise

A man lived in a small house with his wife and seven children. His wife enjoyed inviting friends for cake and a chat; and his children were boisterous. But he loved tranquility, and was becoming utterly distraught. He was too poor to afford a larger house, with a quiet room to himself. So in desperation he went to see Rabbi Schmelke for advice.

'Do you have a goat in your yard?' the rabbi asked. ''Yes,' the man replied. 'Then you must bring it into the house,' the rabbi said. He did as the rabbi instructed. But the goat bleated all day and night, keeping the man awake.

So the man returned to the rabbi. 'The noise in my house is even worse,' the man said, his eyes red with exhaustion. 'Do you have any hens?' Rabbi Schmelke asked. 'Yes,' the man replied. 'Then you must bring them into the house,' the rabbi said. The man brought in the hens, and the cockerel followed them. But the hens cluck all day; and at dawn, just as the man was finally dropping off to sleep, the cockerel crowed.

A week passed, and the man had no sleep at all. He staggered to the rabbi to seek further advice. 'Go home,' Rabbi Schmelke declared, 'and drive the goat, the hens, and the cockerel back into the yard, where they belong.'

The man did as the rabbi instructed. His relief at no longer hearing their various noises was so great, that he hardly noticed the voices of his wife and children. And he could now sleep again. He went back to the rabbi. And exclaimed: 'A thousand blessings on you. My house is like a palace!'

Hasidism

30

Glass and silver

A man asked Rabbi Schmelke: 'We are told to love our neighbors as ourselves. How can I do this when my neighbor is constantly trying to harm me?' The rabbi replied: 'Your neighbor contains God's spirit; and this spirit permeates every part of his body, down to the tips of his limbs. You contain God's spirit; and this spirit permeates every part of your body, down to the tips of your limbs. Sometimes your foot stumbles on a stone, and you fall. Do you beat your foot for causing you pain? No; you remain kind to your foot. Equally, even though he causes you pain, you should remain kind to your neighbor.'

A miser, as he grew older, became more and more unhappy. He was perplexed by his own misery, and said to himself: 'I have every luxury that money can buy. Yet nothing gives me pleasure any more. How can this be?' So he went to Rabbi Schmelke for advice. The rabbi led him by the hand to the window of his room. 'What do you see?' the rabbi asked. 'I see people,' the miser replied. Then the rabbi led him to a mirror, and again asked: 'What do you see?' The miser replied: 'I see myself.' The rabbi said: 'In both the window and the mirror there is glass. But the glass in the mirror is covered with silver. And as soon as silver is added, you cease to see others, and just see yourself.' The miser left the rabbi, and wandered through the town. For the first time he forgot about his own needs, and saw the needs of others. He decided to share his wealth with others, and kept only enough to feed and clothe himself. His misery disappeared, and he was happy.

Whenever a person was worried about some worldly matter, and came to Rabbi Schmelke for advice, he replied: 'Remember, the world belongs to God, not you.'

Hasidism

31

Sabbath blessing

Through the centuries, when the Jews have been dispersed across Europe, Asia and Africa, the rabbis have played a big part in keeping their religion vibrant. But its inner strength has been maintained by the worship that occurs each week within the Jewish family.

On the eve of the day of the rest, the Sabbath, the father leads his family in an act of worship. He begins by praising his wife: 'My wife is worth more than red coral. I trust her without reserve, and her every action benefits our children and me. When she opens her mouth, she speaks wisely; and when she offers advice, it is always sound. Her children extol her many virtues, and my praise can never be too loud. There are many fine women, but my wife excels them all.'

Then he puts his hand on the head of each of his children in turn, and uses the words dictated by Moses:

'May God bless you and protect you. May God make his face shine upon you, and be gracious to you. May God look upon you with kindness, and give you peace.'

Proverbs and Numbers

MONTH

9

EARLY CHRISTIANITY

Introduction

Origins

The first Christian creed was quite simply: 'Jesus Christ is lord.' And the first Christians saw themselves as followers of the 'Way', which Jesus had taught.

Jesus was born into a devout Jewish family in Galilee, a region of the ancient Jewish land of Palestine; and as a child he was taught the ancient Jewish scriptures. His father was a carpenter, or possibly a master builder, and Jesus spent his early adulthood learning his father's craft. But at about the age of thirty he felt called by God to become a spiritual teacher; and he spent the next three years preaching, telling parables, and engaging in religious debates. He attracted large crowds, who were impressed by his wit, eloquence, and air of authority; and he acquired a large body of disciples. His primary mission was to revitalize the Jewish religion, and to re-interpret its teachings for a new age; but he realized that his teachings had universal application.

The Jewish leaders were angered by his disdain for them, and they envied his popularity. Eventually they arrested him on a charge of blasphemy – insulting God – and in a perfunctory trial declared him guilty. Since Palestine was within the Roman empire, they handed him over to the imperial governor for punishment, who allowed them to crucify him.

Initially Jesus' disciples were cast into despair. But two days after his death they experienced his presence amongst them, which they interpreted as his resurrection from death. They formed a community of followers, which expanded with astonishing speed.

Teachings

Jesus summarized his teaching in two commandments: love God, and love other people as yourself. Both these commandments are contained in the Jewish scriptures, but Jesus gave each a deeper meaning. To love God, you should regard him as your spiritual father, and communicate with him with the same intimacy as children communicate with their parents. And you should love your enemies as strongly as you love your friends.

Although he had initially been an enemy of Christianity, Paul, a devout and scholarly Jew, became its most powerful advocate. And he interpreted the death and resurrection of Jesus as the model of the Way: you crucify your sinful desires on the cross with Jesus, and thence rise with him to share his life of love – which is eternal. To most people Christ's death was a sign of defeat, but Paul turned it into his moment of triumph.

Paul conveyed his teachings by means of letters to groups of followers; and through the first three centuries after Christ's death letters and homilies composed by spiritual leaders were the primary means by which Christianity developed and spread its teachings. The spiritual equality of all people before God is constantly stressed, and so is the obligation of the rich to be generous to the poor, in order to bring material equality. When conflict arises, people should be ready to take blame onto themselves, and to forgive those who have wronged them. If people, from an excess of spiritual zeal, start to treat the world with contempt, they should remember that God created all things – and that his 'Word' is present in every living being.

EXPRESSION

Just as the Jewish authorities had felt threatened by Jesus, so the Roman authorities felt threatened by the rapid spread of Christianity. Christians were renowned as upright citizens; but they refused to obey the law that required all people to worship the Roman emperor as divine. Thus by the end of the first century a growing number of Christians were being arrested and executed – often by being thrown to the lions in great arenas, for the entertainment of the populace. But onlookers were so impressed by the courage and serenity of these martyrs that many became Christian themselves, and so Christianity grew even faster.

Apart from its high moral standards, the central feature of Christian life was the weekly meeting for worship. For the first three centuries these meetings took place in people's homes; and their form was taken from Jesus' last meal with his disciples, when he shared bread and wine with them to represent his body and blood. In 312 CE the emperor Constantine declared Christianity to be the official religion of the Roman world; and he authorized the building of churches for worship. Huge artistic skill and expense were devoted to the construction and decoration of churches, and they remain the most visible and beautiful expressions of the Christian faith.

At around this time communities of single men and women, monks and nuns, began to form. And they became the primary means by which the poor and the sick were cared for.

Us

Religion is frequently regarded as a purely spiritual pursuit, which has little connection with daily life. In accordance with his Jewish roots, Jesus teaches that religion must inform and influence every aspect of human existence: in particular, that love for God must be expressed in caring for the needy, in sharing our wealth with the poor, and, above all, in offering the hand of friendship to our enemies.

There may be only a few people, perhaps no one, for whom we habitually feel hostility. But when Jesus speaks of enemies, he refers to those with whom we are temporarily in conflict, or who are our rivals some matter of mutual interest. Jesus urges us to forgive the wrongs that such people may have caused, and to look critically at our own behavior, readily acknowledging the wrongs we have committed. Offering and seeking forgiveness can be astonishingly hard – yet, according to Jesus, without forgiveness love is empty.

The hardness of Christian love is emphasized by Paul in his understanding of the cross: you are required to crucify all the emotions and attitudes which engender enmity. But Paul's understanding of the resurrection points to the reward: this inner death leads to profound and lasting happiness.

1

THE BLESSED

Jesus was the son of a carpenter, and grew up in Galilee. As a young man he felt called by God to travel from place to place, and preach about love. He soon gathered a large number of disciples, who regarded him as a prophet. On one occasion he led his disciples up a mountain; and when they had all sat down, he spoke these words:

Blessed are the poor in spirit; the kingdom of heaven is theirs.

Blessed are those who mourn; they will be comforted.

Blessed are those of gentle spirit; they will possess the earth.

Blessed are those who hunger and thirst to see right prevail; they will be satisfied.

Blessed are those who show mercy; they will have mercy shown to them.

Blessed are those whose hearts are pure; they will see God.

Blessed are the peacemakers; they will be called children of God.

Blessed are those who are persecuted in the cause of right; the kingdom of heaven is theirs.

You are salt to the world. But if salt loses its taste, how can it be made salty again? It is good for nothing, but to be thrown away and trampled underfoot.

You are light for the world. A city built on a hilltop cannot be hidden. When a lamp is lit, it is not put under a tub, but on a lamp-stand, where it shines for everyone in the house. In the same way your light must shine among people, so that, seeing your good works, they may give praise to God.

Matthew: Gospel

2

Love and Enmity

You have been told: 'Do not kill; murderers must be brought to justice'. But I say to you, if you nurse anger against another person, you are guilty of murder.

You have heard been told: 'Do not commit adultery'. But I say to you, if you look at another person's spouse with a lustful eye, you have already committed adultery in your heart.

You have been told: 'Take revenge on those who injure you or your family.' But I say to you, do not resist those who wrong you. If anyone slaps you on the right cheek, turn and offer the left cheek. If anyone wishes to sue you and takes your shirt, let him have your cloak as well. If someone forces you to go one mile, go two miles. Give to anyone who asks you; and if anyone wants to borrow, do not turn your back.

You have been told: 'Love your neighbor and hate your enemy.' But I say to you, love your enemies and pray for those who persecute you; thus you may be children of God, who causes the sun to rise on good and bad alike, and sends the rain on the innocent and the wicked. If you love only those who love you, and if you speak only to your friends, what is special about that?

A healthy tree cannot produce bad fruit, and a rotten tree cannot bear good fruit. Good people produce goodness out of the store of good within themselves; and evil people produce evil from the evil within them.

Be perfect, as your Father in heaven is perfect.

Matthew: Gospel

3

TRUE RELIGION

Do not announce your good deeds with a flourish of trumpets. When you give help, do not tell your left hand what your right hand is doing; let your good deeds be in secret.

Be careful not to parade your religion before others. When you pray, go into a room by yourself, and shut the door; remember that God is everywhere. And in your prayers do not babble; God knows your needs before you ask them.

This is how you should pray: 'Our Father in heaven, hallowed be your name; your kingdom come, your will be done, on earth as in heaven. Give us today our daily bread. Forgive us our sins, as we forgive those who sin against us. Lead us not into temptation, but deliver us from evil.'

Do not judge, and you will not be judged. Do not condemn, and you will not be condemned. Forgive, and you will be forgiven. Give, and there will be gifts for you: a full measure, pressed and shaken down, and running over, will be poured into your lap. Whatever measure you deal out to others, will in turn be dealt to you.

Why do you look at the speck in your brother's eye, but do not notice the log in your own eye? How can you say to your brother, 'Let me take the speck out of your eye', when you are blind to the log in your own eye? First take the log out of your own eye, and then you will see clearly to take the speck out of your brother's eye.

Always do to others as you would wish them to do to you; that is the essence of all religion.

Matthew: Gospel

4

One master

Ask and you will receive; seek and you will find; knock, and the door will be opened to you. Everyone who asks receives; those who seek find; and to those who knock, the door will be opened. Would any father among you offer his son a snake when he asks for a fish, or a scorpion when he asks for an egg? If you, bad as you are, know how to give good things to your children, how much more will your Father in heaven give his spirit to those who ask him?

No one can serve two masters: either he will hate the one and love the other, or he will be devoted to the one and despise the other. You cannot serve both God and money.

That is why I tell you not to be anxious about food and drink to keep you alive, and about clothes to cover your body. Is not life more than food, and the body more than clothes? Look at the birds in the sky: they do not sow or reap or store in barns, yet your Father feeds them. Are you not worth more than the birds? Can anxious thoughts add a single day to your life? And why be anxious about clothes? Consider how the lilies grow in the field: they neither work nor spin; yet I tell you, even a king in all his glory is not clothed like one of them.

Do not ask anxiously: 'What are we to eat? What are we to drink? What shall we wear?' Set your hearts first on God's righteousness, and all these things will be yours as well. Do not be anxious about tomorrow; tomorrow will look after itself. Each day has troubles enough of its own.

Matthew: Gospel

5

The Adulterer and the Prostitute

On one occasion Jesus encountered a group of religious leaders, who were about to stone a woman who had been caught committing adultery. Jesus stood beside the woman, and said to them: 'Is any man here free from sin? Then let him throw the first stone.' One by one the religious leaders slunk away, leaving Jesus alone with the woman. 'Has no one condemned you?' Jesus asked her. 'No one,' she answered. 'Neither do I condemn you,' Jesus said; 'go and do not sin again.'

On another occasion a religious leader invited Jesus to a meal. When Jesus arrived and took his place at table, a prostitute came in. She had heard that Jesus was dining there, and she brought with her a jar of myrrh. She knelt beside him, and wept. Her tears fell on his feet, and she wiped them away with her hair. Then she kissed his feet and anointed them with the myrrh.

When the religious leader saw this, he said to himself: 'If this man were a real prophet, he would know that she is a prostitute, and push her away.'

Pointing to the woman, Jesus said to his host: 'When I entered your house, you provided no water for my feet; but this woman has washed my feet with her tears, and wiped them with her hair. You gave me no kiss; but she has been covering my feet with kisses ever since I arrived. You did not anoint my head with oil; but she has anointed my feet with myrrh.' Then he said to the woman: 'Through the love you have shown me, your sins are forgiven.'

John: Gospel, and Luke: Gospel

6

Eternal life

Jesus was walking along a lane when a man came up to him, and asked: 'What must I do to attain eternal life?' Jesus replied: 'You already know that you should not murder, steal, commit adultery, cheat, or make false accusations.' 'I have avoided all those sins since I was a boy,' the man said. Jesus stared at him, and could see that the man possessed great wealth, to which he was strongly attached. 'You need to do one thing more,' Jesus said; 'sell all you have, and give the money to the poor – and then you will have eternal treasure.' At these words the man's face fell, and he went away with a heavy heart.

A religious leader had observed this encounter, and asked: 'What must anyone do to attain eternal life?' Jesus replied: 'Love God with all your heart, with all your soul, with all your mind and with all your strength. And love your neighbor as yourself.'

Jesus arrived at a village, where the children rushed up to greet him. Jesus put his arms round them, and blessed them. Then he said to the adults: 'Unless you trust God as these children trust me, you will never attain eternal life.'

Two sisters called Mary and Martha welcomed Jesus into their house. Mary sat down at Jesus' feet and listened to his words, while Martha continued with the household chores. Eventually Martha said to Jesus: 'Do you not care that my sister is leaving me with all the work? Please tell her to help me.' 'Martha, Martha,' Jesus answered, 'you worry and fret about so many things, yet eternal life is all that matters. Mary is doing right, and I shall not stop her.'

Mark: Gospel, and Luke: Gospel

7

PARABLES OF THE TRUTH

Jesus led his followers to the shore of a lake. Then he rowed out on a small boat a short distance from the shore, and spoke to them in parables:

'A man went out to sow seeds. Some seeds fell on rocks where there was no soil, and the birds came and ate it up. Some fell on ground where the soil was shallow; it quickly sprouted, but when the sun came up it was scorched, and it withered away. Some fell among thistles; and the thistles grew up and choked it, so it produced nothing. And some seed fell on deep, fertile soil, where it grew tall and strong and produced a heavy crop.'

His followers were perplexed about the meaning of this parable, so Jesus explained it: 'The man is a teacher who sows God's truth in people's minds. Some hear it, but evil thoughts and actions soon eat it up. Some accept it eagerly; but it takes no root within them, so when trouble comes, it quickly withers. Some accept it joyfully, but worldly cares and interests choke it. Some understand it – and it yields an abundant harvest of love.'

Jesus gave them further parables: 'The truth is like yeast, which a woman takes and mixes with three measures of flour until it has all risen. The truth is like treasure that a man finds buried in a field; he sells everything he owns in order to purchase the field. The truth is like a merchant looking for fine pearls; when he finds one of great value, he sells everything he owns in order to buy it. The truth is like a net cast into the sea, where it catches every kind of fish.'

Matthew: Gospel

8

The Samaritan and the Tax Collector

A religious leader asked Jesus: 'What must I do to inherit eternal life?' Jesus replied: 'Love God, and love your neighbor as yourself.' 'Yes,' said the religious leader, 'but who is my neighbor.'

Jesus replied with a story: 'A man was on his way from Jerusalem to Jericho when he was attacked by robbers, who stripped and beat him, and left him half dead. A devoutly religious happened to be traveling along the same road; but when he saw the man, he passed by on the other side. A religious leader also came to that place and saw him, and passed by on the other side. But a man from Samaria, who had little knowledge of religion, saw him, and his heart filled with pity. He went up, bathed his wounds in oil and wine, and bandaged them. Then he lifted him onto his mule, and took him to an inn where he looked after him. Next day he gave two silver coins to the innkeeper, and asked him to care for the man until he had fully recovered.'

Another religious leader asked Jesus: 'How should I pray in order to know God's peace in my heart?' Jesus replied with another story: 'Two men went to the temple. One was a religious leader, who regarded himself as good and holy. He said to God, "I thank you, God, that I am not greedy, dishonest or adulterous like everyone else, that I fast twice a week, and I give you a tenth of all my income." This man left the temple with his heart in turmoil. The other man was a tax collector. He beat his breast, and cried: "God, have mercy on me, a sinner!" And he left the temple with his heart serene and tranquil.'

Luke: Gospel

9

THE GREAT FEAST

A senior religious leader invited Jesus to a grand party. Jesus noticed how the guests were choosing seats near the top of the table. So in a loud voice he said to them: 'If you take a place of honor, and a more distinguished guest arrives, your host may ask you to give up your place – and you will be humiliated. But if you take a lowly place, your host may invite you to come up higher. By exalting yourself, you will be humbled; but by humbling yourself you will be exalted.'

Then Jesus said to his host: 'When you are having guests for lunch or supper, do not invite your friends, your brothers or other relations, or rich neighbors; they will repay you by inviting you back. When you give a party, ask the poor, the lame and the blind. Then you will be blessed, because they cannot repay you.

One of the guests said to Jesus: 'Tell us about God's hospitality.' Jesus replied with a story: 'A man was giving a great feast, and invited a large number of people. But they each made excuses. One said that he had bought a piece of land, and must inspect it. Another said that he had bought five pairs of oxen, and must try them out. Another said that he had just married, and must stay with his spouse. The man was furious. He went out into the streets and alleys of the town, and the lanes around the town, and brought back the poor, the lame, and the blind. Then he welcomed every traveler that passed through the town, until his house was full.'

All those at the party understood that the man in Jesus' story represented God.

Luke: Gospel

10

Prayer and Money

Jesus decided to go to Jerusalem, the capital city. When he came near, he sent two of his disciples to fetch a donkey; and he rode into the city on its back. The people of Jerusalem had heard about Jesus, and were overjoyed at his arrival. They laid their cloaks on the road, and some also cut branches from trees to spread in his path.

Jesus went to the temple of Jerusalem, where merchants sold gifts to pilgrims. He overturned their tables, crying out: 'This should be a house of prayer, but you have made it a den of thieves!'

The religious leaders were jealous of his popularity, and frightened that he would undermine their power. They themselves had no authority to punish him, since their land was part of the Roman empire; so they decided to try tricking him, in order to have a pretext for handing him over to the Roman governor. Pretending to be disciples, a group of them said to him: 'We know that what you preach is right; you show favor to no one, but teach in all sincerity the way of God. Is it right or wrong for us to pay taxes to the Roman emperor?' Jesus realized their intentions, and said to them: 'Show me a silver coin. Whose head does it bear?' 'The Roman emperor's,' they replied. 'Very well then,' Jesus declared, 'pay to the emperor what belongs to the emperor, and pay to God what belongs to God.'

Jesus saw a poor widow put two small copper coins in the temple treasury. 'This woman, he declared, 'has given more money than all the rich donors together. They gave what they could spare; but she gave all that she had to live on.'

Luke: Gospel

11

THE LAST MEAL

Jesus knew that the religious leaders would soon arrest him, and that he would die. So he gathered his closest disciples for a final meal together. When they had sat down, he broke a loaf of bread into pieces, and gave it to them. 'This is my body,' he said, 'given for you and for all people,' he said. Then he poured a cup of wine, and handed it to each in turn. 'This is my blood,' he said, 'poured out for you and for all people.'

After the meal he poured water into a basin, and washed their feet. Afterwards he said: 'You call me your master. Since I, your master, can wash your feet, you also ought to wash one another's feet.'

Jesus now led his disciples out. Darkness had fallen, and he asked his disciples to stay awake, and pray with him. 'My heart is breaking with fear and anguish,' he said; then he knelt down. 'My Father,' he cried out, 'if it is possible, let this cup pass me by. My spirit is willing, but my flesh is weak.' After a long silence he added: 'Not my will, but yours be done.'

At that moment a group of soldiers appeared, sent by Caiaphas, the highest religious leader. They grabbed Jesus, and dragged him to Caiaphas' house. 'You speak of God as your Father,' Caiaphas said; 'do you claim to be his son?' Jesus said nothing. 'Such a claim is an insult to God,' Caiaphas exclaimed; 'you must die!'

At dawn the next morning Caiaphas' soldiers took Jesus to the Roman governor's palace.

Matthew: Gospel, and John: Gospel

12

The death of Jesus

'This man is stirring up rebellion,' Caiaphas said to the Roman governor. The governor turned to Jesus, and asked: 'Are you leading a rebellion? Do you claim to be a king?' 'My task is simply to speak the truth,' Jesus replied. 'What is truth?' the governor asked. But without waiting for an answer he declared: 'I can find nothing wrong with this man.'

In the meantime the religious leaders had gathered a large crowd outside the governor's palace, and at the leaders' instructions they were shouting: 'Crucify him! Crucify him!' The governor was anxious that a riot might break out; but he was also frightened of sentencing an innocent man to death. So he took a bowl of water, and went out the crowd. 'I am innocent of this man's blood,' he declared, washing his hands in the water; 'do with him what you want.'

Caiaphas's soldiers made a crown of thorns, and put it on Jesus' head. 'Hail, king!' they cried; and they spat on him. Then they placed a large cross on his shoulder, and led him to a hill outside the city. A large crowd followed, including many women who wept loudly. As the soldiers nailed him to the cross, he said: 'Father, forgive them; they do not know what they are doing.'

Jesus hung on the cross for three hours. Finally he cried out: 'My God, why have you abandoned me?' There was silence. Then he said: 'Father, into your hands I commit my spirit.' And with these words he died.

A soldier standing nearby said: 'Truly he was a good man.'

Matthew: Gospel, and Luke: Gospel

13

The Rising of Jesus

The body of Jesus was placed in a tomb, and a large stone was rolled across the entrance. But two days later, when some disciples visited the tomb, they found that the stone had been rolled away, and the tomb was empty.

That evening his closest disciples gathered to discuss the disappearance of his body. And as they were talking, Jesus appeared among them. 'Peace be with you,' he said; and he showed them the marks of the nails on his hands and feet. 'Peace be with you,' he repeated. Then he breathed on them, and said: 'Receive my spirit.'

News quickly spread that Jesus had risen from death; and despair amongst his disciples turned to hope. They began to assemble publicly each day in the Jerusalem temple to pray; they also met in each other's homes for meals, and they even shared their property, so no one was in need. And their number rapidly grew. The disciples called themselves followers of the 'Way' – but others called them 'Christians'.

The religious leaders were more frightened than ever. Amongst the Christians there was an eloquent preacher called Stephen, who was winning many new followers. The religious leaders arrested him for insulting God, and they stoned him to death. As he died, he repeated the words of Jesus on the cross: 'Father, forgive them for what they are doing. Into your hands I commit my spirit.'

A supporter of the religious leaders, called Paul, set about arresting more Christians, and bringing them before the leaders for punishment.

John: Gospel, and Luke: Acts of the Apostles

14

PAUL'S PREACHING

Paul decided to go to Damascus, to see if any Christians had escaped there. But on the road to Damascus he saw a flash of bright light, and he fell to the ground. Then he heard a voice: 'Paul, Paul, why do you persecute me?' 'Who are you?' he asked. 'I am Jesus,' the voice replied, 'and I want you to teach people the Way.'

Paul continued to Damascus; but instead of persecuting Christians, he began preaching the Way in the various places of worship. But his reputation as a man of violence made people suspicious of him. So he traveled to other cities. He went to Thessalonica and to Corinth, where he persuaded many people to follow the Way; and he was also accused, like Jesus, of stirring up rebellion.

He continued to Athens. The people of Athens were always interested in new ideas; and when the city council heard of his arrival, they asked him to preach in their hall. 'As I walked through your city,' Paul began, 'I noticed a shrine which bore the inscription, "To the unknown God". If you follow the Way, you will come to know God – who created the world and everything in it. God does not live in shrines made by human hands; he is everywhere, and in every human being. He invites us to search for him, and he promises that we will find him. All of us, of every race and religion, are God's children; and when we find our Father, we attain eternal life.'

At the mention of eternal life some of them laughed. But many of them were convinced by Paul's words, and decided to follow the Way.

Luke: Acts of the Apostles

15

TRUTH AND MONEY

Paul went to Ephesus, where he spent three months preaching. The city contained many silversmiths, and people came from far and wide to buy their statues, which were believed to possess divine powers. Paul taught that people should seek God's power within themselves, and that these statues were useless. The silversmiths became anxious that he would ruin their trade, and they stirred up a riot against him. Paul was undaunted, and continued to preach; and eventually the city authorities quelled the riot.

Eventually Paul decided that he must return to Jerusalem, in order to teach the Way there. He gathered together the followers in Ephesus, and said: 'Although I have devoted much time to teaching you, I have never asked for material support; I have earned my living by practicing the craft which I learned in my youth, making tents. Indeed, wherever I go, I not only look after myself, but I support those in need. I urge you to follow my example: teach others, but do not be a burden on them. Remember always that there is more joy in giving than in receiving.'

When Paul arrived in Jerusalem, he was immediately arrested by the religious leaders, and charged with insulting God. At his trial he said to the religious leaders: 'Wherever people are paid for their religious work, and acquire power and status through it, they start to quarrel. You are no different; there are disagreements amongst you over every aspect of religious belief. For my part, I simply invite people to follow the Way taught by Jesus Christ.'

Luke: Acts of the Apostles

16

Dying and rising with Christ

The religious leaders in Jerusalem quarreled over how to deal with Paul. So they handed him over to the Roman governor. The governor was also uncertain as to what he should do; and after a long delay he sent Paul to be tried in Rome. Paul was kept under guard in Rome for two years; and during this time he wrote letters to Christians in the various cities in which he had preached. To the followers in Rome he wrote:

The proof of God's love for us is that, while we were still sinners, Christ died for us. By his sacrificial death we have now been put right with God.

What are we to say, then? Shall we remain in sin? Certainly not! We have died to sin; so how can we go on living in it? Surely you know that, when we became disciples of Jesus, we were unified with his death; we were buried with him, in order that, as Christ was raised from death by the glorious power of the Father, so also we might begin a new life.

Since we have become one with him in dying, so we shall be one with him in being raised to life. We know that our old self has been crucified with Christ, in order that the power of sin might be destroyed; thus we are set free from slavery to sin. Death, of course, breaks the chains of sin. In dying with Christ, we believe we shall also live with him, because we know that Christ has been raised from death and will never die again. Death can no longer rule over him. By his death he died to sin once and for all; and by his risen life, he lives for God. In the same way you must regard yourselves as dead to sin and alive to God, in union with Christ Jesus.

Luke: Acts of the Apostles, and Paul: Letter to Rome

17

The spirit of God

If we are led by God's spirit, then we are sons and daughters of God. The spirit of God is not a spirit of slavery, causing us to be afraid. The spirit of God enables us to cry out to him: 'Father, Father!' And if we are children of God, then we are heirs of God – and so fellow-heirs with Christ, sharing his suffering in order to share his glory.

I implore you, my brothers and sisters, to offer yourselves to him as a living sacrifice, dedicated to his service and pleasing to God; in offering yourselves you are truly worshipping him. Do not conform to the standards of the world, but let God transform you inwardly by renewing your minds. Then you will be able to discern the will of God, and thus know what is good, pleasing to him, and holy.

Through the grace which God has granted me, I urge each one of you not to think too highly of yourself; but be modest, judging yourself according to the measure of faith which God has given you. In a single human body there are many limbs and organs, all with different functions. In the same way we are one body in union with Christ, joined to one another as limbs and organs. So let us use the various gifts bestowed on us by God's grace. If our gift is prophecy, for example, we should prophesy as our faith prompts us; if it is practical service, we should devote ourselves to serving others; if it is teaching, we should teach; if it is the gift of counsel, we should counsel. When you give to others, do it with a generous heart; when you lead others, do it with enthusiasm; when you help others in distress, do it cheerfully.

Paul: Letter to Rome

18

Love

To the Christians in Corinth Paul wrote:

Let me show the true Way – the path of love.

I may speak in human or angelic tongues, but if I have no love, my speech is no more than a booming gong or a clanging cymbal. I may have the gift of prophecy and the knowledge of every hidden truth; I may have faith great enough to move mountains; but if I have no love, I am nothing. I may give all I possess to those in need; I may give my body to be burnt; but if I have no love, I gain nothing.

Love is patient and kind; love is never jealous; love is never boastful, conceited or rude; love is never selfish or quick to take offence; love keeps no record of wrongs; love takes no pleasure in the sins of others, but delights in the truth. Love is always ready to make allowances, to trust, to hope, and to endure, whatever may happen.

Love is eternal. Prophecies will cease; tongues of ecstasy will fall silent; knowledge will vanish. Our knowledge and our prophecy alike are partial; and when wholeness comes, that which is partial disappears.

When I was a child, I spoke like a child, had childish emotions, thought like a child. When I grew up, I finished with all childish ways. At present we see only dim reflections in a mirror; but one day we shall see face to face. My knowledge now is partial; then it will be whole, like God's knowledge of me.

These three last forever: faith, hope and love. And the greatest of these is love.

Paul: Letter to Corinth

19

DIVINE STRENGTH AND WISDOM

I came to you not with eloquence, nor with words of human wisdom; I came to you weak and nervous, with the simple message of Christ's cross. To many this message is folly; but to us, who are following the Way of love, it is the power of God. Where does that leave the philosophers, the scholars, and the skilful debaters of this world? God has shown up this world's wisdom as folly.

God in his wisdom has made it impossible for people to know him by means of their own wisdom. Instead God chose to save people through the folly of the gospel. Some may demand miracles, and others may look for wisdom, but we proclaim Christ nailed to the cross. To some this is an offense, and to others it is folly; yet to us Christ is both the power of God and the wisdom of God. The folly of God is wiser than human wisdom, and the weakness of God stronger than human strength.

My brothers and sisters, consider what sort of people you are, whom God has called. Few of you are wise by human standards, few of you are powerful or of noble birth. Yet in order to shame the wise, God chose those whom this world counts as fools; and in order to shame the powerful, he chose those whom this world counts as weak. Yes, God has chosen those whom the world despises, treats with contempt and counts as worthless, in order to overthrow the existing order. Human pride has no place in the presence of God. God has brought you into union with Christ Jesus, and he has made Christ our wisdom. In Christ we are holy and free.

Paul: Letter to Corinth

20

Fruits of Freedom

To the Christians in Galatia Paul wrote:

Christ has set us free, so let us remain free. Stand firm, refusing to submit again to the yoke of slavery. My brothers and sisters, you have been called to freedom – the freedom that comes when our sinful passions and desires are crucified with Christ on the cross. The fruits of sin are sexual exploitation, rivalry; jealousy, anger and selfish ambition; while the fruits of freedom are love joy, peace, patience, kindness, goodness, fidelity, humility and self-control.

To the followers in Ephesus Paul wrote:

I fall on my knees before the Father, from whom every family in heaven and on earth receives its name. I pray that he may give you power to be inwardly strong, and that Christ may live in your hearts. May you have deep roots and firm foundations in Christ's love, so, together with all God's people, you may have the power to grasp the breadth and length, the height and depth of that love. May you know Christ's love, even though it is beyond all knowledge. May you be filled with the fullness of God.

Always live up to the standards to which God has called you. Be humble, gentle and patient, accepting one another's weaknesses in a spirit of love. Take every care to make fast with bonds of peace the unity that God forges. There is one body and one soul, just as there is one goal to which God beckons you. There is one God and Father of all, who is over all, through all, and in all.

Paul: Letters to Galatia and Ephesus

21

MESSAGE AND ACTION

The leader of the Christians in Jerusalem, called James, wrote a letter that was sent to Christians everywhere:

Be quick to listen, but slow to speak and slow to become angry; human anger does not promote divine justice. But do not merely listen; when you hear someone explaining the message of Christ, be sure to act on what you hear. Whoever listens to the message, but does not put it into practice, is like a man looking in a mirror at his own features. But those who look closely at the perfect law, which sets people free, and then obey it, will find happiness.

Those who regard themselves as religious, but do not control their tongues, deceive themselves; their religion is futile. In the eyes of God the Father, pure and genuine religion consists in caring for those in trouble, and in remaining uncorrupted by the world.

My brothers and sisters, you must never treat people differently according to their outward appearance. Suppose two strangers came to your meeting, one wearing fine clothes and a gold ring, the other dressed in dirty rags. Would you show more respect to the well-dressed man, offering him one of the best seats, while telling the poor man to sit on the floor. Then you would be making judgments according to corrupt standards, and you would soon be creating similar distinctions among yourselves.

God has chosen the poor to be rich in faith. So let the poor take pride in their poverty; and let the rich regard their wealth as an opportunity for being generous.

James: Letter

22

Life in God

John, a leader renowned for his spiritual insight, also wrote a letter that was widely circulated:

Do not love the world or the things that belong to the world. You cannot both love the world and love the Father. The things of the world, that pander to your physical appetites and appeal to your selfish desires, come not from the Father, but from the world itself. The world with all its pleasures is passing away; but if you obey God, you will live forever.

Dear friends, love one another and all whom you meet, because love comes from God. If you love others, you are a child of God, and know God. But if you do not love others, you will remain ignorant of God, because God is love. God showed his love for us by sending Jesus Christ, that we might have life through him. This is what love is: not that we have loved God, but that he loved us, and sent Jesus Christ to free us from our sins. If this is how God loves us, dear friends, we should love one another. No one has ever seen God, but if we love one another, he himself lives within us; his love is made perfect in us.

God is love; if you live in love, you live in God, and God lives in you. There is no fear in love; perfect love banishes all fear. Love has not been made perfect in anyone who is afraid, because fear implies punishment. We love because God first loved us. Christ has given this command: love one another, as God loves you.

John: Letters

23

A VISION OF A SHEPHERD

An unknown man had a vision of a shepherd, who gave him a series of commandments. The account of this vision was hugely popular among Christians:

While I was sitting on my bed, a man entered the room. He was quite beautiful. He was dressed like a shepherd, his body covered with white goatskin, with a bag on his shoulders and a staff in his hand. He sat beside me, and said: 'I have been sent to live with you for the rest of your life.' I thought he had come to tempt me. 'Who are you?' I asked. 'I am your shepherd,' he said; 'do not be afraid. I shall give you some commandments. These will remind you of what you already know, and enable you to remember what truly matters. If you keep these commandments, and keep your heart pure, you will receive from God blessings beyond measure.' 'So what are these commandments?' I asked. Then he related them.

The first commandment is to believe that there is one God. He made all things out of nothing, and he contains all things, but is himself uncontained. Fear him, and in your fear control your wicked passions.

The second commandment is to be simple and innocent. Be like a child who does not know the destructive power of wickedness. Speak evil of no one, and do not listen to those who speak evil of others. Do good to others with a simple heart; give to those who seek help, without casting doubt on their sincerity. Remember that all your possessions come from God, to be used according to his will.

Shepherd of Hermas

24

TRUTH, PURITY, COURAGE AND CALM

The third commandment is to love truth. Let only truth come from your mouth. The soul, put by God into your flesh, must always be honest. In this way you will glorify God, for God never lies. If you lie to others, you are defrauding God; if you are honest to others, you are honoring God.

The fourth commandment is to be pure in heart. Do not allow yourself to think about another man's wife. Do not think about any kind of immorality. Even thinking about sin, dwelling on its pleasures, is sinful. But if your thoughts are confined to your wife, you will not sin.

The fifth commandment is to be courageous and calm. If you are courageous, you will always respond without hesitation to the guidance that God gives to you; thus you will have power over evil, and always do what is right. If you are calm, no one will be able to distract and disturb you. Moreover, your body will remain strong, your mind will remain alert, and your heart will be full of joy and happiness. But if you are bad-tempered and easily flustered, then your body will weaken, your mind will grow dull, and your heart will be full of anxiety and misery.

The sixth and final commandment is to be straightforward in all you do. Do not try to be devious. Walk on a straight path, and never on a crooked path. The crooked path is rough, with many rocks on which to stumble, and it is steep and thorny; so those walking on it suffer great harm. The straight path is smooth, straight and clear.

Shepherd of Hermas

25

Open confession

Clement, a former slave who became leader of the Christians in Rome, wrote this letter:

You may possess deep insight; you may be capable of expounding many divine mysteries; you may be wise and sound in judgment; you may be an example of virtue in all you do. But the higher your reputation stands, the humbler you should be. Let your eyes always be fixed on the good of others, and your heart filled with love for them; and never consider your own interests.

Who can describe the power of love? Who can express its majesty and beauty? No tongue can relate the heights to which love can carry us. Love binds us to God. Love casts a veil over countless sins. There is no limit to the endurance of love, and no end to its patience. Love is free of both servility and arrogance. Love hates divisions and discord, and takes delight in friendship and harmony. Through love we are made perfect.

Let us beg forgiveness for all our misdoings - for all the sins that the evil within us has prompted us to commit. When there is discord amongst the followers, ask yourself how you may have caused it, rather than point the finger of blame at others; and then admit your faults openly and honestly. Say to the other followers: 'It is I who caused disorder and friction among you. I shall remove myself; I shall go wherever you send me; I shall do anything that you demand. My only desire is that there should be peace.' God will be merciful. And if all of you confess your sins in this manner, then you will be merciful to one another.

Clement: Letters

26

DESIRE FOR MARTYRDOM

Ignatius was the leader of the Christians in Antioch. He was arrested by the imperial authorities for his beliefs, and taken to Rome, where he expected to be martyred. On the journey to Rome he wrote this letter:

God has filled me with courage about my impending martyrdom. But I do not wish to boast, for fear that boasting would undermine me. I tell myself that I should feel apprehensive, and that I should deafen my ears to those who flatter me. Indeed, the words of flatterers are like whips on my back; for although I yearn for martyrdom, I am unsure of whether I am worthy of it. So I desperately need to acquire humility.

The chains binding my body enhance my capacity to understand the divine mysteries; I can see clearly that which is unseen by the human eye. Nonetheless I do not count myself as a true disciple of Christ. I remind myself constantly of how far I fall short - knowing that, if I regarded myself as already perfect, I should indeed fall short of God.

I am utterly serious in my wish to die for God; do not put any obstacles in my way. Let me be a meal for the beasts in the arena, so they will open for me the way to God. I am God's wheat; and the lions' teeth will grind me into the purest flour, to make bread for God. When I face the lions, I shall feel relieved. All I pray is that they may be swift in their work. I shall invite them to attack me, so they might devour me quickly; and if they are still reluctant, I shall compel them. Please forgive me my yearning for a martyr's death; you must trust me to know what is best for myself.

Ignatius: Letters

27

True and false accusations

Justin, a distinguished philosopher, became a Christian, and was then arrested and martyred. Before his death he wrote this letter to the Roman emperor:

We are charged with being Christian. To us that name is gracious. But we do not ask to be pardoned on account of a name. If our conduct is blameless, then any punishment would be unjust.

We are accused of being atheist. We certainly admit to being atheist with regard to the false gods which many people worship. But we are not atheist with regard to the true God, the Father of righteousness, self-control and all other virtues - the God who guides our thoughts towards the truth, and who transmits the truth to others.

We yearn for the life that is eternal and pure; we strive to dwell with God, who created and fashioned all things. We are eager to proclaim our faith to others. And we are certain in our belief that, by obeying God's law of love, all may enjoy eternal bliss.

When you hear that we are looking for a kingdom, you rashly presume that we mean a human kingdom. But we speak of God's kingdom. This is why we are happy to proclaim our faith when we come to trial - even though death is the penalty. If we were looking for a human kingdom, we should deny our faith in order to save our lives; or at least we should try to keep our faith secret. But our faith is not connected with the present political order; so we are not troubled at the prospect of death. Besides, we must all die some time!

Justin: Letters

28

Word of God

A number of Christians in the second century believed that the material world, including the human body, is corrupt, and should be regarded with contempt. Irenaeus, the leader of the Christians in Lyons, opposed this view; and he adopted a concept from Greek philosophy, the divine Word, to explain the holiness of the world:

There is one God, who by his Word and through his wisdom created and ordered all things.

Through the creation, the Word of God reveals the Creator. Through the world the Word reveals the one who is the architect of the world. Through the infinite beauty of the world's design, the Word reveals the one who conceived beauty. Thus the Word reveals God. All creatures, by their very existence, testify to the power and wisdom of God – although not every creature believes in God.

The Word has expressed himself in the words of many prophets; and in this way he has proclaimed the Father. The same Word became visible and tangible in Jesus Christ. Thus by encountering Jesus people encounter the Father.

Thus the Word is the dispenser of the Father's grace to humanity; and he never fails to be generous. He has revealed God to humanity, and thereby raised humanity to God. He shields the Father from human sight, so that human beings will never undervalue God through familiarity, but will always have to reach out to God. Yet he reveals God to humanity in so many ways that human beings have no cause for ignoring God.

Ireneaus: Against Heresies

29

GENEROSITY TO THE POOR

John Chrysostom was leader in Constantinople. He was eventually driven into exile, because in his sermons he urged the wealthy to give generously to the poor:

You should honor Christ in ways of which he approves. When someone is honored, the form of honor should be appropriate to the person receiving it, not to the person bestowing it. God wants you to honor Christ by giving generously to the poor.

But it is not enough simply to give to the poor; you must give without grumbling. It is not even enough to give without grumbling; you must give with a glad and willing heart.

When you help the poor, two attitudes should always be manifest: generosity and joy. Why do you moan about the duty to give to the poor? Why do you express such resentment at having to share your wealth with those in need? If you resist giving to the poor, you are showing no mercy; you are simply exposing your lack of compassion. If you are full of resentment, how you can help someone in the depths of misery?

In fact, giving to others in a spirit of resentment only demeans and humiliates them, because it makes them feel beholden to you. But if you give to others in a spirit of joy, you create no sense of debt, because the receiver can see that you too are benefiting from your gift. A donor's resentment depresses the spirit of the receiver; a donor's joy uplifts the receiver's spirit. If you give gladly, even if the gift is small, it will be munificent. If you give resentfully, even if the gift is substantial, it will be a pittance.

John Chrysostom: Sermons

30

Love and Faith

What do I love, when I love God? Not material or temporal beauty; not some brilliant light that dazzles my eyes; not some sweet melody that captivated my ears; not the fragrance of flowers or perfume; not henna or honey; not a body that arouses sexual desire. It is not any of these that I love, when I love God.

And yet when I love God, I do indeed love a certain kind of beauty, a certain kind of voice, a certain fragrance, and a certain embrace. But these come not from outside myself; they come from within. My soul is bathed in a light that is not bounded by space; it listens to a sound that never dies away; it breathes a fragrance that is not carried away on the wind; it tastes food that is not consumed by eating; it enjoys an embrace which fulfils every desire, and which never ends. That is what I love, when I love God.

What is the connection between faith and love? The purpose of faith is to purify love. The waters of love naturally pour down into the gutter; faith diverts the waters into the garden. Without faith people pour their love into the world; with faith they pour it towards the one who created the world.

Let love be constrained by faith. Love is never idle; and all actions, good and evil alike, are motivated by love. People become thieves, because they love material objects. People commit adultery, because they love sexual adventure. People commit murder, because they love violence. Every kind of wickedness is the expression of some form of love.

Augustine: Commentaries

31

WHEAT FROM MANY FIELDS

Just as Jesus, on the evening before his death, shared bread and wine with his closest disciples, so the followers of his Way met each week to eat bread and drink wine together. At this meeting they said this prayer:

We thank you, Father, for the truth you have taught us through Jesus, your child. As many ears of wheat from many fields have been brought together in this loaf of bread, so you have brought us together and made us one. To you be glory forever.

You have given us food and drink, and given us pleasure in consuming them, that we may have cause to thank you. You have given us Jesus Christ, and given us joy in following him, that we may love you with all our hearts. To you be glory forever.

Save us from all evil, and make us holy by your love. Gather all humanity from the ends of the earth, and bring them together into your glorious kingdom.

Didache

MONTH

10

CHRISTIAN MYSTICISM

Introduction

Origins

As the Christian churches became richer and more powerful, especially after Christianity became the official religion of the Roman Empire in 312 CE, a growing number of devout men and women decided to retreat into the deserts and forests, in order to imitate the material simplicity of Christ. Some lived as hermits, while others formed monasteries; and they dedicated large amounts of time to prayer and meditation. Naturally new monks and nuns sought spiritual guidance; and soon short books were circulating on the art of meditation, showing how an individual may attain direct knowledge of God.

The relationship between the mystics and the church leaders – the bishops and priests – was persistently tense. The monastic way of life was a visible judgment against the church's worldly ambitions; and mysticism itself undermined the spiritual authority of the church, which required people to accept its doctrines about God on trust. As a result many of the greatest Christian mystics, such as Eckhart and Francis of Assisi, were accused of heresy – and some were found guilty, so they and their writings were burned.

Initially the Protestant reformation centered on the same issues. The early reformers taught that the church had lost sight of both the moral and the spiritual message of Christ; and they urged people to seek a direct experience of God, without the mediation of priests. As Protestantism itself became the official religion of much of northern Europe in the sixteenth century, it too sought to suppress spiritual freedom. But new Protestant movements frequently emerged, most of which were inspired by mystical visions.

TEACHINGS

One of the first great mystical teachers in Christianity, John Climacus, taught that mysticism consists in repentance: turning away from all worldly desires and concerns, and directing the heart and mind solely towards the love of God. Such repentance is not a single act, but a matter of constant vigilance, in which people must watch over every feeling and thought, suppressing those that are corrupt, and nurturing those that are pure. And the method of keeping watch is meditation. He recommended a method of meditation, combining particular posture and the repetition of a prayer, which is still widely used.

Isaac the Syrian taught a different form of vigilance, in which the individual welcomes all kinds of thoughts and feelings, and then offers them to God. He also urged people to meditate on the beauties of the natural world, in order to discern the presence of God in all living beings. Love of nature became a recurring theme of Christian mysticism, reaching its height in the life of Francis of Assisi, who sought to communicate with birds and animals, and with the natural elements. Julian of Norwich saw the whole of nature, and thence the nature of God, in even the smallest object such as a hazelnut.

The mystical experience is frequently described as one of spiritual ecstasy – although it may also involve long periods of profound depression, as John of the Cross described. In addition the mystics sometimes speak of physical aspects, such as a taste of sweetness, a sound of singing, or, most commonly, a sense of heat. Richard Rolle wrote of a fire seeming to burn in his body, while John Wesley wrote of his heart feeling warmed.

Expression

The original monks and nuns lived in caves or in simple huts; and, although their spiritual counsel was frequently sought by people from the cities, they offered no practical service. But as the monastic life became more popular, permanent structures were built in stone; and by the medieval period Europe had hundreds of great abbeys and priories, most of which were stunningly beautiful. And in addition to prayer and meditation, the monks and nuns taught the young and nursed the sick - so mysticism and charity become closely allied.

Eventually the abbots of the largest monasteries began to rival the bishops in their influence and splendor; yet this led to a series of reactions, in which new monastic movements sought to revive the original zeal. Hildegard abandoned her first community, to form an alternative one with a more rigorous regime; Francis started an entirely new pattern of monastic life, imitating in almost every detail the life of Christ; and Teresa of Avila and John of the Cross reformed their monastic orders, restoring the founders' ideals. The Protestant reformation was also a reaction against the decadence of both monasticism and the wider church in the late medieval period; but instead of initiating a new monastic movement, the reformers tried to inspire ordinary people in their homes to seek direct contact with God.

The largest body of Christian literature is theological; but much is inaccessible, except to the specialist, and dates badly. The literature of the mystics, by contrast, remains fresh and perennially popular.

Us

Organized Christianity has generally put a heavy emphasis on theological belief: spiritual salvation has often been regarded as a matter of embracing the correct set of doctrines; and people questioning those doctrines have been ruthlessly condemned. Thus in an age when theology of any kind is under heavy intellectual attack, it is hardly surprising that organized Christianity in the western world has declined rapidly; and many young people, who are seeking some form of spiritual wisdom, never bother to explore the Christian tradition.

The Christian mystics offer us a quite different approach. Some mystics simply ignored the doctrines of the church, while others accepted them as spiritual signposts; but all refuted the notion that divine truth can be encapsulated in words and creeds. For them the sole object of religious endeavor is to draw closer to God, and ultimately enjoy a direct vision of him – and such a vision is beyond any kind of human description. The skeptic may ask how mystics can distinguish between a genuine encounter with God and an illusion. The mystics' answer is that the vision of God to the soul, for those who experience it, is as manifestly authentic as the sight of a material object is to the eyes. And as we read the writings of mystics, we are struck by the similarities of mystical experiences between one person and another – and, indeed, between one religion and another.

1

THE SPIRITUAL LADDER

As a child in Egypt John longed to become a leader – a priest or even a bishop – in the Christian church. But when he began to study the life and teachings of Jesus, then, like many others, he was struck by the contrast between Jesus' poverty and humility, and the church's wealth and power. So at the age of sixteen he retreated into the Sinai desert to live as a hermit in a cave. Forty years later a group of monks, from a monastery at the foot of Mount Sinai, found him; and after a long conversation with him, they asked him to come to their monastery as its spiritual guide. He wrote a book for the monks, in which he compared meditation with a ladder, by which you ascend step by step to God; so he became known as John Climacus – John the Ladder. After his death his book was circulated to monasteries throughout the Christian world, and became the main spiritual guide for monks and nuns. It consists of a series of short spiritual reflections:

If you know God's salvation, you strive to live in harmony with his creation, and do nothing to offend him. You try to control your emotions and desires; you make every effort to rise above misfortune and illness; you take every opportunity to do good. In short, you cultivate perfection within your soul.

The primary tool for cultivating perfection in the soul is meditation. And to help you in learning to meditate, let me describe one spiritual exercise you may perform. Lift your arms over your body in the shape of a cross. Then cry out to God: 'Have mercy on me, for I am a sinner.' Repeat those words over and over again until you are exhausted.

John Climacus: Ladder of Divine Ascent

2

The Joy of Repentance

Repentance is the renewal of your contract with God, giving you a fresh start. Repentance goes into the spiritual market place, and tries to purchase humility. Repentance distrusts excessive bodily comfort. Repentance means standing on a watchtower, keeping guard over yourself. Repentance is the daughter of hope, and the son of the refusal to despair. Repentance means acknowledging guilt, and yet not being disgraced.

Those who take pride in their repentance, and who congratulate themselves on their tears of remorse, are like a man who asks his king for a weapon against an enemy - and then turns it on himself.

When people sincerely repent, God does not want them to continue weeping with remorse. He wants them to rejoice that they are reunited with him. He wants their souls to rejoice. After all, if the sin has been taken away, tears are superfluous. Why look for a bandage when the wound has already healed?

Do you imagine that words can precisely, or truly, or appropriately, or clearly, or honestly describe the divine joy that repentance brings. Can words express the purity, the enlightenment, the wonder, and the serenity that comes from a repentant heart? It would be like trying to convey the sweetness of honey to people who had never tasted it.

When you die, you will not be criticized for having failed to work miracles. You will not be accused of having failed to understand theology. But you will certainly be rebuked if you have not frequently repented.

John Climacus: Ladder of Divine Ascent

3

Total trust

Isaac lived in a small hut on the edge of the city of Nineveh, devoting himself to prayer and meditation. Many people came to him for spiritual advice, and he was famous for the depth of his insights. When the old bishop of Nineveh died, the people of the city begged him to take his place; and with great reluctance he agreed. But he hated the administrative tasks that he was required to perform, and was acutely embarrassed by the deference which was frequently shown to him. So five months later, in the middle of the night, he slipped out of the city, and ran into the nearby desert, where he hid in a cave. Hundreds of people went in search of him, and eventually found him. He refused to return to Nineveh as bishop, but he agreed to come to the city once a year and preach a sermon. These annual sermons, which were later copied and circulated, concerned the experience of meditation:

When you start to meditate, come before God like a baby who has not yet learnt to talk. Do not try to speak to God at first; and do not show off any theological knowledge you may have. All the thoughts in your mind should be those of a child. Look upon God as a child looks upon a father or mother, in a spirit of total trust.

Do not be afraid of the emotions that well up in your heart as you meditate. Sometimes you will feel joyful, sometimes sad; sometimes you will feel angry and anxious, sometimes you will feel calm and serene; sometimes you will feel hateful, and sometimes loving. Offer all these emotions to God, because he is their ultimate source.

Isaac the Syrian: Homilies

4

DRUNK WITH LOVE

A moment comes when you cross the boundary from these active forms of prayer and meditation, into the realm of pure meditation. At that moment all mental activity of every kind ceases, and so do both physical and spiritual desire. When the soul enters pure meditation, it ceases to meditate. Before entering this realm meditation is a constant struggle, in which you strive to gain authority over wayward thoughts and feelings. Beyond this boundary prayer is replaced by awestruck wonder, in which the soul marvels at the beauty of God.

You become certain that God loves and provides for every person and every creature on earth. You are filled with wonder at the gracious way in which he governs the world. Gradually the sweetness turns into a spiritual fire that burns within your heart, and spreads throughout your soul and body. You feel a passionate love for every person and every creature you encounter. You become drunk with love, as if you had been imbibing the finest wine. Your limbs grow limp, and your mind stands still in awestruck wonder. Your imagination is transformed, and you can begin to see God himself, as he is.

You may ask why this motionless communion with God is called meditation, if it is not meditation. The reason is that meditation is the means by which the soul attains such a state; there is no other way of reaching it except through meditation. The soul is led by meditation towards it; meditation prepares the soul to receive it; and it occurs during meditation.

Isaac the Syrian: Homilies

5

A MYSTICAL EXPERIENCE

Symeon was born into one of the leading families of Galatia; and he showed such brilliance as a boy, the emperor in Byzantium invited him to his palace, and provided him with tutors. But soon after he had completed his education, he visited a monastery near Galatia, where he met a saintly old monk, also called Symeon. The elder Symeon persuaded him to become a monk himself; and at the age of thirty-one he was elected abbot. He gained such a reputation as a spiritual teacher that people in the region looked to him, not the local bishops, as their leader. The bishops became jealous, and paid a group of criminals to murder him. But he heard of the plot, and escaped into the desert. There he wrote a short letter about a mystical experience, and the advice which his namesake had given him:

One night, when I was still a young man, I went to the place where I usually prayed. As usual I opened my heart to God. But on this occasion I was suddenly moved to tears, and my whole body and soul were seized with desire for God. At first I thought that my tears were from sadness; then I realized that I was filled with joy and pleasure. I fell prostrate to the ground, and at once I saw a huge light. It shone upon me, penetrating my mind and soul. I was utterly amazed and overcome with ecstasy. I became quite oblivious of where I was, or even who I was. I could only cry out: 'Lord, have mercy.'

Eventually I returned to my normal state – and yet I was different. All corrupt thoughts and negative emotions had dissolved. I no longer had any fear of earthly misfortune or even death. My whole being had a sensation of sweetness.

Symeon of Galatia: Reflections

6

A FORETASTE OF DIVINE UNION

After a time the light, which I had seen in that first mystical experience, faded and disappeared. I felt utterly alone, and a terrible pain, like that of grief, gripped me. It seemed to me that the light had represented the infinite love of God, which had wholly captivated my emotions; and now I was separated from this love. So I went to seek advice from Symeon, the old monk who was my spiritual guide.

'My dear son,' he said, 'God wants everyone to reach up to him, and to knock on his door. He wants everyone to see the light that you have seen, to taste the sweetness that you have tasted, and to lose all fear of misfortune and death as you have done. But that light is only a symbol of God, not God himself; and the sensation of sweetness is a foretaste of the joy of union with God, not the ultimate joy. You will not taste the true sweetness while you are still alive on this earth. In the meantime you should do nothing that can hinder you from eventually enjoying that sweetness. Undoubtedly you will fall from time to time, committing some sin. Do not despair; those occasional lapses ensure that you remain humble. So continue to cultivate a spirit of humility, knowing that God alone can blot out past and present failures.'

When I heard these words, I felt a wonderful sense of relief. I recognized that this old man spoke from a great height of spiritual knowledge; and he had acquired that knowledge because he trusted God without reserve. And so from that time onwards I have simply tried to be good to all people, and to avoid sin.

Symeon of Galatia: Reflections

7

Inner understanding

Hildegard started having religious visions when she was a child; and her parents sent her to live with a female hermit, who was attached to a monastery. When she reached adulthood, Hildegard began to speak about mysticism; and although women were not allowed to preach in churches, she frequently gave lectures in barns and town halls. Many women asked to live with her, in order to receive her guidance, and she formed a community at Bingen on the banks of the Rhine. At the age of forty-two she felt a compulsion to express her insights in a book:

Use all your faculties to appreciate God's creation. Use the soul within you to understand the soul within all living beings. Use your body to sympathize with other people's bodily experiences. Use your emotions of anger and revenge to understand war. Appreciate goodness through distinguishing it from evil. Appreciate beauty through distinguishing it from ugliness and deformity. Define poverty by contrasting it with wealth. Rejoice in good health by comparing it with sickness.

Distinguish the various opposites: length and shortness; hardness and softness; depth and shallowness; light and darkness. Enjoy every moment of life by constantly reminding yourself of the imminence of death. And strive for the happiness that is eternal, by contemplating eternal separation from God.

You understand so little of what is around you, because you do not use what is within you.

Hildegard of Bingen: Scrivias

8

THE WISDOM OF GOD

Just as the wisdom of a person is known through the value of what that person does, so the wisdom of the God is known through the value of what he has made. Look around you at the world, and at the different species that inhabit the world. These species all shine with beauty, reflecting the beauty of their origins. They sparkle in the beauty of their perfection, as if they had all been made of burnished copper. Their light shines in every direction, so the whole earth glows with beauty.

When you see God in the beauty of what he has made, you are not looking with mortal eyes, but with the eyes of the soul. When you hear his wisdom within this beauty, you are not using mortal ears, but listening with the ears of your soul to the wisdom he has implanted within you.

The wisdom of God is burning love. This wisdom brings life to those who are spiritually dead. It is a light that exposes sin, and a flame that burns the ropes binding sin to the soul. It exists in all people, whether or not they are aware of it. It is the source of holiness in each person, and makes people desire to become holy. It is magnificent and glorious, and can never be comprehended by the human intellect.

Imagine the highest and widest mountain in the world. Its size reflects the grandeur of God, and thus honors God. It is not greater than God; nothing on earth is greater than its Creator. God is higher and wider than the human mind can comprehend. He is holier than we could possibly understand.

Hildegard of Bingen: Scrivias

9

BROTHERS OF NATURE

As a young man in the Italian city of Assisi, Francis enjoyed a riotous social life, spending the money that his father had earned as a cloth merchant. His father disapproved; but when Francis turned to religion, and gave up all material possessions, his father was furious. Francis' exuberant personality, combined with his passion for all living beings, soon attracted others; and he formed a community of friars, who wandered from place to place, giving sermons and begging for food. The most famous sermon delivered by Francis himself was to a flock of birds that were perched on trees by a road:

My sisters the birds, you have received much from God. You should always praise him for your ability to fly freely, for the songs that you can sing to him, for your vast numbers, and for the air in which you move. You neither sow nor reap; yet God gives you food to eat, rivers and streams in which to drink, mountains and rocks in which to hide, and tall trees in which to nest. And since you can neither spin nor weave, he gives you feathers of bright colors to keep you warm. All these are signs of God's love for you.

Francis also composed a song in praise of nature:

All praise is yours, my God, through all you have made: especially through Brother Sun, who brings the day and gives us light, and through Sisters Moon and Stars, whose beauty entrances us; through humble Brother Air and modest Sister Water, who sustain us; through Brother Fire who keeps us warm, and Sister Earth who provides us with fruit and flowers; through Brother Sickness who teaches us patience, and Sister Death who welcomes us to eternal life.

Francis of Assisi: Little Flowers and Canticle

10

Knowing God and self

Hadewijch lived in a house near Antwerp with a group of other women, devoting the daylight hours to helping the poor and sick, and the hours before dawn and after dusk to prayer and meditation. There were many similar groups in the Low Countries, known as Beguines; and Hadejwich wrote spiritual letters to be circulated among them:

May you come to know God as he is, and may you feel him drawing you into himself. From the depths of his wisdom he will teach you about his love. He will live in you, and you will live in him, so that you will taste his wonderful sweetness. You will be like two lovers. You will be so besotted with God that you will not know where your own self ends, and where God begins. It will seem as if you and God possess one another in mutual delight, mouth in mouth, heart in heart, body in body, soul in soul. The divine nature will flow into you, permeating you. You will find yourself by finding God.

If you want to know God, you must first know yourself. You must understand what you are able to do, and what you are willing to do. You must understand what you love and hate, and how you react emotionally to events. You have to reflect on how you respond to people opposing you, and how you cope in unfamiliar surroundings. You have to ask yourself how you endure the loss of things you like. And you have to examine whether you rise quickly and eagerly to opportunities for good. As you understand yourself, so you will be able to control yourself, remaining serene and tranquil in all circumstances. Thus you will be able to remain constantly close to God - and he will be close to you.

Hadewijch of Brabant: Letters

11

Reborn in God

Eckhart had a brilliant mind and an eloquent tongue, and taught theology in the university of Paris. But he came to regard theology as empty, unless it is based on a personal experience of God. So he returned to his native Germany, where he devoted himself to meditation. After a few years he began preaching in churches and barns, encouraging ordinary people to experience God for themselves. His huge popularity, as well as the substance of his message, evoked the wrath of the local bishops, who sent him to the pope in Rome to be tried for heresy; but he died before the trial was complete. His talks were copied, and circulated in secret:

Inward work - work within the soul - is godly, because it is aimed at making the soul more god-like. If your inward work is feeble and worthless, your outward work will be feeble and worthless too. If your inward work is great, it will make your outward work great as well. If your inward work draws its goodness from the heart of God, and from nowhere else, God is born within you, and you are unified with him

If God has been born within you, then you are estranged from all quantity and complexity; you are even estranged from goodness, truth, and all things that allow any shades of difference or distinction. They are entrusted to God, who cannot be conceived, and who has no complexity and no attributes.

If God has been born within you, he is with you wherever you go. When you are working or relaxing, as well as when you are praying and meditating, he is present.

Eckhart: Talks of Instruction

12

God in all People

You should train yourself to keep God always present in your mind, in your actions, and in your will. Watch over yourself to ensure that God is present - whether you are outside in the clamor of the world, or inside a church. If your attitude of mind is constantly godly, then nothing can disturb your inner serenity.

So how can you develop this serenity; how can you ensure that God is always present within you? Look for God deep within your soul. There you will find a sublime movement towards God; you will observe the soul constantly striving to know him. Do not attempt constantly to think about God; that is impossible, since any train of thought always comes to an end. Rather you should become aware of the soul's innate activity; and you should live in accordance with it.

Some people think that the only way of avoiding evil is to withdraw from the world, and do nothing. But in truth the mere fact of being human compels all of us to engage in some activity. So you should not be afraid of working in the world. Before starting any activity, you should spend some time enlisting God's help through prayer, fixing your heart and mind firmly upon him, and striving to unite your intentions with his. And when you have finished, thank him for what has been accomplished.

The soul is the image of God within you. Thus by becoming aware of the soul, you will see the image of God in all other men and women - and you will naturally behave towards them in a godly manner.

Eckhart: Talks of Instruction

13

THE ACT OF CONVERSION

Johannes Tauler was the son of a wealthy merchant in Strasbourg, and wanted to become a priest. But he was a poor scholar, and failed to master Latin, which was regarded as essential; and he became deeply depressed, hardly coming out of his home. He tried to break though the inner darkness of his condition through meditation, and experienced a conversion in which his entire attitude to life was transformed. Despite being shy, he found the courage to speak at religious meetings:

Your purpose is that God should be born within you. This requires a decisive act of conversion, in which all your powers and faculties, from the lowest to the highest, are directed towards God. It requires a gathering of the whole self, taking away every aspect of the self from worldly distractions, and placing the self in the arms of God. In this way the different aspects of the self no longer conflict with one another, but are brought into harmony.

The act of conversion may be compared with an archer who wants to hit the middle of the target, and closes one eye in order that the other eye can see clearly. In the same way conversion requires total and accurate attention onto the soul, which is the location of divine truth; and this means becoming blind to all else. The act of conversion may also be compared with a tree, in which the sap ceases to flow from the trunk to the branches, but flows back into the trunk. In the same way conversion requires all energy and all life to flow back into the soul, which is the source of life.

Johannes Tauler: Sermons

14

Peace in the Absence of Peace

There are many people who wish to be witnesses of God when their souls feel peaceful, and when their religious observance is giving pleasure. These people want to be holy, so long as their religious efforts do not become burdensome. But when darkness comes, when God seems remote and distant, when they feel lonely and abandoned, when their minds or bodies become sick - then they turn away from God, and show themselves not to be his true witnesses.

It is natural for all of us to seek peace, both in what we do, and in what we are. The true witnesses of God learn to find peace where peace is absent. This is because they are not concerned for peace in itself, but want to discover the source of peace - which is God. They learn to find joy in grief, serenity in disturbance, consolation in bitterness.

If you wish to discover the source of peace, you must do two things. First, you should free your heart from all material and worldly things; you must even free your heart from any concerns about yourself, removing all selfish intentions and desires. In this way you will be able to direct all your heart to God.

Secondly, you must accept all difficulties - whatever their cause, whether they are material or spiritual - as coming from God. In this way you will learn to submit yourself to God, giving yourself totally to him.

When you do these two things, God is born within you. His seed was always there; but now you no longer hinder the seed's growth.

Johannes Tauler: Sermons

15

The fire of love

As a boy Richard Rolle frequently visited a monastery near his home in northern England; and his outstanding intellectual abilities caught the attention of the abbot, who sent him to Oxford to train as a priest. But Rolle hated the arid speculations of the theologians, who, in his view, wanted to define God rather than love him. So he ran away, and lived as a hermit in a hut next to a remote church on the Yorkshire moors. During each summer he toured local villages, singing spiritual songs that he had composed; and when the plague swept through England, he went from house to house to comfort the dying. Eventually he caught the plague himself. But shortly before his death, he described his spiritual experiences in a book:

I cannot describe to you how astonished I was the first time I felt my heart begin to warm. The warmth was real, not imaginary; it seemed as if I were actually on fire. I was amazed at the way the heat surged through me; and this sensation gave me great pleasure and comfort - which surprised me also. I kept touching my chest, to convince myself that there was no physical cause.

Once I was sure that this fire of love was not the result of some illness, bodily or mental, but was a gift from God, I was utterly delighted, and I wished the fire to burn ever brighter. And the desire was enhanced by the wonderful inner sweetness I could taste as the fire blazed. I had never imagined that sinful human beings could enjoy such spiritual warmth and sweetness.

Richard Rolle: Fire of Love

16

Fire, sweetness and song

Let me describe how I first began to receive this fire of divine love, and the other experiences that accompanied it.

I was sitting in church, trying to find pleasure in prayer and meditation, when suddenly I felt within me a strange and pleasant heat. At first I wondered where it came from, but gradually I realized that it did not have a natural cause; it came from God himself. The warmth was extremely intense, and gave me great joy.

Nine months later a wonderful sensation of sweetness was added to the sensation of heat. And I also began to hear spiritual sounds, which seemed to fill the church. These sounds were hymns of eternal praise, sung to a divine melody that I had never heard on earth. Indeed, they cannot be heard except by those who have received them from above.

That night, as I sat in church before supper reciting spiritual poems, I heard above me again the sound of holy words being sung. With all my heart I was reaching out to God; and this symphony seemed to me, in a manner I cannot explain, to be God's response to me. And in my mind I felt myself to be in perfect and delightful harmony with the music.

Then and there my thoughts turned themselves into a divine melody, and my meditation became a poem; every prayer I uttered, and every poem I recited, swelled this wonderful chorus. Through this inner sweetness my whole being began to sing; but I sang without any outward sound, so that only God himself could hear.

Richard Rolle: Fire of Love

17

Creation in a Hazelnut

One spring evening, shortly after the plague that killed Richard Rolle, a young woman lay seriously ill in Norwich in eastern England. Her parents and physician expected her to die. But during that night she had a series of visions, which she interpreted as revelations from God; and the following morning she began to recover. She then became a hermit at a church in the poorest part of the city; a small cell was built on the side of the church, and she was locked in. She spent the rest of her long life there, and became known by the name of the church's patron saint, Julian. She wrote about her revelations in a book that became hugely popular:

Our Lord showed me something small, no bigger than a hazelnut. It seemed to lie in the palm of my hand, and was as round as a ball. I gazed on it with the eye of understanding, and thought: 'What can this be?' I received the answer: 'It is all that is made.' I marveled that it could last; it was so small that I thought it would quickly disappear. And in my understanding I received a further answer: 'It lasts, and will last forever, because God loves it; all things exist through the love of God.'

In this little thing I saw three properties. The first is that God made it; the second is that God loves it; the third is that God preserves it. I saw in it that God is creator, lover, and preserver. And until I am wholly united with him, I can never enjoy true rest or true happiness. I must become attached to him in such a way that nothing stands between me and him.

Julian of Norwich: Divine Showings

18

THE NECESSITY OF SIN AND SUFFERING

I saw nothing hindered me except sin. This is true for all of us. And it seemed to me that if there had been no sin, we should all have been pure, just as God created us. Indeed, prior to this time I often used to wonder, in my folly, why God in his great and prophetic wisdom had not prevented sin from ever existing. If sin did not exist, it seemed to me that all would be well.

These thoughts should have been suppressed. But lacking insight, I felt deeply sad and sorrowful at the existence of sin. God in a vision told me what I needed to know about this. He said: 'Sin is necessary. But all will be well; and all will be well; and every kind of thing will be well.'

It is true that sin is the cause of pain. But all will be well, and every kind of thing will be well. These words were spoken most tenderly, showing that no blame attached to me or to anyone who will be saved. Thus it would be quite wrong for me to blame God for sin, or to criticize him for letting me sin, since he does not blame me.

I saw that God rejoices, with pity and compassion, over the tribulations of his servants. And on all people whom he loves, he imposes some burden that causes them to be scorned, mocked and rejected by the world. God does this to prevent the damage which comes from hubris, pride and self-importance in this wretched life, and thus to prepare the soul for eternal bliss. He says: 'I shall break down within you empty ambition and vanity, and make you meek and mild, pure and holy.'

Julian of Norwich: Divine Showings

19

The Gift of Ecstasy

Teresa's grandparents were Spanish Jews who converted to Christianity. As a teenager she was so unruly that her father sent to a nunnery in Avila, in the hope that its strict discipline would tame her. At the age of twenty she became a nun herself, against her father's wishes. She suffered various symptoms of psychological disorder, including paralysis; but these diminished as she began to enjoy periods of intense spiritual ecstasy. She wrote an autobiography describing her inner experiences, and drawing general conclusions from them:

We may speak of love and humility as the true flowers of spiritual growth; and they give off a wonderful scent, which benefits all who come near. The purpose of spiritual ecstasy is to enable these flowers to bloom.

Unless you have experienced spiritual ecstasy, you can never imagine how much the Lord can accomplish through it, in such a short time. Of course, ecstatic prayer is not essential for spiritual growth; God wants some people to grow more slowly, so he does not bestow on the them this gift. Besides it is extremely exhausting, and leaves little energy for serving others in a practical way.

If you receive the gift of spiritual ecstasy, this does not mean you are spiritually superior to those who do not. Certainly my soul has not merited this gift. God bestows the gift of ecstasy according to his pleasure. No one is ever prepared for it; but God makes the soul ready as and when he wishes.

Teresa of Avila: Autobiography

20

THE EXPERIENCE OF ECSTASY

As spiritual ecstasy sweeps over you, your mind faints away in a kind of a swoon; it feels very calm, and full of joy. The breath and the bodily powers progressively fail, so that you cannot move even the hands without great effort. The eyes close involuntarily; and if they remain open, they see almost nothing. If you try to read in such a state, you can scarcely make out a single letter – you can see that there are letters, but you cannot read them, even if you try. You hear, but you do not understand what you hear.

Your senses serve no purpose; you cannot even distinguish pleasure from pain. Your tongue cannot form a single word, nor would it have the strength to pronounce one. The strength of the body vanishes. As a result your inward strength increases, to enjoy its bliss to the full.

This state of spiritual ecstasy does no harm, however long it lasts. At least it has never harmed me. Even when I have been ill, I can never recall any bad effects from ecstasy; on the contrary, it has always left me feeling much better. What harm could such a blessing do? The effects are so manifest that it is obvious to any observer that a wonderful thing is happening. At the time it robs you of your bodily strength; but afterwards you find your strength has increased.

In fact spiritual ecstasy usually lasts only a very short time. It is so quick that the external signs are not always noticed by others. But once it is over, you are so radiant that it seems the sun is shining from your soul.

Teresa of Avila: Autobiography

21

THE DARK NIGHT OF THE SOUL

John was born only a few miles from Avila, and became a monk at the age of twenty, dedicating himself to the cross of Christ – so he became known as John of the Cross. A few years later, with the encouragement of Teresa of Avila, he started a new monastery in which mysticism was encouraged. He is most famous for describing the profound depression though which many mystics pass, and which he called 'the dark night of the soul':

God cures our imperfections by putting the soul into a dark night. Through pure dryness and interior darkness he weans us away from the breast of earthly gratification and delight, and draws us away from all trivial and childish concerns; and he leads us onto the path of virtue. Even if we practice every kind of self-mortification with great passion and zeal, we achieve nothing until God purges us by means of the dark night and we passively submit.

This night, which is experienced through meditation, causes two kinds of darkness, according to the two parts of the soul: sensory and emotional. In the sensory night the senses are purged, and harmonized with the spirit. In the emotional night the heart is purged and denuded, and thence prepared for loving union with God.

The sensory night is common, and happens to many people; those beginning in the way of mediation experience it. The emotional night is reserved for a few – those who are becoming proficient. The sensory night is bitter and terrible; but is nothing compared with the emotional night.

John of the Cross: Dark Night of the Soul

22

Signs of the Dark Night

It is easy to confuse the dark night of the soul with the mental disturbance that can be caused by sin, weakness, tepidness of spirit, melancholy, or some bodily illness. There are three principal ways of discerning whether dryness and darkness are caused by these problems, or whether they are truly the means of spiritual cleansing.

The first is that during the dark night the soul derives no satisfaction or consolation from worship, nor from material blessings. God puts the soul into the dark night because he wants the sensory appetites to wither away; so he does not allow the soul to find any sweetness or delight in anything.

The second sign is that during the dark night the soul feels it is no longer serving God, but turning away from him. Normally in times of difficulty the soul turns to God for help; but the soul feels such distaste for God during the dark night, that it cannot ask his aid. It is obvious that this aversion to God is not the result of laxity, but is caused by God himself, taking his strength away from the senses.

The third sign is that during the dark night the soul feels utterly powerless. Its efforts to meditate and to use its imagination in order to sense God's presence, which had previously been effective, now prove useless. God no longer communicates through the senses, as he did before, nor through reflection on the doctrines of the faith. Instead he begins to communicate in a purely spiritual manner, directly with the soul; and the form of communication involves neither the heart nor the mind – neither feelings nor thoughts.

John of the Cross: Dark Night of the Soul

23

The will of God

For fifteen years Jean-Pierre de Caussade was an itinerant preacher in his native France, encouraging people to find God in every event and moment of their lives. Then for the last twenty years of life he organized retreats, inviting people to come and stay for a few days in a monastery to learn the techniques of meditation. Shortly before his death he wrote a short book, summarizing all he had learnt and taught:

The will of God is the essence and power of all things; and the will of God harmonizes all things with the soul. Without the will of God all is nothingness and emptiness, lies and vanity, the letter without the spirit, husks without kernels, death. The will of God is salvation and health, life to the body and soul.

The will of God within an object cannot be perceived merely by looking at the object's external appearance; nor can it be perceived by assessing whether the object may be helpful to your body or soul, because that in itself is utterly unimportant. The will of God is the process by which any object or event forms the image of Jesus Christ in your heart. You should not desire one object or event rather than another, because God can bring all things into unity with you.

Sometimes pleasant ideas fill the mind; sometimes the mind is distracted and confused. Sometimes pleasant emotions fill the heart; sometimes the heart is disturbed and anxious. Sometimes the body is well, and sometimes it is sick. Yet in every situation and in every moment the divine will is active, loving you and sustaining you.

Jean-Pierre de Caussade: Self-Abandonment to Divine Providence

24

God is every event

All creatures live in the hands of God. The senses perceive only outward action; but faith perceives the actions of God in every event. Faith knows that God is present in all things, and operates through the course of history – century by century. Faith knows that the briefest moment and the tiniest atom contain a portion of God's hidden power.

If you are able to respond to each moment as a manifestation of God's will, you will find in each moment everything that the heart can desire. What can be more reasonable and more perfect than God's will? Its infinite value could not be increased by some change in time, place and circumstance.

If you have discovered the secret of finding God's will at every moment and in every event, and of finding God's presence in all things, you possess the most precious gift on earth. You do not need to desire anything else. You do not need to hanker after more wealth. Everything you truly want at any moment is contained in the events of that moment.

The present moment is always full of infinite treasure. It contains far more than you can possibly grasp. Faith is the measure of its riches: what you find in the present moment is according to the measure of your faith. Love also is the measure: the more the heart loves, the more it rejoices in what God provides. The will of God presents itself at each moment like an immense ocean that the desire of your heart cannot empty; yet you will drink from that ocean according to your faith and love.

Jean-Pierre de Caussade: Self-Abandonment to Divine Providence

25

THE INNER LIGHT

George Fox, a young weaver in central England, became disgusted at the hypocrisy and spiritual emptiness of conventional religion. He set out on a quest to find someone who could teach genuine faith, but found no one. Then one day he heard God speak directly to his heart; and thereafter he experienced God as an inner light guiding his thoughts and actions. He founded the Quaker movement, which spread rapidly in Britain and north America, with the aim of enabling others to be guided directly by God. He kept a spiritual journal:

I fasted frequently, and walked from place to place alone, filled with sadness and self-pity. I was truly a man of sorrows. I had no respect for priests, and for a time I sought guidance from independent ministers. They usually treated me warmly, but I soon despaired of them; none could speak to my condition. When I realized that no human being on earth could help me, nor even tell me how I could find help, I heard a voice which said: 'There is one, Christ Jesus, who can speak to your condition.' And when I heard this voice in my heart, I leapt for joy.

Then God showed me why no one on earth could speak to my condition – namely, that I should give all the glory to him. All people are imprisoned by sin and ignorance, as I had been, in order that God might save them. For me faith was now a matter of experience. To my eyes all things now seemed new. Creation now had a new fragrance, so sweet that it cannot be described in words. God's light now illuminated my heart and mind, and so shone on everything I perceived. I had been renewed in God's image.

George Fox: Journal

26

Concepts and Experience

Nikolaus Ludwig von Zinzendorf inherited a large estate east of Dresden, where he gave refuge to Protestants from Moravia fleeing persecution. He was struck by their spiritual warmth, which was based on personal experience of God, and came to regard his own faith as too cerebral by comparison. In due course he became their spiritual leader, and the group became know as the Moravian church. He frequently gave lectures in Germany, England and America, outlining his mystical view of religion:

Religion can be grasped without reason; otherwise no one could possess religion except those with intelligence. Moreover, if religion depended on reason, theologians would always excel in holiness; experience tells us this is not so.

The truth of concepts matters far less than the truth of experience. Errors of doctrine matter far less than errors of the heart. An ignorant person is far less evil than a stubborn person.

Understanding reached from concepts changes with time, education, and other circumstances. Understanding reached from experience is not subject to these changes; it simply deepens with time and circumstances.

The experience central to religion is receiving God's revelation of himself. That which God does not want human beings to understand, he does not reveal. That which he does want human beings to understand, he does reveal. It may sometimes be useful to express divine revelations in concepts; it is never necessary.

Nikolaus von Zinzendorf: The German Socrates

27

Implicit and Explicit Faith

We cannot create faith within ourselves. God must work within us, giving us new birth, so that the heart, mind, and all the faculties are transformed. This transformation is the essence of faith. And if faith is to enter us, it must be preceded by distress, which opens our ears to it.

Faith arising from distress may be called implicit faith; it operates within the heart alone, and is not visible to anyone else. It must then lead to explicit faith, which unfolds and manifests itself to others.

Explicit faith has two parts. The first part consists in learning. We want to find out about God. We want to penetrate his nature, both as he is now, and as he was on earth in the flesh. We think deeply about him, and we go and speak to those who have encountered him directly, and are filled with love for him.

Thus we find ourselves falling in love with God, rejoicing in the happiness with which he fills the heart. We take pleasure in meditating on him; and, as we grow to him, our joy is enhanced.

Now comes the second part of explicit faith. Having learned about our faith, we now want to tell others about it. We want to tell others what we have discovered about God, and to share with others the love that God has bestowed upon us. And our faith is so vibrant that we are able to speak with conviction and assurance. Our faith flows out of us with divine power and love, pouring itself at the feet of all we meet.

Nikolaus von Zinzendorf: Saving Faith

28

STRANGE WARMTH

John Wesley, after studying theology at Oxford University, set out for Georgia as a missionary to the native Americans. Yet despite his efforts to serve God, he was beset by guilt, and became convinced that his doctrinal knowledge was worthless. He returned to London, where a Moravian minister, Peter Boehler, taught him to trust God, and thus open his heart to him. This led to an experience that he regarded as his true conversion. He devoted the rest of his life to preaching, and to founding Methodist groups which nurtured similar experiences. He recorded his conversion in his journal:

I came to London, and met a man called Peter Boehler – a meeting that God had planned. Peter Boehler said to me that a true faith invariably has two fruits: dominion over sin, and a constant peace deriving from a sense of forgiveness. I was amazed at this notion, as if it were some new gospel. I said to myself that, if this man was right, I clearly lacked all faith. But I was not willing to admit this. So I argued with him, and tried to prove that faith can exist without these fruits.

That evening I went very unwillingly to a meeting in Aldersgate Street. At about a quarter to nine, while the preacher was describing the change that God makes in the heart through faith, I felt my heart strangely warmed. I felt I trusted Christ, and Christ alone, for my salvation; and an assurance was given to me that he had taken away my sins.

When I returned home, I was greatly buffeted by temptations; but I cried out to God, and they fled away – because Christ was now fighting on my behalf.

John Wesley: Journal

29

Spiritual sunshine

John grew up in a remote village in the far north of Russia, where his father assisted the priest at the local church. He won a place at the theological academy in St Petersburg, and then became priest in the nearby town of Cronstadt. His life was quiet and uneventful; but through his sermons, which were printed and circulated, his reputation as a spiritual guide steadily grew. Two Czars sought his counsel, and one called him to his deathbed. He also kept a spiritual diary, which is a series of short reflections:

Meditation is the living water by which the soul quenches its thirst. When you meditate, think of yourself as alone before God, and bring all your concerns into your relationship with God. Think of God in the world, as the soul is in the body – though he is infinitely higher than the world, and is not limited by it. Your body is small, and is wholly penetrated by the small soul; the world is large, and is wholly penetrated God.Although God already knows our needs, prayer and meditation are necessary for the cleansing and enlightenment of the soul. To meditate is to stand spiritually in the sunshine, feeling the warmth of God, and seeing the world in his light. If we are truly to enjoy life on earth, then through meditation we must learn to see the divine soul in all earthly things. Then we shall be both fully involved in earthly activities, and simultaneously transcend life on earth, rising upwards to our true and eternal dwelling place.

Meditation is necessary for our cold hearts to be warmed, for our hearts hardened by vanity to be softened by humility.

John of Cronstadt: My Life in Christ

30

Breath and Food for the Soul

When you are meditating, convince yourself that God is present, beside you and within you, and that he is hearing your every thought and sensing your every emotion. Speak to God with your whole heart; do not try to justify thoughts and feelings that are wrong. Have faith that your sincere repentance will evoke his forgiveness. And remember that you are a reflection of God.

It is easy to breathe the air around you, and easy to eat the food that is put before you. It is even easier for the soul to receive the love of God. Meditation is the spiritual equivalent of breathing and eating, and divine love is the air and food of the soul.

Meditation is a natural activity. It is the means by which you identify yourself with God, and God unites himself with you. God imbued you with reason, with emotions, and with free will. Thus with your reason, as an act of free will, you can direct your emotions towards him, and acknowledge your total dependence on him.

You will sometimes grow weary of meditating, because the image of yourself as a reflection of God grows dim in your mind, and so you feel alienated from him. Do not stop meditating; and as you continue, so the image will be refreshed.

Sometimes you will plunge into deadly darkness, and experience great anguish. Do not despair when this occurs. Remind yourself that, even if the divine light has ceased to be visible to you, it still shines. Let the darkness be an opportunity for deeper repentance; and soon your spiritual eyes will open once again.

John of Cronstadt: My Life in Christ

31

Enlightened from Within

Thomas a Kempis grew up in Cologne, and spent his adult life in the quiet seclusion of a monastery. He wrote a book of mystical advice for both monks and lay people, which included a prayer for enlightenment:

Dear God, enlighten me with the brightness of your inward light, and cast out all that is dark within my heart. Shed your grace on me from above, and bathe my heart in the dew of your mercy. Lift up my soul that is crushed under the weight of sins; and draw all my desires towards you alone. Let me taste the spiritual pleasures that you provide, that all the material pleasures may become like dust to me. Join me to yourself in the unbreakable bond of love, for you alone can satisfy my yearning for love – and without you life itself has no meaning.

Thomas a Kempis: Imitation of Christ

MONTH

11

ISLAM

Introduction

Origins

At the time of Muhammad's birth in 570 CE, Mecca was both the religious and the commercial center of the vast Arabian peninsula. The Arabs were mostly nomads, with herds of camels, and they came to Mecca both to worship at its Grand Mosque, and to buy the few luxuries that they could afford. Mecca had many wealthy merchants, who sent caravans northwards to buy and sell goods in such cosmopolitan cities as Jerusalem and Damascus; and it also had a body of hereditary religious leaders who exercised power in both spiritual and civil affairs.

Muhammad's family was related to the religious leadership, and had the minor role of supplying water for pilgrims to the Grand Mosque. His father died before he was born, and his mother died when he was aged eight, so an uncle raised him. As a young man he caught the attention of a widow, Khadija, who was a wealthy merchant; and she employed him to lead a caravan to Jerusalem. On this journey he met many Christians and Jews, including a Christian monk, whose ideas made a deep impression on him.

After his return to Mecca he and Khadija married, and he continued to lead caravans for her. But at the age of forty he abandoned this work, and spent much of his time thinking about religious matters. Then, while he was alone for a month on a mountain outside Mecca, he had a vision of the angel Gabriel, who gave him a series of messages from God, and ordered him to convey them to his people. At first he dreaded the ridicule he would encounter; but eventually he felt compelled to start reciting the messages.

TEACHINGS

The messages received by Muhammad on the mountain form the Quran. Its central theme is that there is one God, and that everyone must submit to him. Thus true religion is called Islam, which means 'submission' to God, and a person embracing Islam is a Muslim. Muhammad believed that God sends messengers to every nation in every age, and he recognized the teachings of both Moses and Jesus as divine. He also believed that the traditional Arabian religion was divinely inspired, but had been corrupted by hypocrisy; so he saw himself as a reformer.

The primary religious discipline, prescribed by Gabriel, is to pray five times a day; and Gabriel gave Muhammad the words that people should use in prayer. In addition people should fast during Ramadan, the month that Muhammad spent on the mountain; they should neither eat nor drink during daylight hours. And they should make a pilgrimage as frequently as they can afford; and the main place of pilgrimage is the Grand Mosque in Mecca.

The moral disciplines are equally simple and rigorous. People should be as generous to the poor as their means allow. They should care for their sick neighbors, and welcome strangers into their homes. They never speak harshly, and should readily praise the achievements of others. They should be faithful and tender in marriage. They should cherish all living beings as God's creatures. And they should be indifferent to power and wealth for their own sake, but desire only to do God's will.

Muhammad convinced many people in Mecca that he was God's messenger; but the religious leaders were violently opposed to him, seeing him as a threat to their position. Muhammad and his fellow Muslims were eventually forced to flee to the city of Medina in northern Arabia, where he won many more followers. He now turned himself into a military leader, and waged a war against the religious leaders of Mecca that lasted several years; and finally he marched into Mecca unopposed, and became ruler of all Arabia.

He died two years later in 632 CE. Political and religious leadership now passed to a series of deputies ***(caliphs)***; and the Arabs, united by Islam, became one of the most powerful and energetic military forces that the world has seen. Within a decade of Muhammad's death they had created an empire that controlled most of the Middle East from Palestine to Iran; and this soon extended westwards across north Africa into Spain, and eastwards into the Indian subcontinent. Guided by the principles of the Quran, and the example of Muhammad, Muslim political rule was generally benign and just, although often ruthless. Many in the conquered lands converted to Islam, and those refusing to convert merely had to pay an additional tax.

The caliphs that ruled from Baghdad, from the eighth to the thirteenth century, also encouraged scholarship and the arts. They commissioned Christian, Jewish and Greek scholars to translate the great works of philosophy into Arabic, and to engage in scientific research. And they commissioned craftsmen to build mosques of sublime beauty.

Us

Although we may not support a political party, we probably hold certain views about how a society should be organized and ruled; and we may never have tried to connect these political views to our spiritual attitudes and beliefs. Muhammad and his message challenge us to relate politics and religion. According to Islam God is just as concerned with how merchants conduct their business, judges dispense justice, and soldiers wage war, as with how people pray. Muhammad himself saw no conflict between his role as God's messenger, and his roles as military leader and then as ruler of the Arabian people.

Islam, as taught by Muhammad, allows us a high degree of economic freedom, but requires us to share the fruits of our economic activity with the poor and the sick. It allows rulers to wage war, but with the sole purpose of ensuring religious freedom – and never for the purpose of gaining wealth and power. And it requires everyone, regardless of creed, to be treated with respect. It is no coincidence that the Islamic empire at its height was, by the standards of the time, both tolerant and cultured.

1

A Christian monk's words

Mecca was the commercial center of the Arabian peninsula. Caravans arrived each day to sell their cargoes of precious goods. One of the richest merchants in the city was a widow called Khadija; and she organized caravans to take goods to and from Jerusalem.

She heard people speak well of the intelligence and honesty of a young man called Muhammad, and she invited him to lead one of her caravans; he accepted. As the caravan was approaching Jerusalem, Muhammad saw a monk sitting in a cave near the road. He stopped the caravan, and went to the cave. The monk was Christian, and Muhammad asked him many questions about his faith. The monk's answers impressed Muhammad. The monk then said to Muhammad: 'I can see that you are a messenger from God.'

When he reached Jerusalem, Muhammad sold the goods that he had brought from Arabia, and purchased other goods. And when he returned to Mecca, he handed these goods to Khadija, who sold them at twice the price he had paid. On seeing him again Khadija found herself feeling great love for Muhammad, and she asked him to marry her. He accepted, and his uncle Abu Talib arranged the wedding.

Muhammad thought deeply about the monk's words, wondering if they might be true; and after the wedding he related them to Khadija. She then went to a cousin, a Christian who had studied deeply the teachings of Jesus Christ, and asked whether the monk's words might be true. 'I have long expected God to send a messenger to our people,' the cousin said, 'and I believe that your husband is that person.'

Ibn Ishaq

2

THE ANGEL'S FIRST APPEARANCE

For several years Muhammad continued to lead caravans for Khadija; and she had three sons by him, all of whom died in infancy, and four daughters. But when he reached the age of forty Muhammad grew weary of traveling to and from Jerusalem, and began to spend much of his time alone. He frequently walked out of Mecca to remote hills and valleys; and he felt that every stone and tree was saying to him, 'Peace to you, messenger of God.'

One day, as he was sitting under a tree, he heard a voice. 'Muhammad,' the voice said, 'to each nation and to each generation I send a messenger, who speaks my words. Will you be my messenger to this nation at this time?' Muhammad know that the voice was God's; and without hesitation he replied, 'I will.'

Some time later Muhammad decided to spend the month of Ramadan on Mount Hira. When he was half way up, night fell, and he lay down to sleep. At midnight an angel came, and shook him. When he awoke, the angel said: 'I am Gabriel.' Then Gabriel unfolded a piece of cloth on which some words were written. 'Read!' Gabriel said. 'What shall I read?' Muhammad asked. 'Read the words that are written on this cloth,' Gabriel said. Muhammad looked at the cloth, and could see the words: 'God created all living beings, and he is full of compassion. He will write words that you are to remember, and then dictate to others; these words will conveys truths which the people have forgotten.'

As soon as Muhammad had read these words, Gabriel departed.

Ibn Ishaq

3

Divine messages

At first Muhammad was overjoyed at Gabriel's visit. But then he reflected on its implications. He had seen in Mecca several men who had declared themselves to be messengers of God, and were in a permanent state of ecstasy. Each one had spoken nonsense – and had been treated by most people with contempt. 'If I return to Mecca,' thought Muhammad, 'and say that I am God's messenger, people will treat me with contempt.' This prospect caused him such distress that he decided to go to the top of the mountain, and hurl himself off.

He ran upwards; but when he was about the kill himself, he heard a voice from the sky. 'Muhammad,' the voice said, 'you must not betray God.' He looked up and saw Gabriel, with his feet on either end of the horizon. Muhammad gazed at him for several minutes. Then he turned round; and in every direction he saw Gabriel, with his legs astride the horizon. His heart filled with fear, and he begged God to forgive him.

As he had intended, Muhammad remained on the mountain for a month. Gabriel came many times, and each time fresh words were written on his cloth. Muhammad memorized these words; and he repeated them constantly to himself, so he would not forget a single syllable.

At the end of the month he went back to Mecca, and wrote down what he had heard. He recited the words to Khadija, who knew at once that God was the author. But despite her encouragement, he did not dare recite them to anyone else.

Ibn Ishaq

4

God's love

The following year Muhammad again spent the month of Ramadan on Mount Hira, expecting the angel Gabriel to visit him again. For many days and nights the angel did not appear, and Muhammad wondered if God was angry with him for not having recited his message publicly. Then on the final night of the month, Gabriel came and sat beside Muhammad. 'Do not be anxious, Muhammad,' Gabriel said; 'having once loved you, God will never turn against you. On the contrary, year by year God will draw you closer to himself, so the future will always be better than the past. Eventually God will enter your heart, and then you will have the courage to recite his words to the people.'

For several minutes Gabriel sat in silence. Then he said: 'Your father died before you were born, and your mother died when you were a small child, did they not?' 'Yes,' Muhammad replied. 'Your uncle Abu Talib raised you as if you were his own son, did he not?' Gabriel asked. 'Yes,' Muhammad replied. 'Your wife provides you with every material comfort, does she not?' Gabriel asked. 'Yes,' Muhammed replied. 'Remember,' said Gabriel, 'that God arranged all these things, out of his love for you.'

For several more minutes Gabriel sat in silence. Then he said: 'When you are recognized as God's messenger, do not become proud of your position. Never be harsh to those weaker than yourself. And always give thanks to God for his kindness to you.'

Gabriel now disappeared. Muhammad returned to Mecca, but still spoke to no one apart from Khadija about his encounters with Gabriel.

Ibn Ishaq

5

How to pray

The following year Muhammad again spent the month of Ramadan on Mount Hira. The angel Gabriel arrived on the mountain at dawn two days before the end of the month, and demonstrated to Muhammad how to pray.

First Gabriel taught Muhammad the words that should be used: 'In the name of God, who is compassionate and merciful. All praise belongs to God, the lord of all being. He is compassionate and merciful, and he is our judge. We worship only you; in you alone we seek refuge. Guide us along the straight path, the path of those whom you have blessed – not the path of those who have incurred your wrath, not the path of those who have gone astray.' Gabriel said each phrase, and Muhammad repeated it, until Muhammad knew it by heart.

Then Gabriel told Muhammad that the prayer should be offered five times a day: at dawn, between the time when the sun begins to rise and it has fully risen; at noon, as the sun is beginning to decline; in the evening, when a person's shadow is equal in length to the person's height; at sunset, between the time when the sun starts to set and when it has fully set; and at night, when a third of the night has passed.

Gabriel showed Muhammad the posture for prayer: he laid a mat on the ground, and knelt down with his hands on the ground.

For two days and nights Gabriel prayed alongside Muhammad. Then he disappeared, and Muhammad returned to Mecca.

Ibn Ishaq

6

ALI'S CONVERSION

Muhammad went to see his young cousin Ali, and invited him to pray with him in the manner that Gabriel had taught. Ali greatly enjoyed praying with Muhammad, and was happy to meet Muhammad for prayer five times a day at the times which Gabriel had specified. Muhammad then recited to Ali all the messages that Gabriel had given to him. Ali wept with joy at what he heard.

One day Muhammad's uncle Abu Talib found Muhammad and Ali praying together. He asked Muhammad what religion they were practicing. 'Uncle,' Muhammad replied, 'this is the religion of God and his angels; it is the religion of Abraham and Jesus Christ; it is the religion of all God's messengers through the ages. God has now appointed me as messenger; and you of all people, who has treated me like your own son, deserve to learn the truth from me.'

'My dear nephew,' Abu Talib replied, 'I cannot give up the religion which has been handed to me by my forefathers. But I pray to God that as long as you live, you will not suffer for your faith.' 'My faith,' Muhammad protested, 'is the essence of the religion which your forefathers taught – it is the ancient religion purified of all the hypocrisy and idolatry that corrupts it.' 'I am too old to change my ways,' Abu Talib replied.

Then Abu Talib turned to Ali. 'Do you share your cousin's religion?' he asked. 'Yes,' Ali replied, 'I know that Muhammad's teaching is from God.' 'Muhammad would not ask you to do anything that was not good,' Abu Talib replied; 'stick with him.'

Ibn Ishaq

7

THE FIRST PUBLIC GATHERING

Muhammad now went to a prosperous merchant called Abu Bakr, and recited to him the messages he had received from the angel Gabriel. Abu Bakr was renowned for his courtesy and charm, and also for his knowledge of Arab history and religion. At first Abu Bakr was skeptical as to whether Muhammad's words truly came from God; but by the time Muhammad had finished, he was convinced that Muhammad was indeed God's messenger – and wept with joy.

Many people came to see Abu Bakr for advice on both commercial and matters; and now Abu Bakr told all his visitors about Muhammad. Some of them asked to hear Muhammad themselves; so Abu Bakr organized a meeting at his house, to which eight people came. Muhammad recited the messages, and taught them how to pray. By the end of the meeting they urged him to speak publicly. 'I am frightened,' Muhammad confessed, 'because the leaders of our ancient religion will surely oppose me. And the more people recognize me as God's messenger, the more angry the religious leaders will become.' 'I shall do my best to protect you,' Abu Bakr said.

In the center of Mecca was a large place of worship, called the Grand Mosque. The religious leaders met there every day, and conducted various rituals. Abu Bakr sent a message throughout the city that on a certain day Muhammad would come to the Grand Mosque, and recite messages from God. Since Abu Bakr was so popular, the religious leaders did not dare stop the meeting. And on the appointed day a large crowd gathered.

Ibn Ishaq

8

True religion

These are the words that Muhammad recited:

Your God is one God. There is no god but him. He is merciful and compassionate.

There are many signs of God for men and women who open their eyes to them. There is the creation of the earth and the sky. There is the alternation of day and night. There are the ships sailing the ocean with cargoes that bring pleasure. There is the gift of sleep, by which God revives weary bodies and minds. There is the rain that God sends down from the sky, by which he revives the barren earth and nourishes the creatures living on the earth. And there are the changing winds, which drive the clouds through the atmosphere between earth and sky.

Religion does not consist in whether you face east or west during worship. True religion consists in this: trusting God and praying to him; obeying his commandments; sharing your wealth with your relatives, with orphans, and with the poor; caring for the sick; welcoming strangers into your home; ransoming slaves; keeping your promises; and remaining steadfast in times of distress and adversity. By practicing true religion you honor God.

True religion consists in upholding justice; always telling the truth, even if it puts you in a bad light; showing equal respect to the rich and poor; controlling your emotions; speaking gently, and never using harsh words; and forgiving those who have wronged you. Remember, God knows all that you think and do.

Quran

9

Hypocrites

Avoid those people for whom religion is a hobby, an idle pastime, and whose real interest is in accumulating wealth, glory and power for themselves. They pretend to honor God, but in fact they want only to honor themselves. Avoid those people who claim to love peace, but relish sowing the seeds of conflict and distrust. They pretend to be good, but in fact their hearts are full of evil. Avoid those people who are constantly pointing out contradictions between one person's religion and another's, but ignore the similarities. They pretend to be seeking the truth, but in fact they want to show off their own cleverness. All these people are hypocrites.

Hypocrites exchange guidance for error, the right path for the wrong path. They kindle the fire of faith, but as soon as it starts to emit light and warmth, they smother it and put it out. In their pride they imagine they can look directly on the face of God, but they are blinded by his light.

These hypocrites treat God's messengers with contempt. They say to God's messengers: 'We shall not believe you until you make a fountain spring from the earth before our eyes, or cause streams to reverse their course and flow uphill, or build a house of gold, or fly up into the sky.' When God's messengers say that they can do none of these things, the hypocrites laugh.

And if a messenger from God does not come from a noble family, they say: 'God would only choose a nobleman to convey the truth.'

Quran

10

DEVOUT PEOPLE

Devout people have always fasted, as a means of guarding themselves against evil; and you too must fast. You should fast throughout the month of Ramadan, eating and drinking nothing from dawn until dusk. The month of Ramadan was the time when God revealed his messages to his messenger. But if you are sick, or on a long journey, you may fast the same number of days later on; God does not want to make you ill or weak through fasting, but desires your health and comfort. Set aside the food that you save during the month of fasting, and give it to the poor. Fasting does you great good – but helping others does you even greater good.

Devout people have always made pilgrimages, as a means of reminding themselves of the truth; and you too must be pilgrims. Wherever you live, you should strive to make a pilgrimage each year, so you can meditate on God and his messages. When you begin the pilgrimage, shave your head; and during the pilgrimage abstain from sexual intercourse, obscene language and quarrelling. Provide well for the journey, so that you are not a burden of those you pass; but the best provision is devotion to God. If sickness or any other cause prevents you from making the pilgrimage, then give the fruits of a month's work to the poor.

Devout people always pray at the times specified for prayer. They stop whatever they are doing, kneel down, and say the prayer which God himself has taught. And when they have finished praying, they rise up, and resume whatever they were doing.

Quran

11

GENEROSITY

If you use your wealth in the service of God and other people, you are like a grain of corn that sprouts seven ears, each of which bears a hundred grains. God is abundantly generous to those who are generous; he knows all.

If you use your wealth in the service of God and other people, do not mar your generosity with reproaches and rebukes. The giver is not superior to the receiver, and so has no right to pass judgment on the receiver. Do not mar your generosity with pride. The giver who boasts of the size of the gift, and is eager for gratitude and admiration, is no better than a miser. And do not mar your generosity with resentment. The resentful giver puts a burden of guilt on the receiver, while the joyful giver makes the receiver joyful – and thus bestows a double gift.

A kind word of encouragement, or a selfless word of praise, or a gentle word of forgiveness, is worth far more than a material gift accompanied by insults.

Be generous with your wealth and your words from a desire to please God and to please others – then you will like an orchard that yields abundant fruit. Men and women who give generously with sincere hearts, and ask nothing in return, will be repaid double by God; they will enjoy perfect happiness for all eternity.

Be wise and shrewd in your generosity, so the receivers enjoy the greatest benefit. And do not be so generous that you reduce yourself to penury, and thus depend on the generosity of others – as that will cancel all the good you have done.

Quran

12

Different religions

There are many names for God, and all are equally good. Whenever you speak about God, whichever name you use, speak with reverence and piety. Never abuse a name of God, and keep away from those that do abuse his names. Any of God's names is like a healing balm for the soul: it brings tranquility to the soul in turmoil, and serenity to the soul in distress.

Let there be no compulsion in religion. People cannot be forced to follow the right path; they cannot be forced to renounce idols and worship God. Each person should be free to choose between right and wrong, between the true God and false gods.

God has ordained a form of worship for every nation. There is one way to God, but many different means of following that way; and God gives a different means according to people's customs and needs. If God lacked patience with people's differences – with their peculiarities – then everyone would be damned. But God is infinitely patience, and wants all people to come to him.

God's light can be found in every place of worship in every nation. Wherever people worship God and meditate upon him, his light shines – and nothing can snuff out his light. So every place of worship is sacred, and should be treated with reverence and piety.

God cares not just for every nation, but also for every variety of living being. He provides for animals and insects, birds and fish, just as he provides for you.

Quran

13

Fortune

When people are blessed with good fortune, they say: 'This is from God.' And when misfortune occurs, they blame other human beings. It is true that, when you are blessed with good fortune, it is from God; but when misfortune occurs, you should ask yourself what you have done wrong.

Some people claim to serve God, yet stand on the edge of genuine faith. When they are blessed with good fortune, they are content. But when misfortune occurs, they are angry with God, and turn their backs on him – and sometimes they turn to other gods, who can neither help nor harm them. These people are cheating themselves; by their inconsistency they are denying themselves the inner peace and the freedom from anxiety that true faith brings.

When a ship enters a storm, and the sailors are anxious that it will capsize, they pray to every kind of god; but only God listens to their prayers. When they return to dry land, they rarely remember to thank God for saving them. Are you ungrateful for the many blessings that God has bestowed on you? Remember, whenever God pleases, he can calm the winds, so ships lie motionless in the bosom of the ocean; and he can make the winds rage, so ships are hurled onto rocks.

If you wish to gain God's favor, pray to him, and trust him; avoid sinning against others; be quick to forgive those who sin against you; take advice from people wiser than yourself; and when injustices occur, strive to restore justice.

Quran

14

BEATITUDES

Blessed are the faithful, who are humble in their prayers.

Blessed are those whose speech is always gentle and kind, and who never speak harshly to others.

Blessed are those whose sexual activities are confined within marriage, and who have no desire to commit adultery.

Blessed are those who are worthy of trust, who keep their promises, and fulfill all their duties and obligations.

Blessed are those who strive to honor God in all they do, who believe in his messages, and who worship only him.

Blessed are those who give food to the hungry, drink to the thirsty, clothing to those in rags, and shelter to the homeless.

Blessed are those who are indifferent to the power and wealth that the world can confer, and who want only God's favor.

Blessed are those who are regular in their prayers, who fast at the appointed times, and who make pilgrimages.

Blessed are those who take no pride in their own wisdom or intelligence, and are always eager to learn from others.

Remember that God requires nothing of people that is beyond the strength and abilities that he has given them.

Quran

15

God's creation

It is God who created human beings from dust, and divided them into men and women. No woman conceives without his knowledge and approval. No one grows old and dies, except in accordance with his decree. How can you turn away from him?

It is God who turns night into day, and day into night. He kindles the light of dawn; and at dusk he extinguishes the light so that we can rest. How can you turn away from him?

It is God who put the stars in the sky at night, to give light and guidance to those who travel. It is God who makes the moon wax and wane, so that we can count the months. How can you turn away from him?

It is God who causes the grain and the fruit stone to germinate. It is God who sends rain from the sky, causing the grain to swell, the palm trees to yield dates, the vines to yield grapes, and the olive trees to bear olives. How can you turn away from him?

It is God who makes the rivers and lakes fresh and sweet, and the sea salty and bitter. It is God who fills them with fish that you can catch and eat. How can you turn away from him?

It is God who told the bees to make their homes in the hives that you build, and to feed on every kind of blossom, so that they provide honey to nourish you and heal you from sickness. How can you turn away from him?

No mortal eye can see him, but he created all that you see.

Quran

16

Injury and Forgiveness

God sees all that happens, he hears all that is spoken, and he discerns every thought. If three people talk in secret, he is the fourth. If people plot some evil deed, not a single detail is hidden from him. If malice and hatred stir people's hearts and inspire their actions, they cannot deceive him into believing that their motives are pure. So only use words of which God approves; only make plans that accord with his commandments; and act only with the intention of doing good.

When someone injures you or a member of your family, you may retaliate. But it is far better to go to that person, ask for an apology, and offer forgiveness. Then their guilt and grief will be so great that they will mend their ways. Retaliation is a means of protecting yourself, but forgiveness ensures that no protection is needed.

When you cause injury, whether deliberately or by accident, go immediately to your victim, and seek forgiveness; offer compensation in a spirit of humility and friendship, and strive to make amends.

To endure suffering with fortitude, to forgive those who have wronged you, and to put right the wrongs which you have done – these are the marks of a true follower of God.

To God belongs the earth and all that live on it, the ocean and all that swim in it, and the atmosphere and all that fly through it. He creates whatever he wishes, and destroys whatever he wishes. He bestows male offspring as he chooses, and female offspring as he chooses. God is mighty, and controls all; he is wise, and understands all.

Quran

17

TRUE RELIGION

Many people enjoy speculating about God and about every kind of supernatural being. They invent all kinds of theories and conjectures; some even claim to have calculated the number of angels, and the sex of every angel. On the basis of their theories and conjectures they invent new religions, and appoint themselves as leaders; and they urge people to follow them.

No one can know anything about God except what God chooses to reveal. God reveals himself through what he has created, and through the messages he gives to his messengers. How do you know whether a messenger is genuine, and whether his messages come from God? Search your own hearts. If the messages accord with what your heart already knows to be true, then the messenger is genuine, and his messages come from God. But if the messages contradict what your heart knows, then the messenger is false, and his messages are based on his own theories and conjectures.

I am a messenger sent by God, and I speak only the words that he has given me. Test me by looking into your own hearts. Those who oppose me, and say that my messages are false, are blinded by pride and stubbornness. I do not invent any new religion; my messages are no different from those of every true messenger of God.

God created you. He gave you hearts with which to discern the truth, minds with which to reflect upon the truth, and language with which to understand the truth. Use your hearts to discern, and your minds to reflect upon, the truth of all that I say.

Quran

18

True servants of God

True servants of God are those who walk the earth in humility; who, when they are confronted by hostile people, wish them peace; who, when they are accosted by ignorant people, offer to tell them what they know about God; and who, when they encounter wise people, ask their advice.

True servants of God are those who are neither extravagant or stingy, but are generous according to their means; who, when they sell goods, use honest scales and give full measure; and who keep their promises.

True servants of God are those who never mock other people, but treat all people with respect; who never despise other people, but treat all people as equal; and who never scoff at what other people say, but listen with care and reply with courtesy.

True servants of God are those who never tell lies, but always speak honestly; who never slander others or pass on idle gossip; and who never lose their composure when others insult them.

True servants of God are those who trust others, unless they have good reason not to trust them; who do not spy on others, unless they have good reason for suspicion; and who never call others by rude names.

True servants of God are those who never commit adultery, and are faithful to their spouses; who never abuse their children, but encourage and guide them in the ways of God; who honor their parents, and care for them when they grow old.

True servants of God are 'Muslims' – they have submitted to God.

Quran

19

MUHAMMAD'S POPULARITY

When Muhammad had finished speaking, many people were weeping with joy. But the religious leaders were furious. In their hearts they knew that Muhammad's words came from God; but they feared that, if the common people acknowledged Muhammad as God's messenger, they would lose their power and prestige.

So the following day they went to Abu Talib, Muhammad's uncle. 'If your nephew continues to preach,' they said, 'he will divide our people: some will become Muslims, while others will remain loyal to our traditional religion. You must persuade him to desist – or else we shall have to put him to death.' Abu Talib went to Muhammad, and urged him, for the sake of preserving peace, to stop preaching. 'Uncle,' Muhammad replied, 'I love you as much as my own wife. But if the religious leaders threatened to hurl both the sun and the moon at my head, I should not give up.' A tear trickled down the old man's cheek. 'You must do as God guides you,' he said, putting his hand on Muhammad's shoulder; 'I shall never abandon you.'

Muhammad went each week to the Grand Mosque in the center of Mecca, and recited God's messages. Not only did inhabitants of the city come to hear him, but so also did merchants who were visiting Mecca from other parts of Arabia and beyond; so news of Muhammad quickly spread. Most of his listeners were convinced that his messages were genuine, and became Muslims – and, to the even greater fury of the religious leaders, many people hoped that the whole Arab people would unite under his leadership.

Ibn Ishaq

20

Persecution and Bribery

Muhammad's popularity was now so great that the religious leaders did not dare murder him; they knew that the people would blame them for his death, and turn against them. So they decided to attack his followers, who were still a minority of the whole population of Mecca. They issued a decree making it illegal to buy goods from, or sell goods to, Muslims; in this way they hoped that the Muslims would quickly be reduced to poverty, and would turn against him. But even loyal adherents of the traditional religion regarded this decree as unjust, since the Muslims had done nothing wrong; and they refused to obey it.

The religious leaders now decided to try and bribe Muhammad. A group of them went to his house, and said: 'If you want money, we shall make you the richest man in all Arabia. If you want power, we shall make you the senior religious leader, so that every decision will require your approval. And if you want good health, we shall obtain the best physician's to treat your every illness.' Muhammad smiled, and replied that nothing except death itself would stop him reciting God's messages.

When the group reported Muhammad's answer, one of the religious leaders, called Utba, ran to the market and purchased a sword. Then he went to Muhammad's house, and shouted: 'I have come to stop you preaching.' Muhammad invited him in, and said: 'Before you kill me, let me first recite to you God's messages.' Utba agreed; and by the time Muhammad had finished, Utba was weeping with joy.

Ibn Ishaq

21

GRIEF, DESPAIR, HOPE AND JOY

When Muhammad was aged forty-nine, both his wife Khadija and his uncle Abu Talib died. Khadija had never wavered in her conviction that Muhammad was God's messenger; and, whenever he had felt discouraged by the opposition to him, she had comforted him. Even at his death Abu Talib remained loyal to the old religion; but his love for his nephew remained strong, and he supported his right to speak freely. So Muhammad was overwhelmed with grief.

A number of people from a town to the east of Mecca had become Muslims; and Muhammad decided to go to that town, in the hope of gaining more. The head of the town allowed him to recite God's messages in the market place. But Muhammad's grief at the loss of his wife and uncle was still so great, that his voice was weak and his words jumbled. At the end the head declared: 'Surely a messenger of God would be a more impressive man than you are.' And he ordered Muhammad to be driven away.

A group of young men started hurling stones at Muhammad. He ran away, and they ran after him; he outpaced them, and hid in an orchard outside the town. His grief now turned to despair, and he begged God to appoint someone else as his messenger. A young Christian slave was working in the orchard, and saw Muhammad. He went over to him, and asked him his name. When Muhammad told him, the Christian slave declared: 'You are the spiritual brother of my master Jesus Christ. I thank God daily for you.' With these words hope and joy returned to Muhammad's heart.

Ibn Ishaq

22

DECISION TO EMIGRATE

To the north of Mecca lay the city of Medina, where for many years two clans had vied for supremacy. When chiefs from one of the clans were visiting Mecca, Muhammad went to see them. 'The rancor between the two clans weakens your city,' Muhammad said; 'but if there was peace, Medina could overtake Mecca in power and prestige.' The chiefs asked Muhammad how peace could be achieved. 'Let me come to Medina, and recite God's messages,' Muhammad replied; 'and if people from both clans acknowledge me as God's messengers, then the clans will be united by their common faith.'

The chiefs agreed, and Muhammad went with them to their city. At first the chiefs of the other clan were suspicious of Muhammad, fearing that he would use his eloquence on behalf of their rivals. But when Muhammad began to recite God's messages in the market place, the chiefs and people of both clans were convinced of the truth of his words. Thus Medina was at peace.

In the meantime the religious leaders in Mecca had ordered their servants to injure and kill Muslims at every opportunity. Muhammad thus asked the chiefs in Medina if the Muslims in Mecca could take refuge in their city; and the Medina chiefs readily agreed. Muhammad thus returned to Mecca in order to organize the emigration. He knew that the religious leaders would try to prevent the Muslims from leaving, for fear that they would recruit an army in Medina and attack them; so the Muslims would have to travel under the cover of darkness.

Ibn Ishaq

23

Arrival in Medina

Each day Muhammad visited a small number of Muslims, ordered them to pack their possessions on the backs of camels and donkeys, and leave Mecca six hours after darkness had fallen. Thus night by night groups of Muslims slipped out of the city, and traveled northwards. A few were spotted by supporters of the religious leaders, and were attacked and killed. But most were safe, and assembled by a stream outside Medina. Finally when every other Muslim had departed, Muhammad himself left, riding a camel.

When Muhammad arrived in Medina, he led the Meccan Muslims into the city; and people from both clans greeted him with rapture. Several wealthy merchants begged him to stay in their homes; but Muhammad replied that he would live wherever his camel stopped. The camel continued through the main street of the city until it reached a building used for storing dates; then it stopped, and knelt down. Muhammad climbed off, and declared that a place of worship – a mosque, like the one in Mecca – should be constructed on the site of the date store, with a small house for himself beside it. The owners of the date store were delighted to give it to him; and the following day the Muslims of both Mecca and Medina started to build the mosque and a house.

When the mosque was complete, Muhammad ordered that a tower be built beside it. Five times a day, at the moments specified by Gabriel, a man climbed up the tower and blew a trumpet, to remind people to pray. As soon as the trumpet sounded, all activity in Medina ceased, and people knelt down to offer the prayer that Gabriel had taught.

Ibn Ishaq

24

Prayer and War

After a month Muhammad grew weary of the sound of the trumpet, and decided that a drum should be used instead. But he soon grew weary of this as well; and he asked God for guidance on the best way of calling people to prayer.

The following day a man named Abdullah visited Muhammad, and told him that he had dreamt that night of a human voice calling people to prayer. 'What did the voice say?' Muhammad asked. The man repeated what he had heard: 'God is great. I bear witness that there is no god but God, and that Muhammad is his messenger. Kneel in prayer. Kneel in prayer. God is great. There is no god but God.' Muhammad knew at once that God had composed those words; and he ordered them to be used wherever Muslims live.

Although the religious leaders in Mecca feared that Muhammad would recruit an army, this had not been Muhammad's intention. But he now received a message from God, giving Muslims permission to take up arms against their enemies. The message contained four conditions: they should attack only those who actively persecute them; they should never fight for the sake of gaining wealth or power; they should never exploit or oppress those whom they vanquish; and they should live in peace with anyone who allows them to practice their religion fully and freely.

So Muhammad began to recruit men to serve as soldiers. And, in order to gain experience in fighting, Muhammad decided to attack a caravan owned by merchants in Mecca, led by a religious leader called Abu Sufyan.

Ibn Ishaq

25

THE FIRST BATTLE

A few of the clan leaders in Medina resented the authority that Muhammad now wielded in the city; and they sent a message to Abu Sufyan, warning him that Muhammad intended to attack the caravan. Abu Sufyan then sent a message to the merchants and religious leaders in Mecca, urging them to send an army to protect the caravan. A religious leader called Abu Jahl, who had a violent loathing for Muhammad, recruited an army, and rode towards the caravan.

In the meantime Muhammad and his warriors rode to Badr, a place in the desert that the caravan was likely to pass. As the caravan approached Badr, it crossed a track that Muhammad's army had followed. Abu Sufyan noticed camel dung on the track, and he broke a lump into pieces. 'This contains date stones,' he exclaimed; 'only the people of Medina feed dates to their camels.' Since the dung was fresh, he concluded that Muhammad was near; so he took a long detour, and reached Mecca safely.

Abu Jahl and his army now arrived at Badr, and saw Muhammad's army camped nearby. A messenger had informed him that the caravan had reached Mecca; but Abu Jahl was determined to defeat and kill Muhammad. So at dawn on the following day Abu Jahl and his army attacked. Muhammad had anticipated this, and his men were ready. As Abu Jahl's men approached, Muhammad's men let off several volleys of arrows; and then they fought with great courage. By dusk Abu Jahl and most his men were dead, and the remainder were Muhammad's prisoners.

Ibn Ishaq

26

Mercy on the Enemy

Most of Muhammad's warriors wanted to slaughter the prisoners, but Muhammad insisted that they be taken back to Medina. 'We must never allow the desire for revenge to cloud our hearts', he declared; 'besides, the prisoners' families will pay a large ransom for their return.'

Muhammad ordered that graves should be dug, both for those on his own side who had died, and also for his dead enemies. And then over each grave he offered prayers. 'Why do you pray for your enemies, as well as your friends?' one of his men asked. 'All of us are sinners,' Muhamad replied, 'so all of us depend on the mercy of God.' Then he led his men and their prisoners back to Medina.

Meanwhile in Mecca the religious leaders and merchants were horrified at Abu Jahl's defeat. They persuaded Abu Sufyan to raise another army to attack Medina. Abu Sufyan could not find enough volunteers within Mecca; so a tax was imposed on the people of Mecca, and the money was used to employ warriors from other parts of Arabia and Ethiopia. Abu Sufyan also insisted that the warriors bring their wives, as this would prevent them from running away.

When Muhammad heard that an army from Mecca was approaching Medina, his initial plan was to remain in the city and defend it. But many of his warriors said that this would be interpreted as a sign of weakness and cowardice, and persuaded Muhammad to march out and attack the Meccan army.

Ibn Ishaq

27

VICTORY BY DECEIT

Muhammad's army was far smaller than that of Abu Sufyan; and as the two armies drew close, Muhammad knew that he and his men should turn back – but he was too proud to give the order. As a result most of his warriors were killed, and he was badly injured, losing several of his teeth.

When Muhammad and the other survivors returned, he urged the people of Medina to dig a deep trench around its perimeter; and he worked hard alongside them. So when Abu Sufyan arrived, he realized he would have to besiege the city. The siege lasted many months. The people of Medina had sufficient food; their only hardship was they could not go outside the city to defecate, so the city became quite smelly. But Abu Sufyan had not anticipated a siege, and had not brought sufficient supplies; so his warriors and their wives grew steadily hungrier.

One of Abu Sufyan's warriors, called Nuaym, was secretly a Muslim, and had joined Abu Sufyan's army with the intention of subverting it. Nuaym crossed the trench one night, and came to Muhammad. 'How can I help you?' he asked. 'It is better to win a war by deceit than by fighting,' Muhammad replied. Then he told Nuaym to go to Abu Sufyan, and inform him that his Ethiopian warriors, who were Jewish and Christian, were about to betray him, and join the Muslims.

The next morning Nuaym did as Muhammad instructed; and, fearing for his own life, Abu Sufyan ordered his army to return to Mecca.

Ibn Ishaq

28

A WICKED RUMOR

Muhammad led many expeditions attacking and seizing caravans owned by merchants and religious leaders in Mecca, in the hope of wearing down resistance to him. And on many expeditions he took his young wife Aisha, whom he had married after arriving in Medina.

Aisha traveled in a howdah on top of a camel, to shelter her from the sun. One morning, as they were returning from an expedition, Aisha realized that she had lost a necklace, and went back to the place where they had been camping to look for it. No one realized that she was not in her howdah, and the men with her camel moved on, leaving her behind. One of the members of the expedition, a handsome young man called Safwan, had fallen behind the main group, and was hurrying to catch up. He was astonished to find Aisha sitting alone by the track; he lifted her onto his camel, and walked beside her.

When they arrived back at Medina, a rumor began to spread that Aisha and Safwan had deliberately contrived to meet, and were conducting an affair. When Muhammad heard the rumor, he foolishly believed it, and ordered Aisha out of his house. She returned to her parents; and her distress was so great that she fell dangerously ill.

At first Muhammad had no compassion for her. But he found himself missing her deeply, and eventually he went to see her. He urged her to repent of what she had done, and promised to take her back if she did so. 'I cannot repent of a sin I have not committed,' she cried; 'I would rather die than lie to you.' Muhammad knew at once she was innocent, and took her back. Within a few days she recovered.

Ibh Ishaq

29

THE NEW ORDER

As news of Muhammad's victories reached Mecca, many people concluded that he had divine support, and wanted him to be their ruler; and even some of the religious leaders wanted to make peace with him. So eight years after his arrival in Medina, Muhammad declared his intention to return to his native city. 'I shall go as a pilgrim to the Grand Mosque,' he said to the Muslims in Medina, 'and I invite you to come with me. We shall treat the people of Mecca with courtesy and respect, and fight only against those who fight against us.'

Thus Muhammad led a large body of men, women and children southwards to Mecca. When they entered the city, even his implacable enemies saw that resistance was pointless. Muhammad rode into the Grand Mosque, followed by all the Muslims and most of the inhabitants of Mecca. He ordered everyone to kneel, and offered thanks to God that peace was now restored.

Then he spoke in a loud, clear voice: 'There is no god but God. He has fulfilled his promise by making his messenger your ruler. I hereby abolish all religious leadership in Mecca, and all privileges associated with it. God alone is our leader, and his messages are our guide. God created all people from dust, so in his eyes all are equal.'

He turned to the religious leaders, and asked them if they wished to speak. The oldest one replied: 'We trust you, and we believe you will be kind and merciful to us and to all the people of Mecca.'

Ibn Ishaq

30

Decision to die

Throughout Arabia people had been waiting for the outcome of Muhammad's conflict with the religious leaders in Mecca, before making up their minds about Islam. When they heard of his triumph, they concluded that his claim to be God's messenger must be true; and leaders came from every part of Arabia to pledge their allegiance to Muhammad and the divine messages that he had revealed.

Muhammad ruled in Mecca for two years. Although all the people were now Muslim, they still had disputes and quarrels; and they asked Muhammad to resolve them. Then at the age of sixty-two he began to suffer severe aches in his head. One evening, as he lay on his bed, an angel came to him, and said: 'God is giving you a choice. You may survive into old age, and continue to bear the burden of ruling Arabia; or you may die, and enter the realm of eternal peace and happiness immediately.' 'My task as God's messenger is complete,' Muhammad replied, 'and I am weary of ruling. So let me die now.'

He called his wife Aisha. 'Would it distress you if you were to die before me, so that I might wrap you in a shroud, pray over you and bury you?' he asked her. She was perplexed by the question, but replied: 'If I were to die before you, then you would quickly find yourself a new wife, and forget about me. But if you were to die before me, then I should remember you and mourn for you until the day of my own death.'

Muhammad embraced her, and said: 'You are a truly good person, whereas I am merely someone who does God's will. May you live until you are old, and be an inspiration to many.'

Ibn Ishaq

31

MUHAMMAD'S DEATH

Although his head was aching so badly that he could barely think, he went to the Grand Mosque to speak to the people for the last time.

'When I am dead,' Muhammad said, 'do not turn me into an object of worship. Worship God alone; he will never die. Give honor to God in all you do, praise God for all you see and hear, and thank God for everything that happens to you. Remember that God created all living beings from dust, and he has ordained their destinies. God is one; God is eternal. He gives birth to all, but no one gave birth to him. He has no rivals.'

With these words Muhammad fell silent. He walked slowly from the Mosque, with Aisha supporting him. When he lay on his bed, he said to Aisha: 'My soul is now ready to leave my body.' Then he lost consciousness. She held his head in her arms, and a few moments later he died.

Ibn Ishaq

MONTH

12

SUFISM AND SIKHISM

Introduction

Origins

The territories to the north of Arabia, which formed the heart of the Muslim empire after the death of Muhammad, had contained hundreds of Christian monasteries, in which monks and nuns had devoted themselves to attaining mystical union with God; and around every monastery there were usually many hermits, whose devotion was even more intense. Only a few of these monasteries survived; but the spirit of the monastic life became one of the most powerful and creative currents within Islam – and came to be called Sufism.

The term 'Sufi', derived from the Arab word for wool, refers to the rough woolen robes that Muslim mystics typically wore, which were similar to those worn by Christian monks. Sufis claimed that Muhammad himself was a mystic; and Ibn Ishaq's biography records that a Christian hermit first opened Muhammad's mind to spiritual matters. But as a distinct movement Sufism emerged about a century after Muhammad's death. Unlike conventional Islam, in which leadership was entirely in male hands, Sufism regarded men and women as spiritually equal; and one of the first Sufi teachers was a woman, Rabia, who died in about 800 CE.

In the early centuries Sufism had no formal organization. Anyone was free to adopt the Sufi robe, live simply, and practice contemplation; and it seems that many men and women chose to do this. Some went to live alone in caves, while others built huts for themselves within towns and villages. People sought out Sufis for spiritual advice, and a few Sufis became famous for their teachings and exploits.

Very soon after the death of Muhammad a hierarchy of preachers and theologians grew up within Islam, who formulated precise doctrines and moral laws. And they asserted that Muhammad was the final prophet – the last person in history with whom God would communicate directly. Sufism, by contrast, was based on the conviction that anyone can communicate with God, and that God is present within every human heart. Indeed, the great Sufi Hallaj claimed that every man and woman is God; and the defenders of Muslim orthodoxy crucified him as a heretic.

Sufi teaching is practical, rather than theological, offering spiritual and moral guidance that enables people to discover God for themselves. First, Sufis should restrain their material desires, in order to give their whole attention to the spiritual realm. Some Sufis married, although many decided to remain celibate; but all lived frugally. Secondly, Sufis should love all people, and forgive their persecutors and enemies. Most Sufis believed that God is also present in animals, birds and insects, so they too should be loved. Thirdly, Sufis should learn to give thanks, even when misfortune and illness befalls them.

Most controversially, Sufism taught that theological knowledge is useless, and that the only genuine knowledge is the perception of God in himself. One of the greatest Sufis, Ghazali, was the leading theologian of his time; but he abandoned his post when he realized that he was merely speculating about God – and that mysticism alone can bring certainty.

EXPRESSION

By the eleventh and twelfth centuries CE orders of Sufis began to be formed. Typically an order began when a community of Sufis gathered round a charismatic teacher ***(shaykh)***; then, as the shaykh was dying, the members asked him to appoint a successor – and so the community continued.

The most famous of these orders was the Mevlevi, commonly known as the 'whirling dervishes', founded by Rumi. They developed an elaborate dance around their shaykh symbolizing the rotation of the planets round the sun. As they moved, they stretched out their arms, with their right hands turned upwards to receive divine blessings, and their left hands turned downwards to bestow blessings on the earth. They dressed in long pleated robes, representing burial shrouds, and conical hats, representing tombstones; thus symbolically they were dying to life, in order to enter ecstatic union with God. The tempo of the music gradually increased until they all collapsed in giddy exhaustion.

In addition to transmitting spiritual teaching from one generation to another, the Sufi orders also became a major missionary force. One Sufi order took Islam to west Africa, another to southern Egypt and the Sudan, and another to east Asia. Even in India, where Islam initially appeared through military conquest, Sufis played a large part in winning the adherence of people in the countryside and small towns. The combination of Sufi and Hindu wisdom inspired a young man in northern India, Nanak, to compose hymns that tried to express the essence of all religion. He acquired a growing band of disciples who became known as Sikhs.

Us

At its outset Islam was based on a clear and unambiguous dogmatic assertion: that the Quran was dictated to Muhammad by God himself. For this reason Islam appears the most dogmatic of all the world's religions. But paradoxically Sufism, spawned by Islam, is one of the least dogmatic of religious movements; it appeals to personal experience, not to intellectual belief. Most of the great Sufis were themselves devout Muslims, and did not question the central dogma of their faith; but they attached little importance to it, and did not require others to embrace it. Without doubt the Sufi influence made the Muslim empire remarkably tolerant of religious diversity.

If we are able to believe the dogmas of a particular religion, this may give us great peace of mind. But Sufism and Sikhism tell us that it will not bring wisdom, nor will it bring knowledge of God. And if we are not able – or do not wish – to accept any dogmas, they tell us that this does not exclude us from the highest spiritual experience. The conviction lying at the heart of Sufism and Sikhism, that God is present in all people, is shared by every religion; yet, far from being a dogma, it is an invitation to join a journey of discovery – an invitation to follow the Way.

1

FRIENDSHIP WITH ANIMALS

One of the first Sufi mystics was a woman called Rabia, who lived in Basra. When she was a young woman, there was a terrible famine; and in order to feed their other children, her parents sold her into slavery. Her master forced her to work as a prostitute.

One day, as she stood in the street waiting for clients, she suddenly became aware of God within her own heart. That night, when she had returned to her master's house, she remained awake, and contemplated God. She derived so much pleasure from prayer, that she spent every night in contemplation, only sleeping for a few hours. Her master began to fear that God would punish him for holding her as a slave, and decided to release her.

She ran out of the city to a nearby mountain, where she found a hermit called Hassan living in a cave. He showed her another cave, where she settled. She spent every evening and morning in contemplation; and in the afternoon she went to collect berries from the trees growing on the mountain slopes.

The wild goats and gazelles living on the mountain could sense her love for all living beings. So when she was collecting berries, they followed her from tree to tree; and when she returned to her cave at dusk, many of them spent the night lying down at the entrance. One day Hassan saw the animals following her. 'Why are they so intimate with you, yet dislike me?' he asked her. 'What have you eaten today?' she asked him. 'A stew made from goat's meat,' he replied. 'Would you make friends with a creature that had eaten your brother?' she asked – and he blushed with shame.

Attar: Tadhkirat al-Auliya

2

WATER, AIR, A CANDLE AND A NEEDLE

As a result of devoting themselves to prayer and contemplation, Hassan had acquired the power of floating on the surface of the water, while Rabia could float above the ground. One morning Hassan met Rabia beside a mountain lake. She was sitting on a mat, deep in contemplation; and he was carrying a mat, looking for place to sit. He threw the mat onto the water, and then sat on it. 'Come and join me,' he cried, 'and we shall contemplate God together.' Rabia rose up, threw her mat up in the air, and climbed on to it. Then she said to Hassan: 'If you look around you, you can see countless tiny insects floating on the water. And when I look around me, I can see countless insects flying through the air. So neither of us are any better than insects.'

Hassan realized from this remark that, although he had been a hermit for longer, Rabia had made greater spiritual progress; so he asked her for spiritual encouragement. She led him back to her cave, and found amongst her few possessions a candle and a needle. 'If you are truly devoted to God,' she said, 'you will be like a candle: you will burn with love, and thus give light to the world. If you work hard in your efforts to know God, you will be like a needle: your knowledge will sew together people's hearts.' 'But how can my devotion to God have any effect on the world, and my knowledge have any effect on other people?' Hassan asked. 'How can contemplation enable some people to float on water and others to float above ground?' Rabia asked with a smile. Then she added: 'The effects of contemplation are deep and strange.'

Attar: Tadhkirat al-Auliya

3

People's questions

Rabia soon gained a reputation throughout Basra and the surrounding country for her spiritual insight, and people came to ask her questions.

'Do you see God when you contemplate him?' one person asked. Rabia replied: 'I see God within me, and contemplate him beyond me.'

'How can I be contented and serene?' another person asked. Rabia replied: 'You will be contented and serene when you are as grateful to God for pain and misfortune as you are for pleasure and good fortune.'

'When people repent of their sins, does God accept their repentance?' another person asked. Rabia replied: 'People can only repent of their sins if God gives them a spirit of repentance. When God gives this spirit, and they receive it, then he accepts their repentance. But if people try to repent without receiving this spirit, then he does not accept their repentance.'

'Tell me about love,' another person asked. Rabia replied: 'Love comes from eternity, and returns to eternity.'

'Do you love God because you fear his punishment?' a person asked. Rabia replied: 'You cannot love God through fear.' 'Do you love God because you hope for his reward?' the person asked. 'You cannot love God through hope,' she replied. 'So why do you love God?' the person asked. She replied: 'When you know God, you cannot help loving him; and the more you know, the more you love.'

Attar: Tadhkirat al-Auliya

4

A BANDAGE OF GRATITUDE

Some religious leaders were angry that a woman could gain such a high spiritual reputation. One of these leaders came to her, and said: 'God bestows spiritual gifts on men, not on women. So you have no right to give advice to people on spiritual matters.' Rabia smiled, and replied: 'If women possess no spiritual gifts, that may explain why they are less prone to pride and self-worship.'

Rabia welcomed good and evil people alike to her cave, making no distinction between them – and this made other religious leaders angry. One of these leaders came to her, and said: 'If religion is to remain pure, the good should shun the evil, not welcome them into their homes.' Rabia smiled, and said: 'Happiness comes from God's presence; and, since evil is a sign of God's absence, I feel sorry for evil people.'

A few religious leaders admired her, but were disturbed by the austerity of her way of life. One of these leaders, called Sufyan, visited her regularly. On one occasion he said: 'Your clothes are in tatters, and your blankets are full of holes. There are many people who would be glad to provide you with new clothes and blankets.' 'Everything in this world is on loan to us from God,' Rabia replied; 'I cannot accept the loan of a loan.'

On another visit Sufyan was surprised to find Rabia wearing a bandage round her head. 'Is your head aching?' he asked. 'Most people wear a bandage when they have a complaint,' she replied; 'but my bandage is a sign of gratitude.' When he returned to Basra, Sufyan also tied a bandage round his head.

Attar: Tadhkirat al-Auliya

5

THE NATURE OF FAITH

A young scholar called Malik came to see Rabia. He found that the pitcher, which she used for both drinking and washing, was broken; her reed mat, on which she both prayed and slept, was worn and frayed; and her pillow had disintegrated, so she lay her head on a stone. 'Rabia,' he said, 'I have many wealthy friends. If you permit me, I shall ask them to provide all your material needs.' 'You are mistaken,' Rabia replied; 'your friends and I have the same provider.' 'Yes,' Malik said. Rabia continued: 'Does God forget the poor because of their poverty? Does he forget the wealthy because of their wealth?' 'No,' Malik said. Rabia concluded: 'Since God already knows my circumstances, why should I remind him? Whatever he wills, we should will.'

Some days later Mailk returned, accompanied by two other young scholars, Shadiq and Hussein. The conversation turned to the meaning of faith. 'Having faith means being patient when God inflicts suffering,' declared Shadiq. 'How can you be patient when you are in pain?' Rabia asked. 'Having faith means being grateful for suffering inflicted by God,' declared Hussein. 'How can you be grateful when you are in pain?' Rabia asked. 'Having faith means taking delight in suffering inflicted by God,' declared Malik. 'How can you find pleasure in pain?' Rabia asked.

'Very well,' the young scholars said, 'give us your definition of faith.' Rabia put her hands on the head of each scholar in turn. Then she said: 'Faith means having a clear vision of God, so you are indifferent to the suffering he inflicts.'

Attar: Tadhkirat al-Auliya

6

Illness and Death

When Rabia was old, she fell ill; her stomach swelled,. and she was in great pain. The religious leader Sufyan came to visit her, and was horrified at her appearance. 'Let us pray to God,' he said; 'then the swelling will subside, and your pain ease.' 'God has willed that my stomach should swell,' Rabia replied, 'and he has decreed that my body should feel pain. I refuse to pray for something that is contrary to God's will.'

'Is there anything that you desire?' Sufyan asked. 'Yes,' Rabia replied, 'I desire fresh dates.' 'Then I shall go at once to the market in Basra, and buy some,' he declared. 'No,' said Rabia, 'my desires count for nothing. God's desires are all that matters.'

Sufyan was reduced to silence, and remained silent for a long time. Finally he said: 'Since there is nothing I can do to help your situation, I should like you to say something about mine.' 'You are a good man,' she said, 'but you are discontent. This is because you want to hold a higher position, and are angry with God for not giving you the necessary abilities.' 'Dear God,' Sufyan exclaimed, falling to his knees, 'forgive me!' 'Get up from your knees,' Rabia said; 'God cannot forgive you until you have learnt to forgive him.'

A month later Rabia was on the point of death. A large number of religious leaders and scholars gathered in her cave. When she knew that death was imminent, she asked them to leave. From outside the cave they heard her say: 'May my soul be serene and happy, and be pleasing in your sight.' When they came back in, she was dead – with a broad smile on her face.

Attar: Tadhkirat al-Auliya

7

Pride and Secrecy

Junayd grew up in Baghdad, the capital of the Muslim empire. His father, Ahmad, was a successful merchant; and his uncle, called Sari, was a Sufi, who lived in a hut on the edge of the city. Although Sari had gained great spiritual insight, he was still very proud; and in his pride he refused to accept gifts from Ahmad; and this caused Ahmad much grief.

When Junayd was a young man, he said to his father: 'Give me a bag of gold coins, and I shall give them to my uncle.' His father gave him a bag of coins, and Junayd went to Sari's hut. 'In the name of God,' Junyad said, 'I beg you to take these coins. God has dealt graciously with you and justly with my father.' 'What do you mean?' Sari asked. 'He was gracious with you in giving you poverty,' Junayd replied; 'and he was just with my father in giving him great wealth. In your poverty you are free to accept or reject these coins, as you please; but my father is obliged to share his wealth with those who need it.' Sari took the coins.

Junayd knew that he too was called by God to be a Sufi; but he dreaded being treated with respect by others, because he feared this might make him proud like his uncle. So he decided to make spectacles by day, and only devote himself secretly to prayer and contemplation at night. He lived like this for forty years. Then one day he happened to be walking through the city square when a thief was being hanged. Junayd rushed over to the thief, and kissed his feet until he died. Some were indignant at Junayd's action, while others recognized it as a mark of holiness – and so began to visit him for advice.

Attar: Tadhkirat al-Auliya

8

Patience in prayer

A man came to Junayd, and said: 'Through the years I have listened to many spiritual teachers, in the hope that they would give me faith; but none has succeeded. Can you give me faith?' 'Dear friend,' Junayd replied, ' you have been looking for someone to carry your burdens – and such a person is indeed hard to find. Instead, start carrying the burden's of others; then you will find faith.'

Another man came to Junyad, and said: 'God has bestowed many gifts upon me, but my heart is filled with bitterness and resentment, so I cannot feel grateful to him. What can I do?' Junayd replied: 'God does not demand your gratitude. He simply wants you to use his gifts in the service of others. If you do that, bitterness and resentment will dissolve, and gratitude will take their place.'

An elderly woman came to Junayd, and said: 'My son went on a journey, and was due to come back several days ago; but he has not appeared. What should I do?' 'Pray to God for his safe return,' Junayd said. The woman came to Junayd the following day, and said: 'I have prayed all day and all night for my son's return, but still he has not appeared.' 'Be patient in your prayers,' Junayd replied. The woman came to Junayd every day for a week saying that her son was still missing; and each time Junayd told her to be patient. Finally she said: 'My patience is exhausted; pray to God on my behalf.' 'If your patience is truly exhausted,' Junayd replied, 'then God must no longer want you to pray. That means your son is about to return.' The woman went back home, and found her son waiting for her.

Attar: Tadhkirat al-Auliya

9

Lessons learnt

Whenever Junayd went to purchase anything, he always made his request with the words, 'For the sake of God.' And when he went to his barber, he always asked him to cut his hair for the sake of God. His barber, who admired Junayd's holiness, refused to take payment. Since Junayd was offered many gifts, he at first gave little thought to the barber's kindness. But then he felt an urge to reward him; so he decided to pass on to him the next gift that he received. It so happened that the next gift was a large bag of gold from a wealthy merchant. He immediately took it to the barber, and offered it to him. The barber was angry. 'You ask me to cut your hair for the sake of God,' he exclaimed, 'and now you offer me money! If I do something for God's sake, I cannot accept payment.'

Junayd often recounted this incident, and added: 'I learnt true faith from that barber.' He also recounted another incident from which he learnt a lesson. A man came to him, and asked for money. 'You are perfectly healthy,' Junayd replied; 'you should live by working, not by begging.' The following day the man returned, and offered Junayd a bag of gold. Junayd was surprised, and asked the reason for the gift. 'Yesterday I judged you as generous,' the man replied, 'but you judged me as greedy. So today I judge you as greedy, and hope that you may judge me as generous.' 'And where did you get that bag of gold?' Junayd asked. 'From a man who passes no judgments,' the man replied. Junayd fell to his knees and begged forgiveness. 'I shall only forgive you if you accept my gift,' the man said. So Junayd accepted it.

Attar: Tadhkirat al-Auliya

10

God's closeness

Junayd acquired a small number of disciples, who built themselves huts near his hut. He loved all of them, but he loved one of them, called Haddi, above the rest. His preference for Haddi made the other disciples jealous; and one day Junayd heard some of the disciples making rude remarks about Haddi. So Junayd called the disciples together, and gave them each a piece of cake. 'Go away,' Junayd said, 'and find a place where no one can see you – then eat your piece of cake. Afterwards come back to me.' A few hours later the disciples returned. All of them had eaten the cake except Haddi. 'Why have you not eaten the cake I gave you?' Junayd asked him. 'Master,' Haddi replied, 'you said that it should eaten where no one can see me. But wherever I went, God was watching.' Junayd turned to the other disciples, and said: 'Now you understand why Haddi has a special place in my heart.' They fell on their knees, and begged his forgiveness.

When Junayd knew that he would soon die, he invited his disciples to have a meal with him. After the meal he offered his final insights: 'When people speak about God with clarity, it's a sign that they do not know him; the closer you approach God, the more bewildered you become, and the less you are able to speak coherently about him – it's as if you were permanently drunk. When people have a clear sense of their own identity, it is a sign that they are far from God; as you draw near to God, you lose your own identity, and regard yourself as part of him – it's as if you had ceased to exist. With God all rational knowledge dissolves, and spiritual knowledge takes its place.'

With these words he became unconscious; and a few moments later he died.

Attar: Tadhkirat al-Auliya and Junayd's Tawhid

11

Lecturer and traveler

Shortly before Junayd's death, a young man called Hallaj visited him. Hallaj was the son of a weaver in a town called Tostar; and at the age of eighteen he was filled with the desire to become a Sufi. So he walked to Baghdad in order to seek Junayd's guidance. Junayd told him to spend a year in solitude; and Hallaj went to live in a cave near the top of a mountain. But when he returned to Junayd for further guidance, Junayd had died.

Hallaj returned to Tostar; and, inspired by what he had learnt about the soul during his year of solitude, he began to give lectures on the soul in the town square. He was a brilliant speaker, and drew vast crowds. His popularity made the local religious leaders envious; and they told people not to trust his teaching, because he had no religious training. But their opposition made him even more popular.

After a further year Hallaj became worried that the public adulation would make him proud. So one night he slipped out of Tostar, and he spent the next five years wandering from place to place as a beggar. Then he settled in the town of Ahwaz, where again he gave lectures about the soul. As in Tostar he was hugely popular.

Another year passed. Then he announced to the people of Tostar that he now intended to visit India and China, and listen to their spiritual teachers. So he set off eastwards, and traveled throughout those vast countries, listening with deep respect to Hindu, Buddhist and Taoist teachers; he also shared his own insights with them. Then he returned to Baghdad.

Attar: Tadhkirat al-Auliya

12

The Divinity of All

News of Hallaj's brilliance as a speaker had reached Baghdad; and now news of his return from India and China spread through the city. So numerous people came to him, and begged him to give a lecture. At first he refused, because the religious leaders were extremely powerful in Baghdad, and he knew they would oppose him. But finally he agreed. A special podium was erected in the city square for him; and on the appointed day the square was packed.

'I am God,' Hallaj declared in a loud voice; 'and you are God. All living beings, all material things, and all events are divine. God is deep in the earth, and he is high in the sky. He is in the water of every lake; and, when a lake has dried up, he is in the cracks of its bed. God is in the abundant harvest; he is also in the famine that occurs when the harvest has failed. God is in the lightning; he is also in the darkness when the lightning has faded. God can be seen in the rain, when it falls from the sky like nails; and he can be heard in the thunder. God is the eyes of the blind, and he is the ears of the deaf.

'People ask me how God can be known. Any method of knowing God can only yield intellectual knowledge; it cannot penetrate the heart of his being, which is the heart of all being. People may spend their whole lives seeking God through intellectual endeavor; they may speculate about God, and concoct theories about him. But their speculations are no more than guesses, and their theories no more than dreams.

'God can only be known by looking within – looking within you and me, within animals and trees, within rocks and sand. I am God, you are God, all is God.'

Attar: Tadhkirat al-Auliya and Hallaj's Tawasin

13

Arrest and Death

The religious leaders of Baghdad were incensed at Hallaj's claim to be God, which they regarded as blasphemy. They reported him to the caliph, who ordered him to be arrested and imprisoned.

Hallaj remained in prison for a year. At first many people came to visit him and seek his guidance; but when the caliph heard about this, he ordered that Hallaj be kept locked in a cell on his own. A religious leader, who secretly admired Hallaj, sent him a message, urging him to renounce his claim to be God and to ask for a pardon, so that he might be set free. Hallaj sent a reply, urging the religious leader to ask God's pardon for such cowardly advice.

One of the prison guards, who also secretly admired Hallaj, gave him the keys to his cell and the prison gates, so he could escape. Hallaj used the keys to release all the other prisoners, but remained in the prison himself. When the caliph heard what had happened, he realized that Hallaj was blessed by God, and wanted to release him. But the religious leaders told the caliph that Hallaj would stir people into rebellion, and they persuaded him to order Hallaj's death.

The caliph, at the religious leaders' suggestion, decided to crucify Hallaj. So Hallaj was wrapped in thirteen heavy chains, and dragged to a hill outside the city, where he was nailed to a cross. The crowd shouted to him: 'Give us a final message.' Hallaj replied: 'To love God is to be God.' The guards now cut out his tongue – so he said nothing more.

Attar: Tadhkirat al-Auliya

14

Truth and Knowledge

Ghazali grew up in northern Iran. As a young man he longed to find the truth for himself. So he refused to accept any ideas on the authority of others, and he cast aside the religious beliefs that he had been taught as a child. He observed that the children of Christians grow up to be Christian, the children of Jews grow up to be Jews, and the children of Muslims grow up to be Muslims. He wanted to find the inner, universal truth that lies behind all religions.

He decided that knowledge can only be certain if it is disclosed in such a way as to dispel all doubt. So he reflected on the knowledge he already possessed, and concluded that none of it was certain except the perceptions of the senses – and even they may be open to question, since, for example, shadows appear stationary, but are in fact constantly moving. So he became totally skeptical.

He went to Baghdad where he studied theology. He was impressed at logical coherence of theology, and its capacity to defend orthodox religion against heretics who oppose it. And he became such a brilliant exponent of theology that at the age of thirty-three he was appointed a professor.

But theology failed to satisfy him. It convinced him that God probably exists, but it did not lead to a direct encounter with him that was beyond doubt. So he turned to the study of mysticism. He read many books by Sufi mystics, and within a short time he had an expert knowledge of Sufi teaching.

Ghazali: al Mundqidh min ad-Dalal

15

Agony of indecision

Ghazali was now felt like someone who knew the physiology of drunkenness, but had never been drunk; or who knew about health and contentment, but was ill and unhappy. While knowing about mysticism, he had experienced nothing of the inner ecstasy that mystics describe – and which, they claim, is the consequence of direct awareness of God.

As he reflected on his predicament, he realized that his way of life prevented him from following the mystics' path. While the mystics detach themselves from worldly concerns, he was caught in a web of worldly attachments. In particular, he enjoyed the social status and the public influence that his professorship gave him, as well as the grand house and servants that he was able to afford.

Thus he was faced with a choice: to abandon his career and its privileges, and become a Sufi; or to cling onto his career, and abandon the pursuit of truth. Day by day he grappled with the choice. One day he would decide to abandon his career, and the next day he would reverse the decision. For six months he dithered; and he felt both his physical and mental energy ebb away.

Finally the decision was taken for him. He stood one morning in front of his students, about to deliver a lecture, and found himself unable to speak. And the same illness prevented him from swallowing food, so he could only consume thin soup. During the following weeks his body wasted away, and the physicians gave up hope of treating him. So he was compelled to resign his professorship.

Ghazali: al Mundqidh min ad-Dalal

16

Divine ecstasy

When he was close to death, Ghazali: illness suddenly vanished, and he found himself able to talk and eat normally. He now sold his house and possessions, and gave the proceeds to the poor. Religious leaders were astonished at his conduct, because they regarded teaching theology as the highest calling; and they urged him to return to his professorship. Government officials, who had often sought his advice, were offended that that he showed no interest in their affairs. This opposition forced him to leave Baghdad

He traveled first to Damascus, where he lived in a small hut near a mosque. At dawn each day he went to the mosque, and tried to contemplate God; and at dusk he returned to his hut to eat and rest. After two years he had not experienced a single moment of ecstasy. So he decided to go on a pilgrimage to Mecca, in the hope that this would bring greater spiritual reward; but it too proved fruitless.

By now his appearance had changed completely: he had grown a long beard, and his smooth pale skin had turned rough and ruddy. So he was able to return to Baghdad without being recognized. As in Damascus, he lived in a hut near a mosque, and spent the daylight hours in the mosque contemplating God. At last he began to perceive light within himself; he realized that this light signified God's presence, and he was overwhelmed with joy. Then he heard voices that sang the most enchanting melodies; he realized that the voices belonged to God's angels, and his joy intensified. Finally he encountered God directly, and he attained the summit of ecstasy. Unaware of himself, he danced around the mosque, to the astonishment of the other people present.

Ghazali: al Mundqidh min ad-Dalal

17

The mystical path

When Ghazali finished dancing, the people in the mosque asked him his name; and without anticipating the consequences, he told them. News of his presence in Baghdad quickly spread; so a few days later a group of young people came to the mosque, and asked him to start lecturing again. 'I have no interest in theology any more,' he replied, 'so my words would bore you.' 'We shall be interested in anything you say,' they replied. So he agreed to give a single short lecture.

'My friends, 'he said, 'I shall tell you what I have learnt since I have followed the mystical path. I have learnt that the mystical path is the highest path – that if the intellect of intellectuals and the scholarship of scholars were combined, they could not improve on the life and character of mystics.

'I have learnt that there are two parts to the mystical path. The first is the attainment of purity. Mystics must banish from themselves all impure thoughts and feelings; they must never utter impure words or engage in impure actions. This requires great effort. The second involves waiting and watching. Mystics make themselves available to God by sitting in silence; and at the times of his choosing he reveals himself.

'I have learnt that all religions are based on direct knowledge of God, which is the only truth of which anyone can be certain.'

At the end of his lecture twenty young people asked to be his pupils. For four years they lived with them, and he taught them to be mystics. Then he died.

Ghazali: al Mundqidh min ad-Dalal

18

From Theologian to Mystic

Rumi was born in Balkh in Afghanistan, where Rumi's father was a teacher of theology. But when Rumi was aged twelve, the Mongol army led by Genghis Khan overran the city. Rumi's mother was killed, but he and his father escaped. They walked to Baghdad, which Genghis Khan would also conquer, but they were disgusted by its decadence. So they traveled northwards to Konya, the capital of Turkey, where the sultan appointed Rumi's father as his spiritual advisor.

Rumi devoted his time to theological study, and at the age of thirty-three became a teacher himself. He won respect for the sharpness of his intellect, which he used against anyone who opposed religious orthodoxy. Four years later a wandering Sufi called Shams came to Konya. Most people were repelled by his wild behavior and shabby appearance; but Rumi, to his own surprise, was fascinated. He invited Shams to live in his house, in order to teach him Sufi ideas. Shams remained with Rumi for a year, at the end of which Rumi gave up his teaching post, and spent every day in mystical contemplation.

His students, and the religious leaders of Konya, were angry at Shams' influence, and chased him from the city. Rumi was distraught, and went after him. He eventually found him in Syria, and brought him back; but a few months later Shams was murdered.

Rumi remained in Konya for the rest of his long life. He continued to follow the mystical path that Shams had shown him. He also married and had a son, who also became a mystic. His son organized a school of mysticism at which Rumi taught; and he also persuaded Rumi to write down his insights, which were then widely circulated.

Rumi: Masnavi

19

THE CREED OF LOVE

The creed of love is separate from all religions; the creed of love is God.

If you want to sit with God, sit with those who love God. If you do not consort with God's lovers, you will be lost; you will be separated from the whole.

Your must turn your intelligence into ignorance; you must become mad. Whenever you see something that may yield material profit, flee from it. Curse anyone who praises you. Lend your wealth to the poor and the feckless. Abandon the security of your home, and live in places of danger. Throw away your reputation, and embrace dishonor and disgrace. I shall test my intellect to the limit; and then I shall make myself mad.

If you want your misery to vanish, then try to banish your worldly wisdom. This is because worldly wisdom belongs to the lower nature, which is not illuminated by God's light. The wisdom of the world makes you both more opinionated, and more doubtful about your beliefs. But the wisdom of faith carries you beyond the sky.

Existence is illusory and appearances are deceptive; the true essence of all living beings and all objects is hidden. Look at dust blowing in the air: you see the dust, but the wind blowing the dust is invisible. Existence and appearance varies from one living being and object to another; but the true essence is one – and is divine. So do not love outward forms, but love the inward essence; then you will love God.

Rumi: Masnavi

20

TWO KINDS OF KNOWLEDGE

The outward forms of religion are like signs on the road, guiding travelers who do not know the way. But if you truly love God, you have no need for signs; the divine lamp shines in front of you, and guides you. When God's lovers engage in outward religion, they are trying to guide those who are uncertain of the way. Remember that the parents of a newborn child utter babbling sounds, even though they can speak clearly.

When you have attained direct vision of God, you do not need the support of doctrines and rituals. Having seen the spiritual beauty of God, you are bored by religion, and only engage in it for the sake of others. Truth transcends all doctrines; vision transcends all rituals.

There are two kinds of knowledge. The first kind is acquired from books and teachers; it consists of definitions which you learn by rote, and concepts which your grasp by reflection. This kind of knowledge is a burden; and the more you acquire, the greater the burden becomes. The second kind of knowledge is a gift from God. It springs up from the soul, and flows through the breast. This kind of knowledge lifts from your heart every anxiety and all sadness.

When you know God, your personal attributes have been subsumed into the attributes of God. Consider a candle: in the night it shines brightly; but when dawn breaks, its flame is subsumed into the light of the sun. In the darkness of ignorance individuals shine brightly; but in the light of divine truth, their individuality disappears.

Rumi Masnavi

21

THE PURPOSE OF SUFFERING

Melancholy may enter your soul, and ambush your happiness; but it will prepare you for true joy. Melancholy drives out all other emotions and feelings, so the source of all goodness may occupy the whole house. It shakes the yellow leaves from the tree, allowing fresh leaves to grow. It pulls up old bodily pleasures by the roots, allowing divine spiritual pleasures to be planted. Melancholy takes many things from the soul, in order to bring better things in return.

Human beings are created from the dust of the earth; but do they resemble dust? Grapes come from vines; but do grapes look like vines? Does theft have the same shape as gallows? Does piety resemble eternal life? Nothing resembles its consequences. So the root of pain and torment is not evil.

Where there is illness, God will find the cure. Where there is poverty, God will supply what is needed. Where there is confusion, God will bring clarity. Spend less time worrying, and more time trusting.

The prospect of dying in union with God is sweet; but the prospect of eternal separation from him is horribly bitter.

God created suffering and heartache, so that joy and happiness might be known as their opposites. Hidden things become manifest through their opposites. But God has no opposite, so he remains hidden. Light is known as the opposite of darkness; but God's light has no opposite. Thus we cannot know him through our eyes.

Rumi: Masnavi

22

True religion

When love for God has doubled in your heart, you know without doubt that God loves you. You have never heard one hand clapping without the other.

Love cannot be contained in words; it cannot be conveyed through speaking and listening. Love is an ocean whose depths cannot be plumbed. Would you try to count the drops of water that a sea contains? In comparison with the ocean of love, the seen oceans of the world are nothing.

Love is an attribute of God, who himself has no need of love. Love for any other being derives from the love of God. My religion is to live in the service of love.

If you wish to know God, your intelligence must be broken. If you wish to love God, your heart must be broken.

Since your intelligence puffs you up with pride, become a simpleton; then your soul will remain healthy. Sacrifice your intelligence for the love of God, who is your friend; after all, he gave you your intelligence in the first place. If your intelligence departs from your head in confusion, then every hair on your head will know truth.

Hearsay is for those who are absent, not for those who are present. When you attain vision, have no more need of hearsay. When you sit with your beloved, you send away the go-betweens.

How should we seek truth? By no longer trying to possess knowledge. How should we seek love? By no longer trying to possess the objects of love.

Rumi: Masnavi

23

Kindness to sinners

Sadi grew up in the ancient Persian town of Shiraz. As a young man he decided to become a Sufi; but he could find no one in Shiraz who could teach and guide him. So he decided to wander across the world in search of wisdom. He spent several years in north Africa, several more years in India, and then traveled through central Asia. Finally as an old man he returned to Shiraz, and he told people numerous stories about the wise men and women that he had met. People suspected that the stories were really about himself, and often recounted them with Sadi as the subject.

Sadi was living in a simple hut, where he spent most of his time in contemplation. One night a thief entered his hut. The thief searched everywhere, but could find nothing worth stealing. Sadi saw the expression of disappointment on the thief's face; so he rose up, and gave the thief the mat on which he had been lying.

A man, who had been falsely accused of some sin, came to Sadi in state of indignation. 'I want to make my accuser pay for his slander,' the man said. 'Be especially kind and generous to him,' Sadi replied; 'then his conscience will punish him.'

Sadi was addressing a group of worshippers in a mosque. But he could make no impression on them; it was like trying to ignite wood that is still green. Then a passer-by entered the mosque, heard Sadi's words, and was so enthralled that he applauded. The worshippers now listened with greater attention, and they too became enthralled. At the end Sadi said to himself: 'Unless hearts are open, words are useless.'

Sadi: Gulistan

24

THE APPEARANCE OF WISDOM

Sadi was working as a cook for a man who took great pains to appear wise and devout; he dressed in simple clothes, frequently quoted words from spiritual books, and uttered long prayers on the roof of his house where passers-by could see and hear him. The king invited this man to dine with him. The man ate very little, and spent much of the time praying. When the man returned home, he ordered Sadi to prepare a large meal. 'But you have just eaten with the king,' Sadi protested. 'I hardly ate a thing, but prayed a great deal instead,' the man replied. 'In which case,' Sadi said, 'you must first repeat your prayers – but this time say them with your heart. Only then shall I satisfy your stomach.'

Sadi was walking along an especially dangerous road, where thieves and wild animals frequently attacked travelers. He met a group of wealthy merchants who were traveling together for mutual protection; and he asked if he could join them. They refused, and told him to keep a distance from them. Sadi was angry. 'You are judging me by my ragged tunic,' he said, 'and you assume that I am poor and feckless. But in fact I am a man of wisdom, and you would gain greatly by listening to what I have learnt.' 'Please don't be offended by our answer,' one of the merchants replied; 'but only yesterday we were robbed by someone dressed just as you are.' So Sadi was forced to continue traveling alone, and to trust in God alone for protection. And as he walked, his anger turned to shame. 'I took pride in my wisdom,' he thought, 'and I insulted all who are poor. From now on I shall take pride in my poverty, and regard myself as a fool.'

Sadi: Gulistan

25

Praise and Thanksgiving

Sadi was wounded by a leopard. He tried every kind of medicine to heal his wound, but none was effective. Yet he never ceased to give thanks and praise to God. People frequently said to him: 'You are suffering greatly, and yet you constantly thank God. How is this?' 'I give thanks to God,' Sadi replied, 'because I am suffering a physical wound caused by an animal, and not a spiritual wound caused by sin.'

Sadi was traveling with a large group of people from one city to another. The journey took two days, and they spent the night on the edge of a forest. As soon as dawn broke, Sadi awoke, and started singing and dancing. The other travelers asked why he was behaving in this manner. Sadi replied: 'The nightingales are singing in the trees; the partridges are calling from the mountains; the frogs are leaping in the water; and the wild beasts are howling in the forest. When all these creatures are engaged in praising God with their movements and noises, how can I remain still and silent?'

On another journey Sadi traveled with a group of young men who aspired to be holy. They rode camels, while Sadi walked at their side; and they constantly sang hymns and recited religious texts. One evening they arrived at a certain village. A rough uneducated boy began to sing a hymn in a loud raucous voice. The pious young men looked at the boy with contempt, and exchanged rude remarks; and they were so absorbed by their own contempt that they did not notice their camels wandering off into the desert. 'Why does this boy's praises move your camels,' Sadi asked, 'yet leave you unmoved?'

Sadi: Gulistan

26

DIGNIFIED RELIGION

A middle-aged man, who was wondering whether to become a Sufi, came to Sadi, and said: 'Sufis like yourself, who devote themselves to prayer and contemplation, seem very virtuous. But do they have any faults?' 'The greatest fault of Sufis,' Sadi replied, 'is that they place greater importance on the wishes of others than they do on their own wishes. If you live with a Sufi, this drives you mad – and that's why most Sufis live alone.'

Sadi lived for a time in a hut on the edge of a forest. The king and his principal officers were out hunting one winter's day; and they were so absorbed with their sport, that they failed to notice time passing. When dusk fell, they found themselves near Sadi's hut. 'It's too dangerous to return to the palace in darkness,' the king said; 'we must spend the night in this peasant's hovel.' 'It would be beneath your majesty's dignity to stay with a peasant,' one of the officers protested; 'it would be better to kindle a fire, and spend the night huddled around it.' Sadi overheard this conversation, and rushed out. He bowed before the king, and declared: 'The dignity of a king cannot be lowered, but the dignity of a peasant can be raised.' The king was so pleased with these words that he overruled his officer, and accepted Sadi's hospitality.

In the morning Sadi revealed to the king that he was a Sufi; and the king invited Sadi to dine at his palace. When Sadi arrived, the king said: 'The religion of a Sufi cannot be diminished, but the religion of a king can be increased.' Sadi was so pleased with these words that he insisted on serving at the king's table.

Sadi: Gulistan

27

THE ILLUSION OF SEPARATENESS

When Sadi was quite old, he fell sick; and the people of Shiraz realized that he would soon leave them. So they asked him to give a lecture, summarizing the wisdom he had acquired. Sadi agreed; and on the appointed day he was carried on his bed to the market square. Then he uttered seven simple aphorisms in a frail, rasping voice:

Let the words between enemies be such that, if they were to become friends, they would not be ashamed of what they had said. When you are in doubt about a decision, choose the course that is least likely to cause injury to others. The enemy of good order is a king without mercy; the enemy of good religion is a teacher without wisdom. The greedy are never satisfied, even if they have all they want. If you wish to be contented, you must be satisfied with just a crust. If you do not put into practice what you have learnt, you are like a man who ploughs a field but does not sow seeds. God is in every living being: so when we pray, he is speaking to himself; and when our consciences prompt us, he is acting on his own behalf. Life hangs on a single thread; so if you barter the eternal joy of God for the transient pleasures of the world, you are a fool.

Sadi was carried back to his house. The following day it was clear that he was about to die, and a large crowd gathered round his bedside. 'How do you feel?' someone asked. 'You have all had the agony of a bad tooth,' he replied; 'you long for the tooth to be pulled out.' Then with his final breath he spoke to God: 'Now in death may the illusion of my separateness be shattered forever; may I know you as me, and me as you.'

Sadi: Gulistan

28

ETERNAL TRUTH

Armies from Muslim lands invaded and conquered northern India, and large numbers of Hindus were converted to Islam by Sufi preachers. A young man called Nanak, the son of a tax official, listened carefully to both the Sufis and to the Hindu gurus; and he concluded that at heart Hinduism and Islam are the same. He composed hymns expressing the common spirit of religion, and for twenty years he toured India singing them. His followers became known as Sikhs, who continue to sing his hymns:

There is one God. Eternal truth is his name. He is the maker of all things.

God fears nothing, and hates no one. He is immortal and unborn; he is his own being.

In the beginning he was the truth; and he has been the truth throughout all ages. Here and now he is the truth; and he will be the truth for all eternity.

It is not through thought that you can understand God - even if you strive to grasp him with your mind a thousand times. It is not through sitting in silence, engaging in lengthy meditation, that you can reach the inner silence of God. You cannot satisfy your hunger for God by amassing great wealth - even the wealth of several worlds. If you possessed innumerable clever devices, none would assist you in obtaining God.

How can you know God? How can you tear away the veils of falsehood, and see him for yourself? By obeying his will. And if you obey God's will, then you shall be true to yourself.

Nanak: Japji

29

DIVINE TRUTH AND LOVE

Some people possess the strength of God; and they sing of his might. Some possess understanding of God; and they sing of the signs of God on earth. Some possess the virtue of God; and they sing of his love. Some possess knowledge of God; and they sing of his deepest thoughts. Some possess the cycle of birth and death; they sing of his creative and destructive power. Some possess a sense of the transcendence of God; and they sing of his glory. Some possess a sense of the immanence of God; and they sing of his compassion.

People of religion preach countless sermons about God; there are discourses and expositions without number written by religious scholars. Day by day generous people give to the needy, and day by day the needy receive their gifts. All this is good, because it refreshes the human spirit. Yet no sermon, no discourse and no exposition can encompass the truth of God; and no act of generosity compares with the justice of God.

God is truth; and truth leads to understanding. So if you wish to understand the world, turn to God. The language of God is love; and love leads to happiness. So if you wish to be happy, listen to God.

We pray to God, and he answers our prayers. Yet what can we offer him in return? What words can we utter that are equal to his love? As the dawn rises each morning let us meditate upon him, reflecting on his greatness.

No image of God can be made, because God is beyond our imagination. God is as he is, and we are as we are.

Nanak: Japji

30

The Countless Names of God

If you believe in God, sing of his truth. Sing of his many gifts, and the many signs of his love. Sing of his greatness, and his acts of kindness. Sing of his wisdom, which is hard to comprehend. Sing of the beauty of what he has made, and sing of how he destroys what he has made. Sing of how he takes life, and then restores it anew. Sing of the infinity of God. Sing of how he is both far away and near. Sing of how he is both transcendent and immanent - far above us, and meeting us face to face. To sing truly of God would exhaust the vocabulary of every language; God is beyond all human expression.

Let every voice sing God's praises. Let young men leap with joy, and young women dance in his honor. Let sages speak of his mysteries, and let priests of every religion perform their rituals.

Countless are the worshippers of God in every land, who do good works in order to please him. Countless are those who turn their backs on worldly wealth and success, and devote their lives to finding him.

Countless are the names of God, and the places where he is present. He made the world as it is, and as it shall be. He will never depart from this world, and no one can force his departure. You created all living beings and all objects, giving to each its own color and form. His handiwork is a visible testimony of his greatness. He does whatever pleases him, and no one can control him; all are subject to his will. He is the King of kings.

Nanak: Japji

31

The world as a thread

As he lay dying Nanak, whose followers had given him the title 'guru', gave these final instructions:

Make contentment and modesty your ear-rings, self-respect your purse, and meditation the ashes with which you smear your body. Make self-control your coat, faith your staff, and wisdom the path on which you walk.

Make divine knowledge your food, compassion your larder, and the promptings of conscience the pipe with which you call people to eat. Regard the world as a thread, and the living beings in the world as jewels strung on the thread - making a divine necklace.

Remember that God rules the world, allocating pleasure and pain according to his will.

Nanak: Japji

Index and Guide to Sources

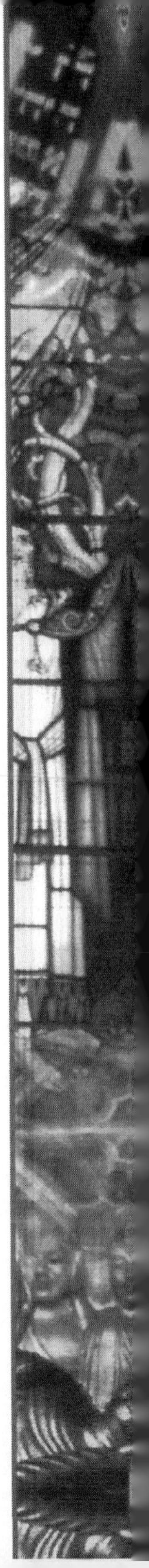

Late c4 BCE. Taoist teacher in China. The book of his exploits, written by him or a follower, is possibly the most popular Taoist work.

Clement, Early Christianity 25.
Died circa 100 CE. Leader of the Christian community in Rome, who was probably originally a slave.

Crow, Native American Religion 19.
A tribe native to the upper Missouri area.

Dabistan, Zoroastrianism 1-5, 29-31.
Circa c17 CE. A Persian account of eastern religion, containing a biography of Zarathustra based on older sources, and a Zoroastrian mystical work of unknown source.

Dadistan-I Dinik, Zoroastrianism 18-20.
Circa c9 CE. An account of the teaching of Manuskihar, a Zoroastrian priest.

Delaware, Native American Religion 31.
A group of tribes native to an area from Maryland to Long Island.

Diamond Sutra, Zen 2-4.
Circa c2 CE. A Buddhist treatise composed in India, which became highly influential in China and Japan. It is sometimes attributed to Bodhidharma, a possibly mythical figure credited with having brought Buddhism from India to China.

Didache, Early Christianity 31.
Early c2 CE. Short book on morality and worship given to new converts to Christianity.

Dina-I Mainog-I Khirad, Zoroastrianism 21-28.
Circa c9 CE. An account of the teaching of an unnamed Zoroastrian sage.

Ecclesiastes, Judaism 14-15.
Circa c3 BCE. A series of reflections by an old man, who had possibly held a high position in society.

Eckhart, Christian Mysticism 11-12.
Died 1327. A leading theologian in Germany, who was condemned in Rome as a heretic.

Ekoi, Traditional African Religion 15.
A tribe on the Calabar coast of Nigeria, western Africa.

Exodus, Judaism 2-4.
Circa c13 BCE. The first book of the Jewish Bible, traditionally attributed to Moses, and concerned mainly with his life and the events surrounding him.

Ezekiel, Judaism 12.
Circa c6 BCE. A Jewish prophet.

Fox, George, Christian Mysticism 25.
1624-1691. A wandering preacher and the founder of the Quakers.

Francis of Assisi, Christian Mysticism 9.
1182-1226. The founder of a large order of wandering preachers who lived by begging. He became especially famous for his love of Nature.

Ga, Traditional African Religion 31.
A tribe in Nigeria, western Africa.

Ganda, Traditional African Religion, 3-8.
A tribe in Uganda, eastern Africa.

Gemara, Judaism 21-25.
Circa c5 CE. A collection of wise sayings and stories of Jewish rabbis.

Genesis, Judaism 1.
Circa c13 BCE. The first book of the Jewish Bible, traditionally attributed to Moses, but based on at least two sources.

Ghazali, Sufism and Sikhism 14-17.
1058-1111. A leading theologian in Baghdad, who abandoned his career to adopt the ascetic life of a Sufi mystic.

Hadewijch of Brabant, Christian Mysticism 10.
Early c13. A member of a Beguine community of single women.

Haida, Native American Religion, 23.
A tribe native to Alaska.

Hakuin, Zen 27-28.
1685-1768. A Japanese Zen teacher, who remodeled the method of teaching to make it fiercer and more direct.

Hasidism, Judaism 29-30.
Circa c18 CE. A movement against religious legalism amongst Jews in eastern Europe, which yielded many parables and wise sayings.

Hausa, Traditional African Religion 16-20.
A tribe in northern Nigeria, western Africa, who converted to Islam in c14.

Heart Sutra, Zen 5.
Circa c2 CE. A Buddhist treatise composed in India, which became highly influential in China and Japan. It is sometimes attributed to Avalokita.

Hildegard of Bingen, Christian Mysticism 7-8.
1098-1179. Founder and abbess of a convent, who also preached in churches, gave spiritual counsel, composed music and studied medi-

cine.

Hillel, Judaism 18.
Late c1 BCE. A Jewish rabbi who was the foremost member of the Pharisees, a school of rabbis who dominated Jewish life for more than five centuries.

Hosea, Judaism 7.
Circa c8 BCE. A Jewish prophet.

Hui-neng, Zen 8-11.
637-713. The sixth patriarch of the Chinese school of Zen Buddhism.

Ibn Ishaq, Islam 1-7, 19-31.
Died circa 770 CE. Collector of accounts of the life of Muhammad, the founder of Islam.

Ignatius, Early Christianity 26.
Died circa 110 CE. Leader of the Christian community in Antioch, who was taken to Rome to be martyred.

Irenaeus, Early Christianity 28.
Died circa 190 CE. Leader of the Christian community in Lyons, who opposed heresy amongst Christians.

Isaiah (First), Judaism 8-9.
Circa c8 BCE. A Jewish prophet.

Isaiah (Second), Judaism 13.
Circa c6 BCE. A Jewish prophet.

Issac the Syrian, Christian Mysticism 3-4.
Circa c7 CE. A hermit in the Syrian desert. A monastery formed around him, and his sermons to the monks were widely circulated.

James, Early Christianity 21.
Mid c1 CE. A Christian leader, possibly of the community in Jerusalem.

Jeremiah, Judaism 11.
Circa c7 BCE. A Jewish prophet.

Jesus Ben Sirach, Judaism 16-17.
Circa c2 BCE. A scholar in Israel who traveled widely.

John, Early Christianity 5, 11, 13, 22.
Late c1 CE. Writer of a Gospel, an account of the life and teachings of Jesus Christ, and of letters to Christian communities.

John Chrysostom, Early Christianity 29.
Died circa 407. Patriarch of Constantinople, who was driven into exile for preaching against the greed and wealth of many Christians.

John Climacus, Christian Mysticism 1-2.
Died c.650. Hermit and later abbot of a monastery on Mount Sinai. His book of spiritual guidance has been widely used in Eastern Orthodox monasteries.

John of Cronstadt, Christian Mysticism 29-30.
1829-1908. A priest near St Petersburg in Russia. He was widely sought as a spiritual counselor, including by two czars.

John of the Cross, Christian Mysticism 21-22.
1542-1591. A monk in Spain. He was much influenced by Teresa of Avila.

Julian of Norwich, Christian Mysticism 17-18.
Died circa 1416. After recovering from a serious illness, during which she had a number of visions, she lived as an anchoress attached to a church in Norwich, England.

Justin, Early Christianity 27.
Died circa 155 CE. A philosopher who converted to Christianity, and was martyred in Rome, after writing a personal letter to the emperor.

Kamba, Traditional African Religion 21.
A tribe in Kenya, eastern Africa.

Kempis, Thomas a, Christian Mysticism 31.
Died 1471. A monk, whose writings had a huge influence for many centuries.

Lao Tzu, Taoism 1-8.
Late c6 BCE. Taoist teacher in China. Most accounts of his life are speculative, but his book, Tao Te Ching, is generally regarded as the basic text of Taoism.

Lieh Tzu, Taoism 21-31.
Early c2 BCE. Taoist teacher in China. Although he is the central figure in the book ascribed to him, the tales may have more ancient sources.

Lin-chi, Zen 12-14.
Died 866 CE. A Chinese Zen master whose teachings had particular influence in Japan, where he is known as Rinzai.

Lotus Sutra, Zen 6-7.
Circa c2 CE. A Buddhist treatise composed in India, which became highly influential in China and Japan. It is sometimes attributed to Avalokita.

Luke, Early Christianity 5-6, 8-10, 12-16.
Late c1 CE. Writer of a Gospel, an account of the life and teachings of Jesus Christ, and of the *Acts of the Apostles,* an account of the early

Christian communities.

Mark, Early Christianity 6.
Late c1 CE. Writer of a *Gospel,* an account of the life and teachings of Jesus Christ.

Masai, Traditional African Religion 9-10.
A tribe in Kenya, eastern Africa.

Matthew, Early Christianity 1-4, 7, 11-12.
Late c1 CE. Writer of a *Gospel,* an account of the life and teachings of Jesus Christ.

Mensa, Traditional African Religion 25-26.
A people in northern Ethiopia, eastern Africa.

Mbundu, Traditional African Religion 22-24.
A tribe in Angola, southern Africa.

Micah, Judaism 10.
Circa c8 BCE. A Jewish prophet.

Midrash, Judaism 26-28.
Circa c13 CE. A collection of wise sayings and stories of Jewish rabbis.

Milarepa, Zen 21-26.
1038-1122. Tibet's greatest saint and writer, credited with having spread Buddhism throughout the country. His biography may have been written by him, or by his pupil Rechung.

Mirabai, Hinduism 30.
Late c14. A devotional poet in northern India, reputed to be the daughter of a king.

Mishna, Judaism 19-20.
Circa c3 CE. A collection of the wise sayings of Jewish rabbis.

Mumon, Zen 15-20.
1184-1260. A collector of stories about Chinese Zen teachers.

Nanak, Sufism and Sikhism 28-31.
1469-1539. The founder of Sikhism.

Numbers, Judaism 31.
The fourth book of the Jewish Bible, traditionally attributed to Moses.

Origen, Early Christianity 29.
Died circa 254 CE. Philosopher in Alexandria, who ran a school for aspiring converts to Christianity. He was severely tortured for his faith.

Patanjali, Hinduism 28-29.
Circa c4 CE. Composer of the *Yoga Sutra* that gives instruction on how to meditate.

Paul, Early Christianity 16-20.
Mid c1 CE. Theologian and preacher, who took Christianity to cities in the eastern Mediterranean.

Pawnee, Native American Religion 15.
A tribe native to the Platte River area of Nebraska.

Penobscot, Native American Religion 20-21.
A tribe native to the area around the lower St. Lawrence River.

Proverbs, Judaism 31.
Circa c5 BCE. A collection of Jewish proverbs.

Quran, Islam 8-18.
Early c7 CE. Words of revelation given to Muhammad, the founder of Islam from about 610 to his death in 632 CE.

Red Jacket (Chief), Native American Religion 1-3.
Early c19. Chief of the Seneca tribe, located west of the Seneca Lake in upper New York State.

Rig Veda, Hinduism 1-4.
Circa c13 BCE. A collection of hymns and meditations by unnamed Hindu gurus.

Rolle, Richard, Christian Mysticism 15-16.
Died 1349. A hermit in Yorkshire, England. He frequently left his hermitage to sing and preach in local villages.

Rumi, Sufism and Sikhism 18-22.
Died 1273. The most highly regarded of all Sufi writers.

Sadi, Sufism and Sikhism 23-27.
Died circa 1290. Persian writer who traveled widely in India, Africa and the Arab world.

Samuel, Judaism 5.
Circa c11 BCE. Israelite prophet and judge.

Seattle (Chief), Native American Religion 8-12.
Mid c19. Chief in the Puget Sound tribes in western Washington.

Setcho, Zen 1-2, 15-20
980-1052. A collector of stories about Chinese Zen teachers.

Serrano, Native American Religion 26.
A tribe native to California.

Symeon of Galatia, Christian Mysticism 5-6.
949-1022. An abbot of a monastery, who became famous for his spiritual direction. He was driven into exile for a period by jealous church leaders.

Sioux, *Native American Religion 16.*

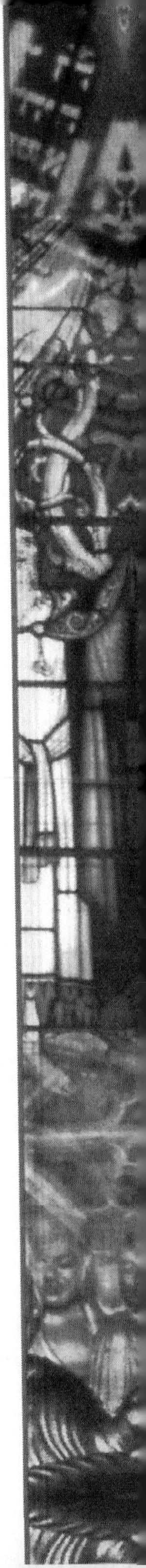

A misnomer applied to the Dakota people of the northern Great Plains.

Smohalla (Chief), *Native American Religion 6-7.*
Late c19. Chief of the Wanapum tribe, located on the Oregon-Washington border.

Snohomish, *Native American Religion 25.*
A tribe native to the Olympic Peninsula of western Washington.

Sutta Pitaka, *Buddhism 25-31.*
Circa c1 BCE. One of the three divisions of the Buddhist scriptures, written in Pali. It consists mainly of sermons and discourses by the Buddha.

Tauler, Johannes, *Christian Mysticism 13-14.*
Died 1361. A preacher in his native Strasbourg. He was much influenced by Eckhart.

Tenkswataya, *Native American Religion 4-5.*
Mid c19. A prophet, who sought to forge a federation of the tribes east of the Mississippi to prevent further white encroachments on tribal lands.

Teresa of Avila, *Christian Mysticism 19-20.*
1515-1582. A nun in Spain. She founded a new convent where she encouraged the nuns to seek mystical experiences.

Togo, Traditional African Religion 27-30.
A people in western Africa.

Upanishads, Hinduism 5-16, 31.
Circa c4 BCE. Collection of meditations and stories by Hindu gurus.

Vinaya Pitaka, Buddhism 11-24.
Circa c1 BCE. One of the three divisions of the Buddhist scriptures, written in Pali. It is addressed primarily to Buddhist monks and nuns.

Wapakomo, Traditional African Religion 31.
A tribe in Kenya.

Washakie (Chief), Native American Religion 17.
C19. Chief of the Shoshone group of tribes who lived throughout the Far West.

Wesley, John, Christian Mysticism 28.
1703-1791. Founder of Methodism, and tireless outdoor preacher.

Winnebago, Native American Religion 13-14.
A tribe native to eastern Wisconsin.

Zarathustra, Zoroastrianism 6-17.
Circa c12 BCE. The founder of Zoroastrianism. His hymns, the

Gathas, form the basis of Zoroastrian teaching.

Zinzendorf, Nikolaus von, Christian Mysticism 26-27.
1700-1760. Founder of the Moravian church, and pioneer of evangelical Christianity.